F. Scott Fitzgerald's Short Fiction

Modern American Literature
Series Editors: Martin Halliwell and Mark Whalan

F. Scott Fitzgerald's Short Fiction

From Ragtime to *Swing Time*

JADE BROUGHTON ADAMS

EDINBURGH
University Press

Edinburgh University Press is one of the leading university presses in the UK. We publish academic books and journals in our selected subject areas across the humanities and social sciences, combining cutting-edge scholarship with high editorial and production values to produce academic works of lasting importance. For more information visit our website: edinburghuniversitypress.com

Edinburgh University Press Ltd
The Tun – Holyrood Road, 12(2f) Jackson's Entry, Edinburgh EH8 8PJ

Typeset in 10/13 ITC Giovanni Std Book by
Servis Filmsetting Ltd, Stockport, Cheshire,
and printed and bound in Great Britain.

A CIP record for this book is available from the British Library

ISBN 978 1 4744 2468 4 (hardback)
ISBN 978 1 4744 2469 1 (webready PDF)
ISBN 978 1 4744 2470 7 (epub)

CONTENTS

LIST OF FIGURES

ACKNOWLEDGEMENTS

I wish to begin by thanking my series editors, Martin Halliwell and Mark Whalan, for their encouragement and support during the course of my work on this book. Edinburgh University Press have been a pleasure to work with, and my thanks go to Ersev Ersoy and Michelle Houston for their patience and assistance.

I am grateful to the following people and institutions for their invaluable help: the University of Leicester, the British Association for American Studies, the Eccles Centre at the British Library, the F. Scott Fitzgerald Society, AnnaLee Paul at the Rare Books and Special Collections Library at Princeton University, and the Billy Rose Theatre Division at the New York Public Library. I would like to thank Eleanor Lanahan, Blake Hazard and Chris Byrne, the Trustees of the F. Scott Fitzgerald literary estate, for their assistance.

I want specifically to thank William Blazek, Kirk Curnutt, Horst Kruse, Philip McGowan, Catherine Morley, Laura Rattray, Walter Raubicheck, Lauren Rule Maxwell and Bonnie Shannon McMullen for their warmth and willingness to make time to speak with me about my project, which was invaluable. Anthony Berret's stimulating correspondence with me about our shared interest in Fitzgerald's musical fiction was indispensable to this book. Will Friedwald was generous with his boundless knowledge of the music of the 1920s and 1930s, which was much appreciated. Helen Turner never fails to stimulate my thinking and make me laugh, often simultaneously: 'Many fêtes', Old Sport. Emily Wingfield generously read a draft of this book and I am eternally grateful for her patient and longstanding friendship. I would also like to thank Martin Halliwell for his continued support, sage advice and friendship over the years.

I am indebted to my wonderful family and friends for their love and support: Jessica Broughton, Cai Broughton, Lloyd Broughton, Sarah Broughton, Suzanne Phillips, Jennifer Broughton, Jon Humphries, Nigel and Celia Adams, Nick, Kate and Rose Greenwood, Elma, Jon and Oliver Balkwill, Owen Jones and Jeremy Zheng. To my parents, Desirée and Nick: thank you for your unwavering belief and support. Your courage and creativity are humbling and inspiring.

This book is dedicated partly to Patrick Broughton (1936-2008), who first introduced me to Fitzgerald's short stories. It is also partly dedicated to my boys, Matthew and Otis, who are both my biggest inspirations and best distractions. Thanks for adventuring with me 'up an erroneous Alp, an unmapped Savoy river'. My greatest debt is to my husband Matthew. Thank you for all you have done to support the writing of this book: I couldn't have done it without you.

'Harlem On My Mind' by Irving Berlin
© Copyright 1933 by Irving Berlin
© Copyright Renewed
International Copyright Secured. All Rights Reserved. Reprinted by Permission.

'Remember' by Irving Berlin
© Copyright 1925 by Irving Berlin
© Copyright Renewed
International Copyright Secured. All Rights Reserved. Reprinted by Permission.

'Blue Skies' by Irving Berlin
© Copyright 1926, 1927 by Irving Berlin
© Copyright Renewed
International Copyright Secured. All Rights Reserved. Reprinted by Permission.

'Puttin' On the Ritz' by Irving Berlin
© Copyright 1928, 1929 by Irving Berlin
© Copyright Renewed
International Copyright Secured. All Rights Reserved. Reprinted by Permission.

Rest of World
'Grizzly Bear'
Words & Music by Irving Berlin
© Copyright 1910 Irving Berlin Music Corporation, USA
Universal Music Publishing Limited
All Rights Reserved. International Copyright Secured.
Used by permission of Music Sales Limited.

'Harlem On My Mind'
Words & Music by Irving Berlin
© Copyright 1933 Irving Berlin Music Corporation, USA
Universal Music Publishing Limited
All Rights Reserved. International Copyright Secured.
Used by permission of Music Sales Limited.

ABBREVIATIONS

The following abbreviations are used to refer to Fitzgerald's short story collections and editions of his short stories and essays. These references are given in parenthesis in the text. All editions are from the *Cambridge Edition of the Works of F. Scott Fitzgerald*, edited by James L. W. West III, unless otherwise specified. References to West's Introductions and critical apparatus are given in the endnotes.

Note that the Cambridge editions of each of Fitzgerald's four collections (*Flappers and Philosophers, Tales of the Jazz Age, All the Sad Young Men* and *Taps at Reveille*) contain 'Additional Stories' that are included in the volume but which did not appear in Fitzgerald's original selection for each volume.

See Appendix for Fitzgerald's original selections.

ACC	*A Change of Class*
ASM	*All the Sad Young Men*
BJG	*The Basil, Josephine, and Gwen Stories*
F&P	*Flappers and Philosophers*
LK	*Last Kiss*
MLC	*My Lost City: Personal Essays, 1920–1940*
TAR	*Taps at Reveille*
TJA	*Tales of the Jazz Age*
TLD	*The Lost Decade: Short Stories from 'Esquire', 1936–1941*

Introduction: Not 'a Sincere and Yet Radiant World' but 'Trashy Imaginings' – Representations of Popular Culture in Fitzgerald's Short Fiction

Updating his editor, Maxwell Perkins, about his progress on *The Great Gatsby*, F. Scott Fitzgerald wrote, 'So in my new novel I'm thrown directly on purely creative work – not trashy imaginings as in my stories but the sustained imagination of a sincere yet radiant world.'[1] Fitzgerald's classification of his stories as 'trash' recurred throughout the course of his twenty-one-year professional career, but the interplay between art and commerce in Fitzgerald's œuvre is complex. Fitzgerald resented having to pause his novel-writing efforts in order to earn cash from the magazines to which he sold his stories, but he was also proud of the high fees his work commanded, reaching his peak price, $4,000 per story, at the *Saturday Evening Post* in 1929. Though often written out of financial need, Fitzgerald's short fiction served vital purposes in his career: he built a brand with his early, effervescent flapper stories, and he began to use the medium to develop ideas and to workshop characters that were to appear in his novels, even exporting phrases from stories verbatim. From 1937 until his death in 1940, working in Hollywood, he experimented with the medium, adopting a distinctively terse style of writing and turning to a fragmentary short story form that reflected an intensifying exploration of the themes of alienation and loneliness.

Fitzgerald's reference to 'trashy imaginings' apparently shows him dismissing the popular culture that infused these short stories, despite the fact that it is this same vivid interpretation of popular culture which he uses to create his 'sustained imagination of a sincere and yet radiant world'. In particular, four major leisure pursuits of the interwar period – jazz dance, jazz music, musical theatre and film – impacted upon Fitzgerald's literary aesthetics. In his integration of these media into his short fiction, we can trace a recurring ambivalence towards them: Fitzgerald is torn between embracing these modern leisure pursuits and rejecting them on account of their hedonism. This ambivalent response to modernity can be elucidated through readings of his invocations of dance, music, musical theatre and film as parodic. Often, Fitzgerald presents the enticing glamour and moral vacancy of these pursuits simultaneously. This tension manifests itself, for example, in Fitzgerald's exaggerated portrayals of jazz performers, in his satirical treatment of 'reformers' who were opposed to the proliferation of jazz expression in its many guises, and in the complex and shifting parody of the flapper figure that pervades his fiction, especially in the 1920s.

Fitzgerald's relationship with the popular culture of the 1920s and 1930s was not dissimilar to his relationship with the genre of short fiction: he was alternately dismissive of it and excited by it. In the modern dances that led to rising hemlines and new degrees of publicly displayed corporeal intimacy, Fitzgerald simultaneously saw progress and moral decay. Jazz music, its near-ubiquitous syncopation punctuating daily life, seemed to Fitzgerald both quintessentially native and resolutely foreign. His ambivalence reaches its zenith in his intellectual and artistic assessments of the film industry, which seemed to him to embody the best and worst of American cultural practice, but which he believed had the potential to be 'a more glittering, a grosser power' than the novel, as he stated in 1936 (*MLC*, 148). This ambivalence has not been fully accounted for in Fitzgerald studies. Five years after Fitzgerald's death, Malcolm Cowley originated the term 'double vision' to describe how Fitzgerald 'surrounded his characters with a mist of admiration and simultaneously he drove the mist away'.[2] Cowley's conception of this 'double vision' denotes Fitzgerald's ability to function simultaneously as an observer and a participant, a doubleness which seems to stem from a deep-seated insecurity about being 'a poor boy in a rich man's club at Princeton'.[3] Nowhere is this duality more present than in Fitzgerald's representation of the leisure pursuits of the interwar social worlds he inhabited, the four foremost among them being dance, music, musical theatre and film.

Fitzgerald's career spans two decades in which there was a great upheaval of cultural values, and, in these four related popular cultural forms, we can trace responses to these changes. The interwar period bears witness to a national debate about leisure and its purpose in society, and the widening chasm between popular culture and so-called 'high' culture. Contemporary criticisms of jazz music and dance reflected 'anxieties about rapid and monumental cultural changes', whilst the rise of celebrity as a cultural currency after the First World War consolidated ideas around the importance placed upon social success and helped to fortify the idolisation of youth.[4] As many cultural and literary critics have chronicled, the early 1920s heralded the ascendancy of youth culture for the first time, and Fitzgerald documented this movement. Young America was listening to jazz and dancing new dances (many of which had emerged from African American culture and were enthusiastically adopted by African Americans and white Americans alike), and people of all ages were watching motion pictures that celebrated innovation whilst revolutionising social and cultural life.[5]

But this excitement was to be tempered by the midpoint of Fitzgerald's two-decade career with the Wall Street Crash of October 1929. Scott and Zelda Fitzgeralds' finances did not suffer directly, but Fitzgerald's career (and indeed his posthumous reputation) was deeply affected by his widespread association with the years of excess he so glamorously depicted. After October 1929, Fitzgerald's depictions of the wealthy, and especially the expatriated wealthy, had a new and contentious cultural resonance, given that the very legitimacy of leisure itself as a pursuit was now being debated at home, while Fitzgerald spent the period of the Crash living in France and Switzerland.[6] Through prolific letter-writing, mixing with fellow Americans who were newly expatriated, and reading the international editions of American newspapers, Fitzgerald kept a close eye on shifting cultural trends back in the United States during his four sojourns in Europe.

Fitzgerald's own personal crash began with Zelda's deteriorating mental state and hospitalisation in spring 1930 and continued until the mid-thirties. In early 1936, he published a series of three essays detailing his artistic and psychological 'Crack-Up', before he journeyed back to Hollywood, and subsequently began work on *The Last Tycoon*. Despite Fitzgerald's personal life being especially fraught in the period between 1929 and 1936, stories like 'The Bridal Party' (1930) show a sense of optimism in the wake of the Crash. However, such depictions of wealthy American expatriates did not sit well with all of Fitzgerald's large reading public: the conservative, commercial magazine, the *Saturday Evening Post*, had an audience of approximately 2.5 million people in the mid-1920s. Fitzgerald himself acknowledged, in an abandoned preface to his final published collection of short stories, which were composed between 1927 and 1935, 'Before the last of these stories were written the world that they represented passed' (*TAR*, 402).[7]

During the Depression, discussion of what Susan Currell has termed the 'new "problem of leisure"' led to leisure becoming 'a battleground for widespread ambivalence about technology, social change, economic change, and new social habits, as well as a domain in which older ideas about individuality and democracy could be mediated or challenged'. The majority of Fitzgerald's stories were written between 1920 and 1933, and were marketed to widely circulating magazines; inasmuch as they frequently depict members of the leisured class – as well as middle- and working-class citizens partaking in leisure activities – we can read them in Currell's terms, as 'narratives of crisis that can be fruitfully dissected to reveal the class, race, and gender discourses contained within them'.[8] Fitzgerald's portrayals of popular cultural pursuits as more than frivolous ephemeral pastimes provide insight into perceptions of national identity in this period, as well as into responses to modernity and the mechanisation of culture.

What follows is an examination of the wide-ranging ways in which the popular culture of the 1910s, 1920s and 1930s impacted upon Fitzgerald's short stories. I consider how the increasing mechanisation of daily life and the work efficiency models known as Taylorism influenced Fitzgerald's young heroes and heroines, and I examine the indispensable role that African American culture played in shaping modernism, especially in terms of performance and parody, both of which permeate

Fitzgerald's writing. I demonstrate how the ubiquitous theatricality of the 1920s is central to any discussion of Fitzgerald's short fiction, and how the concept of performance infused many strata of experience throughout the period in which Fitzgerald was writing. I consider the vital influence of parody on Fitzgerald's short stories, in which he depicts jazz, motion pictures and other leisure pursuits as simultaneously fun and dangerous, before outlining Fitzgerald's conflicted relationship with high-paying popular magazines such as the *Saturday Evening Post*. Fitzgerald used these lucrative magazines to help him establish his brand in his early career but grew wary of being closely identified with these commercial magazines in lieu of finding critical acclaim as a 'serious' author. Finally, I situate Fitzgerald's literary modernism on a spectrum between two key models of short story writing: those of Anton Chekhov and O. Henry. The contrast between these two influences represents the fluidity with which Fitzgerald navigated between popular and high culture in his fiction, often destabilising our expectations of his lyrical style with metafictive experiments or by importing popular cultural references that work on both thematic and formal levels.

Popular cultural references in the 'trashy imaginings' of Fitzgerald's short fiction tell us more than what he thought of the Charleston, of 'Cheek to Cheek' and of *The Four Horsemen of the Apocalypse* (1921): they encapsulate Fitzgerald's racially and sexually coded response to modernity itself, a response which permeated deeply into his literary aesthetics of both novel- and story-writing. In 'Myra Meets His Family' (1920), Myra Harper is unambiguously introduced as a stock character. She is one of the notorious debutantes who has attended one prom too many in her search for a husband, leading to a reputation as a fortune hunter at the grand old age of twenty-one: '"the famous coast-to-coast Myra"' (*F&P*, 229). After a whirlwind romance, she finally becomes engaged to 'sweetly shy' Knowleton Whitney, who hears a rumour that Myra is only after his family wealth and conceives of a scheme to prompt her to break off their engagement (*F&P*, 232). Whitney stages a preposterous series of interventions which include tricking Myra on to the stage at a vaudeville show, forcing her to improvise a performance of a popular song in front of an audience made up of her fiancé's family and neighbours, later revealed to be actors who were employed by Whitney:

> As she sang a spirit of ironic humor slowly took possession of her – a desire to give them all a run for their money. And she did. She injected an East Side snarl into every word of slang; she ragged; she shimmied; she did a tickle-toe step she had learned once in an amateur musical comedy; and in a burst of inspiration finished up in an Al Jolson position, on her knees with her arms stretched out to her audience in syncopated appeal. (*F&P*, 244)

This extract shows how Fitzgerald's work is infused with the popular culture of his day: the 'East Side snarl' with which Myra enunciates her slang words references 'the Lower East Side of Manhattan, where working-class immigrants lived', and Al Jolson, a famous Lithuanian immigrant himself, had recorded his signature song, 'Swanee', in January 1920, just two months before 'Myra' was published.[9] Myra's familiarity with dance steps like the Tickle Toe show her engagement with musical theatre, this particular step having featured in the 1918 musical comedy *Going Up*. Her Shimmy shows an awareness of the very latest dances, as the Shimmy had been introduced to white New Yorkers for the first time in 1919, despite having existed in African American communities for much longer.[10] The 'spirit of ironic humor' that possesses Myra is apt: it undermines the 'burst[s] of inspiration' she experiences as she presents her jazzy repertoire, rendering readers somewhat confused and perhaps reluctant to respond to her performance – in other words, mirroring the reaction of her audience in the story.

My reading of Fitzgerald's short fiction develops John Kuehl's reading of irony as a method by which Fitzgerald can mediate his 'double vision' and protect it from rendering his work contradictory: 'This personal ambivalence or double-mindedness is kept under control by irony, Fitzgerald's means of achieving distance in third-person narratives.'[11] I argue that we can reframe Fitzgerald's ambivalence to his contemporary culture not solely as a means of achieving critical distance, but also as a route to more thoroughly interrogating his own responses to modernity. The lens of irony allows Fitzgerald to examine his subjects – that is to say, jazz dance, popular music, musical theatre and film – with a simultaneous critical detachment and an emotional investment. His parodic portrayals of popular culture are laden with value judgements, but this innately critical viewpoint coexists with giddy celebration of the whirling cadences of the Black Bottom and the howl of saxophones. My approach follows Linda Hutcheon's definition of parody as 'imitation with critical ironic distance'.[12] This parodic mode often sits in tension with the commercial publication contexts of his stories: beyond merely setting the scene, Fitzgerald uses popular cultural references to enhance his literary aesthetics in unexpected, sometimes jarring ways. The parody inherent in many of his stories offers two readings: the surface interpretation and the parodic reading, which is often critical of popular culture even when published in the most popular magazines of his time, his stories appearing alongside adverts for Tin Pan Alley records and movie stars endorsing face creams.

Fitzgerald's writing often undermines and even rewrites short story formulae that were commonly found in popular magazines of the 1920s and 1930s. Charles R. Hearn has surveyed a sample of fiction (focusing on stories with a theme of success) from four magazines dating from the 1920s with wide circulations, including three magazines in which Fitzgerald's fiction was regularly published. He finds that Fitzgerald utilises (and manipulates) several common story formulae, including 'the conventional rags-to-riches myth', reaching success as a sign of moral virtue, the 'wrongness, even sinfulness, of not having any particular ambition' resulting in losing (or almost losing) a love interest, and the Golden Girl story, in which a girl 'symbolizes all that is beautiful and glittering and desirable in the world' with 'a hero who is irresistibly attracted by the glitter of the girl and her world, but too poor to court her'.[13] Fitzgerald uses the Golden Girl formula in many stories, including '"The Sensible Thing"' (1924), 'A Penny Spent' (1925), 'Love in the Night' (1925), 'Presumption' (1926), 'The Last of the Belles' (1929), 'A Freeze-Out' (1931) and perhaps most famously, 'Winter Dreams' (1922). Some of these stories are notable for their unhappy endings, deviating from the Golden Girl formula. In '"The Sensible Thing"', George O'Kelly attains financial success and wins his golden girl, only to find that the reality of achieving this goal is not as fulfilling as he had hoped. In 'Winter Dreams', Dexter Jones's profoundly sad realisation that he can never recapture his lost love (a golden girl who prefigures Daisy Buchanan in 1925's *The Great Gatsby*) is presented in a lyrical crescendo:

> The dream was gone. Something had been taken from him. In a sort of panic he pushed the palms of his hands into his eyes and tried to bring up a picture of the waters lapping on Sherry Island and the moonlit veranda, and gingham on the golf-links and the dry sun and the gold color of her neck's soft down. And her mouth damp to his kisses and her eyes plaintive with melancholy and her freshness like new fine linen in the morning. Why, these things were no longer in the world! They had existed and they existed no longer. (*ASM*, 65)

Fitzgerald's lyrical style can be deceptive, distracting the reader from the modernist techniques at work in his stories: in this case, the bittersweet yet ambiguous ending Fitzgerald gives us in place of a closed, obviously happy ending. Fitzgerald's lyrical style can often cloak such innovation, and he also frequently employs themes of disguise and identity, which in certain readings can work to further obscure aspects of his literary modernism. I show how his use of dance, music, musical theatre and film, centred around the concepts of performance and leisure, can subtly undermine our expectations of his short fiction. My approach is primarily literary, examining the cultural discourses surrounding the popular cultural forms Fitzgerald has chosen through a literary analysis of their depiction in his stories. I argue that Fitzgerald innovatively imported practices borrowed from other popular cultural media into his short stories, deploying threads of ambiguity and parody that sit in tension with reader expectations of his lyrical style and the commercial publication contexts of his stories. In the extract from 'Myra Meets His Family', above, the irony becomes a feature of Myra's performance – she is giving her audience what they requested, regardless of their reactions. This results in an enthralling one-woman vaudeville show in microcosm.

Aspects of Myra's performance in 'Myra Meets His Family', and indeed many of the modern dance steps, were influenced by new industrial practices of streamlining. Felicia McCarren has explored the relationship between dance and mechanisation, especially in terms of the Taylorist principles of minimum gesture and maximum productivity. Frederick Winslow Taylor's influential 1911 book, *Principles of Scientific Management*, adopted a scientific approach to improving efficiency and productivity in the workplace, and thus sought to refine processes to the minimum effort in gesture that retained maximum efficiency.[14] The often tense relationship between movement and machines, McCarren argues, culminated in the creation of the cinematograph, which 'would seem to return to dance its mechanical, time-transcending, perpetual movement while promising to safeguard the anti-mechanical naturalness of dancing'.[15] We can see, in turn, how these social and economic pressures exert an influence over a range of Fitzgerald's characters.

In effect, when Myra does the 'Shimmy' in 'Myra Meets His Family' – that is to say, when she shakes her shoulders and chest without moving any other part of her body – she is enacting Taylorist–Fordist principles by distilling movement to one gesture: we can read her Shimmy as either 'a minimalist machine aesthetic or a parody of mechanistic madness'.[16] This is more than just an image of a girl singing and dancing to jazz: Fitzgerald is referencing a complex cultural web of associations, from Taylorism to 'savage' modernity and sex, via performative identity, character archetypes familiar to magazine audiences, and metafictive literary techniques. Elsewhere in Fitzgerald's œuvre, the Shimmy is associated with a heightened sense or display of sexuality, such as when Marcia Meadows in 'Head and Shoulders' (1920) 'did a shaky, shivery, celebrated dance' that provoked 'remarks about [her] bosom' from the audience, causing her to 'blush fiery red' (*F&P*, 62, 69–70). Also, in 'Benediction' (1920), Lois declines one of the seminarians' requests to 'show us what the shimmy is' on the basis that 'the Father Rector would send me shimmying out the gate' (*F&P*, 144). Both examples show a strange cohabitation of minimum movement with maximum impact. As with many new dances of the 1920s, the shimmy was considered risqué, and even faced various bans voted for by dancing masters across Europe and the United States, as dramatised in the Universal film *Stop That Shimmie* (1920).

Myra's performance is also consistent with a major feature of 1920s self-presentation: theatrical identity. The story calls to mind Kirk Curnutt's assessment of what he calls 'performative personality':

> Identity in the 1920s assumed an unprecedented performative dimen-
> sion [. . .]. What flappers were 'performing', of course, was an unabashed
> embrace of their sexuality. [. . .] As much as Fitzgerald celebrated perform-
> ative personality, he also cautioned against the identity confusion arising
> from its theatricality.[17]

Whilst many scholars have identified the repeated presence of performance in Fitzgerald's short fiction, this is seldom related in detail to the popular culture of the 1920s and 1930s themselves, in which performance, in all its guises, was almost ubiquitous.

As Irving Berlin's 1919 song admonishes, 'You Cannot Make Your Shimmy Shake on Tea', and the prohibition of alcohol brought with it a culture of disguise and concealment that had social and political repercussions.[18] The National Prohibition Act, or Volstead Act, of October 1919, born as an act of apparent patriotism, in fact resulted in widespread rebellion, with otherwise law-abiding citizens flouting the law and imbibing alcohol. From secreting gin in teacups to evade prohibition laws to performers in blackface makeup, and from immigrants Anglicising their names to the millions of Ku Klux Klan members (many of whom wore masks and hoods), conspicuous disguise and performance were rife.[19]

Myra's performance is one of multiple performances in the story, which is full of actors and disguise. Beyond demonstrating that she is a good sport for having the song performance unexpectedly thrust upon her and going through with it anyway, Myra's performance of the song 'Wave That Wishbone' presents her as a character who is able to take on personae and to switch between roles easily. This raises questions about who the real Myra is, and also how genuine she is, in a story that is built on the suspicion of whether or not she is a fortune hunter. She is introduced as a kind of archetypal figure: one of 'the Myras', who 'live on the Eastern colleges, as kittens live on warm milk' (*F&P*, 229). Fitzgerald describes her life as a progression of predictable actions, from attending Ivy League proms, to taking a suite at the Biltmore where 'invariably she has a somnolent mother sharing a suite with her' (*F&P*, 229). Having introduced the exemplar, Fitzgerald sees fit to introduce 'the particular Myra', Myra Harper, by giving her 'a paragraph of history'. In a playful authorial interjection that draws our attention to the literariness and therefore mimetic function of the story (another type of performance), he adds that 'I will get it over with as swiftly as possible' (*F&P*, 229). It is apparently difficult for Fitzgerald to begin to explain the real Myra, as he seems to feel that she expresses herself more effectively through the roles she plays, both wittingly and unwittingly.

Ironically, the people in the audience of Myra's impromptu recital are also actors, as she has been tricked, but Myra has the last laugh, participating in a fake wedding and then surreptitiously deserting her 'husband' on a train heading to their 'honeymoon'. It is a twist ending that has frustrated some critics whilst being celebrated by others.[20] It is only through performative personality that Myra gains the self-understanding she needs to realise that she does not want to marry Knowleton Whitney, despite his wealth and her advancing years (she has reached the grand old age of twenty-one), revealing herself – through layered role-playing – not to be a fortune hunter after all.

The twist ending recurs throughout much of Fitzgerald's early fiction, especially when the trick involves a beautiful young woman. In many of Fitzgerald's stories based around disguise motifs, the expression of the authentic self through role-playing leads to crisis. In calling upon popular culture to aid her in expressing her authentic self, Myra gives us an insight into how Fitzgerald himself was grappling with the many radical cultural changes of his time. Fitzgerald's role as animated chronicler of 'the Jazz Age' sits in tension with his anxieties about shifting moral codes and the widening gap between popular and high culture that characterised the 1920s, and we can trace his attempts to resolve this profound ambivalence towards Jazz Age popular culture in his stories written for popular magazines such as the *Saturday Evening Post*.

When Myra lands in 'an Al Jolson position', she is drawing upon shared popular knowledge of Jolson's signature move at the end of a performance, iconically captured on film in *The Jazz Singer* (1927). Jolson, born Asa Yoelson, famously appears in blackface in the film, a practice that obviously calls upon its historical use in minstrelsy to bring its complex significations into play. Myra's reference to Jolson, the Shimmy and her 'East-side snarl' all contribute to the richness of her performance, but these references also serve to demonstrate the palimpsest of past and present in the era. Even in the most modern of pursuits, like Al Jolson's crowd-pleasing song and dance routines, or the Shimmy's scandalous quivering, the American cultural practice of minstrelsy, and therefore by association, slavery, sit just below the surface, latent reminders of American entertainment's complex issues of authorship, ownership and cultural inheritance.

The American theatrical tradition of minstrelsy directly or indirectly infused much of the entertainment of the 1920s. Ann Douglas explains:

> Minstrel shows were first performed for largely white audiences by white actors in blackface who claimed to have learned their art by observing Southern blacks. Then, in the 1860s, black minstrel artists began to put on shows for white and black audiences. [. . .] But for black minstrels to succeed, they had to meet the expectations of their white audiences. [. . .] The Negro minstrel performer donned blackface himself and perforce imitated, with variations, the white performers playing, and distorting, blacks.[21]

The layers of performance and disguise are multifarious. Minstrelsy was built upon the mimicry of others for artistic and oppressive reasons and remained central to American artistic expression throughout the second half of the nineteenth century, its influence to some extent diverted into vaudeville at the turn of the twentieth century. Mimicry and impersonation were deep-rooted aspects of the nation's drive to create its own, native, art and the influence lingered on into the 1920s and 1930s, when improvisatory practice became mainstream, thanks to the influence of the new music. Repetition, ragging, variations and quotations are all essential facets of jazz in both musical and dance forms, and these techniques were appropriated by white performers and marketed to white middle-class Americans. In popular music from Tin Pan Alley and on Broadway, repetition was a major feature of the song lyrics in the period, partly to encourage sales of sheet music and, later, radio airplay. Even the film industry indulged in extensive quotation of itself, from repeated plots, to serial instalments of film franchises, and remakes of films released only a few years before. The quotation of culture was not a mutually exclusive process: black culture called upon white, as well as white drawing upon African American influences. But the power dynamics involved in a country where slavery had been abolished only fifty years before meant that cultural appropriation was of significant concern when black culture was invoked for white pleasure and profit.

As a site of 'safe' interaction with African American culture, minstrelsy was the precursor to the Harlem nightclubs of the 1920s that catered to a mainly white clientele. To enhance the theatricality of racist spectacle, many of these clubs, as Lewis Erenberg has demonstrated, created colonial and antebellum settings.[22] Though, in Paul Gilroy's phrase, 'performance was central to the process of cultural intermixture' in the United States, tracing a diachronic genealogy of such performative cultural forms is unfeasible because of the slippery synchronic and diachronic borrowings and influences that have been practised over the years.[23]

Fitzgerald, then, in his popular cultural references, is drawing upon an already 'promiscuous' set of cultural media, a set of cultural media that originates in a culture other than his own. It is hard to untangle Fitzgerald's creative decisions from the widespread cultural appropriation that is present in the period in which he was writing. His often seemingly ambivalent references further complicate the significance of his allusions. Aside from this sense of ambivalence also being characteristic of the age, as Douglas's survey of the centrality of performance and disguise demonstrates, ambivalence also serves as a strategy of black resistance in some African American cultural contexts.[24] In Fitzgerald's work, ambivalence has two major functions: it operates as a representation of his inability to reconcile his identity as an entertainer and as a 'moralist' (which itself is ineffably linked to his two identities as a commercial short storyist and a critically acclaimed novelist); and secondly, ambivalence as expressed in his literary technique, through the extensive use of disguises, personae and stereotypes, destabilises our readings of Fitzgerald because it makes it difficult to interpret his popular cultural references.[25]

'Myra', for example, opens with a description of one such stereo-type: the flapper, or to be more specific, the husband-hunter flapper. Rena Sanderson and Curnutt have both written about Fitzgerald's ambivalent portrayal of the flapper, detecting a response in which Fitzgerald both was drawn to, and recoiled from, the 'modern young woman who was spoiled, sexually liberated, self-centered, fun-loving, and magnetic'.[26] Both critics reach the conclusion that Fitzgerald ultimately feared the moral confusion that the flapper represented.[27] A major plot pattern in flapper films of the 1920s concludes with flappers being 'domesticated', the protagonists returning home after a period of hedonism in order to be married and to settle back into the established order that they had previously rebelled against. This common plot arc is visible in the film titles of the popular Joan Crawford trilogy *Our Dancing Daughters* (1928), *Our Modern Maidens* (1929) and *Our Blushing Brides* (1930). Zelda Fitzgerald, in a *McCall's* essay from October 1925, reflects on how

> the flapper has come to none of the predicted 'bad ends', but has gone at last, where all good flappers go – into the young married set, into boredom and gathering conventions and the pleasure of having children, having lent a while a splendor and courageousness and brightness to life, as all good flappers should.[28]

There is an analogue to be drawn with Scott Fitzgerald's portrayals of dance, music, musical theatre and film. He fears the moral reper-cussions of these jazzy innovations but is still irresistibly drawn towards them. However, there was no such domesticating prece-dent in these forms. In fact, ragtime dance and music had become even more wild and revolutionary by the 1920s, the First World War having instilled a new attitude of *carpe diem* opportunism in Fitzgerald's generation, and youth culture was ascendant. He cele-brates these developments at the same time as fearing the results.

In an essay published in 1931, written after the Stock Market Crash, Fitzgerald identifies satire as being symptomatic of 'the Jazz Age': 'It was an age of miracles, it was an age of art, it was an age of excess, and it was an age of satire' (*MLC*, 131). Fitzgerald enjoyed satirising this combination of excess, art and miracles, as did many of his peers such as Dorothy Parker and Ring Lardner, but it was perhaps within the African American community that satire served the most significant purpose. Satire flourished in the Harlem Renaissance, with some black writers criticising institutions and individuals in an attempt to confront the prevalence of racism in a society that increasingly prided itself on its modernity.[29] The hypocrisy of this so-called progress was borne out by the popularity of minstrelsy-infused entertainment, and the white appropriation of black culture for both entertainment and profit. Myra, who is white and from the East Coast, impersonates Jewish Al Jolson, who is in turn acting as Jakie Rabinowitz, impersonating a stereotype of an African American, singing a song, 'Mammy', about another racist archetype of an African American as imagined and shaped by whites.

To complicate this multi-layered role-playing further, we see black entertainers themselves engaging with these stereotypes, reappropriating the satirical distance in order subtly to disrupt the status quo whilst seemingly reinforcing it. Thus satire and parody operate, at face value, both as apparent endorsements of racist stereotypes, and as simultaneous strategies of black resistance when critically unravelled.[30]

Eric Lott has analysed in detail the problematic relationship between white Americans and African American culture in which white ridicule actually often represented a deep fascination with black culture that became, by the 1920s, a vital element of white American identity itself. His study of blackface minstrelsy, which emerged as a cultural practice in the early 1830s and reached its peak in the 1840s and 1850s, shows how white men 'caricatured blacks for sport and profit', mainly in the urban North, relying on 'ridicule and racist lampoon' to create entertainment thematically infused with the practice of slavery, and provide a site to 'facilitate safely an exchange of energies between two otherwise rigidly bounded and policed cultures'.[31] Parody, satire and the perpetration of stereotypes fuelled these practices. Lott suggests that

> by the 1920s an imaginary proximity to 'blackness' was so requisite to white identity and to the culture industry which helped produce that identity – witness the sudden vogue of the suntan – that the signifier of blackface had become redundant; the apposite development of forceful

public black cultural production in the Harlem Renaissance also made itself felt.[32]

Fitzgerald frequently draws upon this 'imaginary proximity to "blackness"' in his short fiction, especially in his presentation of popular culture. Michael North reconceptualises the impetus towards primitivism expressed by many white artists and writers in the pre-war years and into the 1920s as a 'rebellion through racial ventriloquism', arguing that this 'rebellion' was born of an attraction to a dialect that offered an arresting alternative to conventional expression, rather than simply as a reaction against the rapid cultural and technological changes that characterised the period.[33] North explores the ways in which artists and writers were reaching for solutions to 'the crisis of representation that Picasso purposely provoked in paintings like *Les Demoiselles d'Avignon* (1907)' and finds that figuratively reimagining themselves as black, and adopting black voices, was a defining characteristic of American culture in the 1920s.[34]

Sieglinde Lemke's assertion that 'black, or African-inspired, expressions have played a seminal role in the shaping of modernism' is upheld in Fitzgerald's choice of allusions and referents.[35] The racial politics in play for white and black entertainers show the complexities of the cultural exchanges of the period. Without a doubt, black culture was intrinsic to the shaping of a modernism that superficially presents itself as white, from Irving Berlin to Paul Whiteman, Irene and Vernon Castle to Greta Garbo. As deeply ingrained elements of African American culture, parody and satire were vital forces in the shaping of modernism, and Fitzgerald's work is no exception.

Brian Harding has suggested that in Fitzgerald's magazine writing for the *Saturday Evening Post*, Fitzgerald self-consciously parodied himself in some of his love stories, which have been habitually criticised for being 'formulaic'. Harding suggests that 'gestures towards romance that were made "for the trade" were undercut by ironies of characterization and plot' and that there is 'a tendency towards self-parody in the commercial fiction'.[36] Parody performs a wider function in Fitzgerald's work than simply assuaging the potential tedium of conforming to formulaic expectations and is in fact a central facet of Fitzgerald's literary modernism, in commercial and non-commercial stories alike.

In his references to popular culture, Fitzgerald operates on two levels: he calls upon the cultural media to demonstrate their attractiveness, their glamour and their fun; and secondly, he shows how they can be dangerous, overly relied upon and misused. As discussed above, this has usually been read as evidence of ambivalence, or as characteristic of Fitzgerald's habitual 'double vision', but a reading of these references as parodic can enhance our understanding of Fitzgerald's literary aesthetics. Parody dictates that one has a mastery of the subject being parodied, before revealing something new about it by showing it from a different or exaggerated angle. Even if it is not always intentional, this is what Fitzgerald does with his popular cultural references in his commercial short fiction.

Simon Dentith stresses that 'parody includes any cultural practice which provides a relatively polemical allusive imitation of another cultural production or practice'.[37] Fitzgerald's use of parody thus elucidates his response to certain aspects of modernity and popular culture, but his satirical eye is deployed more frequently than much current criticism acknowledges. Fitzgerald deploys parodic treatment of popular cultural forms, but also utilises self-parody, both in the short fiction, in which self-parody was sometimes a by-product of Fitzgerald's desperation to provide the popular magazines with the types of stories that had previously commanded high fees, and in the non-fiction representations of his public persona as manifested in his essays. In non-fiction pieces such as 'How to Live on $36,000 a Year' (1924) and 'How to Live on Practically Nothing a Year' (1924), Fitzgerald lampoons his own spendthrift tendencies, solidifying the Fitzgerald brand for which he had become famous at his debut: 'I was now a successful author, and when successful authors ran out of money all they had to do was to sign checks [. . .] it was impossible that I should be poor! I was living at the best hotel in New York!' (*MLC*, 28).

In a similar vein to his use of self-parody, metafictive devices are a prominent feature of Fitzgerald's modernism, and his forays into metafiction are often enriched by his use of parody. Through his parodic and self-parodic allusions, he draws attention to the conventions of short-story writing, and literature itself, and so we notice the literariness of the works, especially through comparison with the other modes of expression he draws on, such as the cultural forms examined here. In this parodic mode, Fitzgerald often writes about writing, just as professional dancers, singers and actors consciously perform their performances.

In *Terrible Honesty*, Douglas argues that 'American popular arts had originated in parody, a parody in which high European art was spoofed and replaced by low American art'.[38] Yet Fitzgerald enjoyed parodying the American popular culture of his time: to take his first full year of professional authorship, 1920, he satirises sensationalist pamphlets that condemn the modern dancing styles in his characterisation of the chorus of older women in 'Bernice Bobs Her Hair'; in 'May Day', he spoofs the craze for orchestras with unique attractions when he describes 'a famous flute-player, distinguished throughout New York for his feat of standing on his head and shimmying with his shoulders while he played the latest jazz on his flute' (*TJA*, 91); and he brutally satirises the flapper film vogue in 'The Offshore Pirate' when Ardita insolently suggests: 'Have it filmed. Wicked clubman making eyes at virtuous flapper. Virtuous flapper conclusively vamped by his lurid past. Plans to meet him at Palm Beach. Foiled by anxious uncle' (*F&P*, 8).

In addition, Fitzgerald's own writing style was itself parodied in the 1920s: in 1921, Dorothy Parker wrote a parody of the first verse of 'Old Mother Hubbard' in the style of *This Side of Paradise* (1920) for *Life* magazine; and *The Beautiful and Damned* (1922) found itself lampooned by Christopher Ward as 'Paradise Be Damned! by F. Scott Fitzjazzer' in 1923.[39] The incorporation of 'jazz' into Fitzgerald's name in Ward's piece emphasises the centrality of jazz in this period, with its multiple cultural resonances.

Fitzgerald himself deployed two modes of parody throughout his career: firstly, he adopted parodic plotting and characterisation practices that subtly undermined the formulaic constraints of magazines such as the *Saturday Evening Post*; and secondly, he embarked upon self-parody, both intentional and subconscious, in an effort to ensure his stories would continue to be sold and enjoyed, especially to the high-paying 'slicks'. The name 'slicks' derives from the glossy paper (as opposed to cheaper pulp) that the magazines were printed on. 'Slicks', especially the *Saturday Evening*

Post, were vital to Fitzgerald's livelihood as well as his literary development.[40]

The *Saturday Evening Post* was a widely circulating publication that specialised in delivering to the American public what Jan Cohn has described as 'an image, an idea, a construct of America [. . .] a model against which they could shape their lives'.[41] This model included a mixture of fiction and non-fiction articles, its glossy pages heavily punctuated by advertisements, which also contributed to the aspirational model.

Fitzgerald quickly established that the 'slicks', like the *Saturday Evening Post*, *Collier's Weekly* and *Liberty*, offered the most profitable home for his fiction and set about establishing what they enjoyed in a story, by going through back issues and noting down recurring themes and patterns.[42] He diligently completed his homework in a similar way when appointed as a screenwriter in Hollywood in the 1930s. Writing stories with a particular publication in mind, often the *Saturday Evening Post*, led to a mutually beneficial and profitable relationship, but also to great personal anxiety for Fitzgerald, who feared being known as 'only a writer of *Post* stories'.[43]

The genre of '*Post* stories' which Fitzgerald contributed to in his early career was anointed flapper 'confections' by H. L. Mencken, who published some of Fitzgerald's more heavily realistic efforts of the period in the *The Smart Set*, the magazine he edited along with George Jean Nathan.[44] Flapper 'confections' habitually made use of mistaken identity tropes or twist endings, and involved glamorous young debutantes who were courted by handsome young men.

As James West explains, the brand of 'formula story' favoured by mass-circulation magazines, of which 'flapper confections' were a subset,

> began typically with action or dialogue in order to capture the attention of a reader paging through an issue; [. . .] was rigidly plotted and moved relentlessly toward an artificial climax; and [. . .] ended with a 'final suspiration', often faintly saccharine in tone, usually in the advertising pages at the rear of the magazine.[45]

To apply West's summary to an example, Fitzgerald's story 'Two Wrongs' appeared in the *Post* on 18 January 1930. It opens with the exclamation, 'Look at those shoes,' on page 8 of the magazine, and the story continues on to page 9 before breaking and resuming on page 107, alongside an article about the Federal Government's efforts to stimulate construction and a column advertisement: '17 shades of Venus black provide the perfect pencil for the business man, the architect, engineer, artist and other craftsmen' (*TAR*, 24). After this half-page continuation, the story again pauses for a page to accommodate a full-page advertisement for Champion spark plugs, continues for another page and then is again interrupted, this time for a double-page spread advertising Philco Radios, immediately succeeded by a one-page ad for 'The New Elgin Lady Watches'. The story finally concludes on page 113, alongside a column ad for Dixon's Ticonderoga – another brand of craft pencil. The effect of these circumtextual interruptions is to disrupt the story quite significantly, and Fitzgerald is thus tasked with gaining and maintaining his readers' attention over the course of a 105-page span between the story's opening and its conclusion.

Fitzgerald organises the story in his favoured five-part struc-ture, drawing upon German novelist Gustav Freytag's 'pyramid' consisting of exposition, rising action, climax, falling action and dénouement (although Fitzgerald's sectioning of the story into parts does not necessarily correlate with Freytag's units of dramatic structure).[46] The opening of the story tells how Bill and Emmy (a producer and an aspiring actress) meet and start work on a show together. The show is declared a hit, and the 98-page break occurs. As the story continues, they are married, and the climax builds: Bill stays out all night, drunk, and Emmy goes into labour alone, tripping as she exits the cab at the hospital and losing the baby. The falling action (here ironically following a fall) describes Emmy's determination to take up dance, and the story breaks again. When it resumes, we find that Bill has been diagnosed with tuberculosis and sent to Denver for the winter to recover. The short dénouement – Part V consists of just three paragraphs – relates that by allowing Emmy to stay in New York and take up a role she has been offered in the ballet, he considers them to be even, the two wrongs of his drunken spree and her selfishness in taking the job cancelling each other out. The morose ending suggests that Bill half-hopes that he will die in Denver because that will ensure that Emmy comes back to him. The melodramatic story adheres to the fairly rigid plotting of which West complains: the patterning of job offers, deaths and ebbing vitality is neatly inverted by the story's end, and Bill's melodramatic wish for death sits incongruously next to an advertisement for pencils, inadvertently undermining the melodrama. The familiar five-part structure, encompassing Freytag's five components of drama, gives readers an anchor amid the potentially confusing and destabilising reading experience.

Many other magazine short storyists followed a similar pattern – but some followed the pattern too prescriptively and were thus were accused of producing formulaic fiction, a charge levelled at both Fitzgerald and the prolific O. Henry, who often followed the five-part structure to build towards a twist ending, as in his 1905 story, 'The Gift of the Magi'. As mentioned above, Harding's 1989 essay on the 'Radicalism of Fitzgerald's *Saturday Evening Post* Love Stories' mounts a convincing defence against such charges of structural formalism, suggesting that Fitzgerald self-consciously parodied himself through his 'ironies of characterization and plot' and use of 'the ominously happy ending', which technically fulfilled the *Post*'s requirements but allowed discerning readers to appreciate their ironic nuances.[47]

As early as the mid-1920s, Fitzgerald began to resent the stigma attached to being a successful '*Post*' author. He felt that this label meant his stories would be automatically judged as being formulaic and conceived of himself prostituting out his talent. His famously vivid grumble, in a letter to Ernest Hemingway of September 1929, recounted that 'the *Post* now pay the old whore $4000. a screw. But now its [sic] because she's mastered the 40 positions – in her youth one was enough.'[48] Read in isolation, this is a damning indictment of the short story market – both magazine editors and readerships – as he rails at them for the prostitution of literary talent. But read in context, it appears as a postscript to a letter in which Fitzgerald confesses to 'nervous depressions', 'moods of despair' and 'collaps[ing] about 11.00 [. . .] with the tears flowing from my eyes or the gin rising to their level and leaking over'. Hemingway, his old friend and rival, had sent him the promising typescript of his novel *A Farewell to Arms* in June, and Fitzgerald, who had not published a novel since *The Great Gatsby* in April 1925, was understandably feeling frustrated and depressed. This was the context in which his dismissive boast appeared.

Elsewhere, he sometimes accords his story-writing higher esteem. In any case, by the mid-1930s, he struggled to produce this 'formulaic' fiction that had appealed to the *Post*'s editors in the peak years of his close association with the magazine, between 1925 and 1933. Seven months before his death in December 1940, he wrote to Zelda:

> As soon as I feel I am writing to a cheap specification my pen freezes and my talent vanishes over the hill and I honestly don't blame them for not taking the things that I've offered to them from time to time in the past three or four years. An explanation of their new attitude is that you no longer have a chance of selling a story with an unhappy ending (in the old days many of mine *did* have unhappy endings – if you remember). In fact the standard of writing from the best movies, like Rebecca, is believe it or not, much higher at present than that in the commercial magazines such as Collier's and the Post.[49]

Ironically, whilst Fitzgerald chided himself for being unable to write 'to a cheap specification', the Chekhovian model of story favoured by writers such as James Joyce and Sherwood Anderson was becoming increasingly commonplace, and was also accused of being formulaic, despite its association with literary modernism. According to Charles May, 'the inconclusive incident and the unresolved impasse' became customary features of what many critics regarded as 'a new formula to replace the old trick-ending story of O. Henry'.[50] Fitzgerald was undoubtedly influenced by O. Henry, and yet, despite charges of being hackneyed, Fitzgerald actually parodied himself innovatively in his short fiction.

O. Henry (William Sydney Porter) was a prolific short storyist born in 1862 and living until 1910, at one point producing a short story every week for the New York *World*. He is famous for his frequent use of the trick ending, in which a plot twist occurs. This fame was cemented by the many imitators who seized upon the surprise ending as the fundamental feature of 'the O. Henry story'.[51] What is less often remembered is his virtuosic grasp of rhetorical devices, his humour, and his sensitive portrayals of multiple strata of life. O. Henry's stories usually involve simple plots that are none the less carefully constructed to feed into their habitual 'sting in the tail' twist endings, which, along with his fast rate of production, inevitably necessitated some repetition and reuse of plot, setting and character.

O. Henry's style of writing contrasts greatly with the short stories of his contemporary, Anton Chekhov, who was born two years before O. Henry, in 1860 and who died in 1904. Chekhov's stories are most frequently described as 'plotless'. They explore the stasis between character and action in the seemingly mundane lives of ordinary people. This leads to an interrogation of the properties of language itself, as well as to an exploration of the episodic nature of experience, which, taken together, are fundamental concerns of later writers such as Joyce, Hemingway and Sherwood Anderson. The plotless Chekhovian model was in large part a reaction to the modern condition in which artists turned inward to depict interior experiences of reality rather than demonstrating a reliance on social authority over phenomenological factors. Though Chekhov's first collection of short stories was published in 1884, around twenty years before Joyce finished the stories that would eventually be published as *Dubliners*, Chekhov's short stories shared many concerns with this group of authors and their influence was felt by Fitzgerald for his whole career: he recommended that Zelda read Chekhov's story 'The Darling' (1899) in a letter of May 1940, six months before he died.[52]

Drawing upon both of these schools, Fitzgerald combined the use of so-called 'formulaic' constructed plots favoured by O. Henry, complete with forays into trick endings, with a new, modernist emphasis on introspection and an interrogation of the possibilities that were inherent in the form of the short story itself. Of course, Fitzgerald's style varied over the course of his career, between his more commercial, traditional, fiction that was published in the 'slicks' (mainly the *Saturday Evening Post*) in the period between 1920 and 1934, and his later fiction, from 1934 to 1940, which was published in several magazines, leading up to an almost-exclusive association with *Esquire* from 1936 to 1940. Early stories such as 'The Camel's Back' (1920) and 'The Popular Girl' (1922) utilise plot twists and other 'formulaic' devices, whilst a Chekhovian lack of plot can be identified in later stories, such as 'Thank You for the Light' (1936) and 'The Lost Decade' (1939), but later stories also make use of formulae, like the Pat Hobby series of stories (1940–1).

Milton Stern argues that the modernist movement generally used irony to 'replace . . . coincidence, contrived twist, and dramatic convenience', but, in stories such as 'The Swimmers' (1929), we can see Fitzgerald straddling both schools of thought, where coincidences coexist with modernist synaesthesia like 'that very blue color of four o'clock' (*TAR*, 236). He uses, in Stern's terms, 'conventional and chronological development of narrative progress', and does not exclusively focus on the 'episodic and epiphanic nature of experience', but his use of irony is extremely important in understanding the intertextual dialogue that took place in the 1920s and 1930s between Fitzgerald and other modernists' attempts to confront modernity.[53] Fitzgerald's use of irony, parody and satire, particularly in his depictions of popular culture, is vital to an understanding of his modernist aesthetics, though it is often obscured or even latent.

Although his use of parody is often obscured, Fitzgerald's authorial persona is frequently visible in his fiction. Certain of Fitzgerald's peers – for instance, Ernest Hemingway – often tried to eliminate authorial presence so as to provide no intervention between the reader and character and to retain an objectivity in their presentations. A reader is rarely able to gauge how the author feels about their subjects. Fitzgerald, however, enjoys using omniscient narrators, who interject, comment on the action and break the fourth wall on occasion. This is especially true of his early fiction. For example, in 'The Smilers' (1920), Fitzgerald introduces Sylvester Stockton in a playfully irreverent way: 'Accusing eyes behind spectacles – suggestion of a stiff neck – this will have to do for his description, since he is not the hero of this story' (*F&P*, 254). He creates a lively rapport with the readership which was useful in a popular magazine context, where his authorial voice was a valuable commodity to sustain readers' attention across a potentially disruptive reading experience.

Rather than trying to cloak his authorial presence, Fitzgerald chooses to make a feature of it in his work, especially enjoying metafictive asides in his early work. Famously, he wrote that 'the test of a first-rate intelligence is the ability to hold two opposed ideas in the mind at the same time, and still retain the ability to function' (*MLC*, 139). Cowley succinctly calls it Fitzgerald's 'double vision'.[54] The object of this narrative stance is to ensure the reader's simultaneous emotional immersion and objectivity. This is a pervasive image in the stories themselves – for example, Dexter Green in 'Winter Dreams' (1922) is both within and without the world he aspires to. This division of self results in dramatic tension, but also a unique authorial point of view. The image of the poor boy looking through the window at the prom is a poignant one that Fitzgerald revisits in various stories, conferring a universal status on the cast of poor boys yearning after rich girls that mark them out as identifiably Fitzgeraldian.

Andy, the narrator of 'The Last of the Belles' (1929), comes to represent not just himself, but all of the many suitors of Ailie Calhoun, and indeed all of the Belles: through Fitzgerald's rendering, he becomes archetypal. Fitzgerald poignantly ends the story with Andy's acceptance that he cannot relive the past: 'I stumbled here and there in the knee-deep underbrush, looking for my youth in a clapboard or a strip of roofing or a rusty tomato can.' Andy contemplates how 'in another month Ailie would be gone, and the South would be empty for me forever' (*TAR*, 66). This bittersweet self-knowledge is also common to Fitzgerald's 'poor suitor' set of characters, and through Fitzgerald's lyricism, as well as the abbreviated form of the short story, Andy's experiences take on an aura of universality. This use of symbolism is a prominent feature of the modernist short story.

In criticism of the modernist short story, the form has often been deemed to be an ideal conduit for modernist innovation, and cited as innately representative of episodic experiences of modernity.[55] Modernists' interest in the possibilities of symbolism are accommodated by the short form, which, as many critics repeat, implies the typicality of a specific episode, and the ensuing compression demands use of image and symbol, which are more economic methods of narrative exposition, to suit the abbreviated form.[56]

Echoing earlier critics, Heidi Kunz Bullock finds Fitzgerald's portrayal of Southern belle Ailie Calhoun to be ultimately satirical.[57] Ailie's entrance into the story, on 'the obligatory white-pillared, vine-covered veranda', sets the scene for a cavalcade of Southern 'clichés appropriated from popular fiction and regional convention'.[58] The narrator's proclamation, 'There she was – the Southern type in all its purity' (*TAR*, 51), recalls the introduction of Myra as an archetype, but here Ailie fails to assert the individuality that would emancipate her from such a stereotype. Unlike Myra, who rebels against her label, Ailie's 'mythic stature' renders her vulnerable to misreadings: when Andy laments that 'the South would be empty for me forever', his metonymic use of Ailie as a representative of the South leaves her open to the projection of meanings on to her (*TAR*, 66). Such deciphering misses the distinctly satirical note with which Ailie is presented in the story. Bullock convincingly argues that 'Like Andy, everybody "knows" that Ailie Calhoun is "The Last of the Belles" – until Fitzgerald's satire reminds us that, like Andy, nobody really knows Ailie'.[59] In 1929, the South is empty for Andy, but this parallel, satirical reading shows how the golden girl flapper, especially in her irresistible Southern incarnation, has evolved a great deal since her outings as Myra and Ardita. Both losses are difficult blows to bear, and this sense of bittersweet nostalgia pervades many of Fitzgerald's stories. Aside from the golden girl flapper figure, others who are given the self-parodic treatment include showgirls and blues singers, socially mobile young heroes, and filmmakers.

Like many other literary modernists, Fitzgerald was influenced by developments in other art forms, such as the collage aesthetic in fine art and the legacy of vaudeville, mixing these influences with aspects of his modernist literary sensibilities to explore the potential of the short story form. In Fitzgerald's œuvre, modernist short story features are deployed on a regular basis. For example, plastic spatiality and the abandonment of temporality are explored in stories like 'Babylon Revisited' (1931), where the past and present exist in a precarious palimpsest, constantly threatening to collapse into each other. Similarly, in 'The Ice Palace' (1920), the South is temporarily psychically transplanted into the North, with disastrous results. These two stories have recourse to musical references to achieve these spatial and temporal effects. Another common theme of the modernist short story – loneliness in an increasingly competitive society – is extensively explored by

Fitzgerald in the stories which depict Hollywood, such as 'Jacob's Ladder' (1927), 'Magnetism' (1928) and the Pat Hobby stories (1940–1). Dislocation from collective experience is often present in stories that contain dance-floor scenes, which cultivate a sense of social belonging and exclusion experienced by characters in stories such as 'Dice, Brassknuckles and Guitar' (1923) and 'The Perfect Life' (1929). Additionally, moments of epiphany are also often provoked by popular culture: for example, in 'The Ice Palace', where Sally Carrol realises that she has made a mistake whilst watching a vaudeville performance of 'Dixie' at a Minnesotan theatre, and in 'Emotional Bankruptcy' (1931), when Josephine Perry realises her incapacity to feel love, only an hour after she had been 'singing for the first time in weeks' (*BJG*, 282). Songs themselves can function as episodic micro-narratives embedded within the stories. Fitzgerald interrogates the value and purposes of popular culture, exploring authorship and the function of art in a modern world in which sensibilities had been drastically altered in the wake of the First World War. Fitzgerald employs the figures of the dancer, the musician, the songwriter and the filmmaker in order to explore his own role as an author who courted both critical acclaim and popular success. Fitzgerald calls upon all of these popular cultural forms to explore these modernist aspects of the short story.

Working within the constraints of his commercial employers (whilst playing to his strengths as a literary craftsman), Fitzgerald achieves many modernist aims. He interrogates authorship and choreography, questioning the purpose of art in a modern world in his representations of dance in his short fiction. The episodic and epiphanic experience of modern life is encapsulated in the micro-narratives of quoted songs and musical theatre allusions in his stories. His representations of film show him exploring the juxtapositional marriage of visual, auditory and linguistic art, as well as interrogating the relationship between art and commerce in a modern mass-market setting.

Fitzgerald renders the extravagance of his characters to examine how money affects morality, and he repeatedly explores the dangers inherent in the conflation of the material and the spiritual. His world is filled with natural and manufactured objects that he can use as symbols to convey emotion, and in the magazine contexts of his stories, his characters were likewise surrounded (on the page) by advertisements for consumer goods and services.

Several of Fitzgerald's contemporary critics fashioned an opposition between Fitzgerald's style and the commercial medium of his short fiction, invoking the emotive language of volition and 'dignity' to imply that Fitzgerald's style was suited to loftier climes than the *Saturday Evening Post* and the other slicks. Reviewing the 1926 collection, *All the Sad Young Men*, Frances Newman laments, 'Mr. Fitzgerald is really a poet himself, and [. . .] only the twentieth century could have forced him into the more profitable medium of prose.'[60] His 'mastery of style', according to another reviewer, this time of *Taps at Reveille* (1935), 'swift, sure, polished, firm – is so complete that even his most trivial efforts are dignified by his technical competence'.[61] Evidently, for most of his career, Fitzgerald was capable of achieving the double aim of satisfying the demands of his marketplace and developing his own distinctive and appealing literary style.

Riddled with parody, ambiguities and narrative experiments, Fitzgerald's stories consistently use songs, music, dances and film references to destabilise our expectations of his lyrical style, and the conventions of the magazine short story itself, such as when, at the end of 'The Offshore Pirate' (1920), the heroine Ardita is described 'reaching up on her tiptoes [and] kissing [Curtis] softly in the illustration' (*F&P*, 35). The impact of popular culture on Fitzgerald's stories is both thematic and formal, the formal aspects often being bound up in performance. He takes the classical ballet position of the arabesque and transforms it into a conceptual motif linking disparate time frames and bridging high and low culture. He reimagines the flapper archetype time and time again, creating a thematic syncopation of his own golden girl figure that is comparable to the musical practice of ragging so enjoyed by these same flappers. He imports filmic technique into his stories, utilising close-ups, soundtracks and dream sequences to show how daily life is a theatrical experience. Invoking these popular cultural forms, Fitzgerald meditates upon the possibilities of each medium.

With these literary, cultural and publishing contexts in mind, each of the chapters that follow will explore Fitzgerald's contrapuntal short story prose, examining in turn how he uses ragtime and jazz dance, popular music, musicals and film references to subvert our expectations of a commercial short story, at the same time as scrutinising popular culture by deploying the parodic mode that was so central to his modernist literary aesthetics.

CHAPTER 1

'Dancing Modern Suggestive Dances that are Simply Savagery': Fitzgerald and Ragtime Dance

'There were couples dancing flat-footed in the corner to a phonograph record made by Rastus Muldoon's Savannah Band; there were couples stalking a slow Chicago with a Memphis sideswoop solemnly around the room' (*TJA*, 463).[1] Jim Powell, protagonist of Fitzgerald's 1923 story, 'Dice, Brassknuckles and Guitar', named his dance academy after three of the courses offered alongside dance lessons. This quotation exemplifies the need for annotation within scholarly editions of Fitzgerald's works. Who is Rastus Muldoon? And what is the difference between a slow Chicago and a Memphis Sideswoop? These details are important: they establish the socio-cultural milieu in which we find these characters, and as a 'social realist', in Matthew Bruccoli's phrase, Fitzgerald was constantly drawn to the popular culture of the 1920s and 1930s in his fiction.[2] He was especially interested in leisure activities: popular music, musical theatre, film, dance and sport references litter his stories. When Fitzgerald refers to the musical *The Midnight Sons* in 'The Captured Shadow' (1928), his contemporary audience would presumably have known that the famous British dancer Vernon Castle is one of the 'three men in evening clothes and opera hats sauntering jovially along Broadway' (*BJG*, 101). For the modern reader, these references need to be teased out for a full appreciation of Fitzgerald's artistry, and to ensure that Fitzgerald's own playfully stated aim of writing 'for the youth of his own generation, the critics of the next, and the schoolmasters of ever afterwards' is fulfilled.[3]

James West has written about the difficulties associated with annotating Fitzgerald's works, since Fitzgerald clearly intends for his readers to appreciate his references to song lyrics, dances, films and celebrities, but identification is the tip of the iceberg, and the particular resonance Fitzgerald was reaching for by selecting a reference often lies dormant within the annotations. Although determining Fitzgerald's intentions presents West with an unwelcome (and editorially precarious) task, investigation of these reference points yields new readings. West writes of his difficulties in deciding how much readers needed to know about the references he had identified, but he also had to consider more practical factors such as the number of pages the publisher would print, as well as the anticipated shelf-life of the editions in libraries around the world. Tasked with taking over as general editor of the Cambridge Edition of Fitzgerald's works, West began with a conservative strategy focused only on elucidating lost references with facts, and over the past twenty years has gradually moved towards notes which flirt with literary analysis. In his later editions, from the year 2000 onwards, he has 'slipped in a few hints about how a reference might illuminate a passage'.[4]

West's explanatory note glossing the above quotation from 'Dice, Brassknuckles and Guitar' reads: 'These steps and styles of dancing . . . were southern dances, often of African American origin, performed to jazz or ragtime music.'[5] Indeed, 'flat-footed' dancing was a Southern phenomenon, which evolved into flatfoot tapdancing. Combined with the Savannah Band, the dance's Dixie origins are clearly presented. The reader is thus shown that Jim Powell is introducing Southern musical and dance influences to his prosperous Hamptons students. The slow Chicago, a bluesy slow dance actually born in Harlem, has its Northeastern roots violated by the Memphis Sideswoop, a kick and dip step which originated in New Orleans. The name Rastus Muldoon combines a common Irish surname with a reference to the racist portrayal of an African American character named Rastus, who is lazy and unreliable, in a series of films from 1910 to 1917.[6]

In his study of the five mythic types of stereotypical African American characters portrayed in film, Donald Bogle identifies the Rastus figure as belonging to the 'coon' racist stereotype: 'Those unreliable, crazy, lazy, subhuman creatures good for nothing more than eating watermelons, stealing chickens, shooting crap, or butchering the English language.'[7] Fitzgerald's Rastus is certainly meant to evoke the stereotypically racist Rastus of the 1910–17 film shorts, but his Irish surname renders him representative of both racial otherness and immigrant stock. In a letter of 1933 to John O'Hara, Fitzgerald described his own family heritage as 'half black Irish and half old American stock'; though 'black' here refers to brunette and dark-eyed Irish, it is clear that Fitzgerald identified with the ethnic outsider, as Michael Nowlin has argued.[8]

Fitzgerald's seemingly innocuous scene-setting reveals an artist who is conscious of the influence of new cultural developments upon modernist aesthetics. Jim Powell's dance school is a place where the African American band facilitates dancing, which in turn is inspired by dance steps originating in African American communities. What initially appears to be a description of couples dancing modern dances in a room is actually a complex interplay between North and South, showing imitative identity in action. The description is subtly critical of the popular trends: the somnambulant dancers fail to live up to the Fitzgeraldian stereotype of flaming youth, instead embodying the move from individualist craftsmanship to production-line philosophy popularised by Henry Ford's ideas on mass production which filtered down into the arts. Felicia McCarren has explored this intersection between philosophies of work and the arena of leisure. In *Dancing Machines: Choreographies of the Age of Mechanical Reproduction*, she analyses the 'fragmented gesture' of modern dance as performed by artists such as Josephine Baker, in the context of 'the European Science of work and American Taylorism', finding that Baker's 'clowning' and riffing on industrial streamlined and optimised gesture can be read 'as a parody of modern times: imitating the frenzy of the assembly line; mimicking the chorus-line engine; dancing the human motor that made these industry and entertainment teams run' (Figure 1.1).[9]

The relationship between machines and the new jazz dances was complex, but the most important common ground they occupied was their democratising drive along with their very novelty. Sieglinde Lemke asserts that 'modernist aesthetics and the assembly line were often conflated in the popular imagination', and Ann

1.1 Josephine Baker and Joe Alex perform the 'Danse Sauvage' at *La Revue Nègre* (Paris, 1927), and Baker rotates like a cogwheel.

Douglas compares the cabaret revues of Broadway in the 1920s to 'the new accelerated assembly lines'.[10] As Ford's production lines began to displace individual craftsmanship, dances and music that were once improvisatory began to be packaged and prepared for the mass market, through mechanistic standardisation of organic dance steps via dance manuals, as well as instruction films and advice columns in newspapers and magazines. During the peak of Vernon Castle's fame, from 1912 to 1916, 'the cabaret and the dance craze extended the leisure patterns of the very wealthy to the middle class and to the Americanized children of the immigrants'.[11] Vernon and his wife Irene's packaging of their dances as refined, almost aristocratic, yet accessible to all for the cost of entering a *thé dansant* or a cabaret contrasted with the lower-class, African American origins of the new dances the Castles were advocating.

In the early 1920s, Fitzgerald persistently uses descriptions associating 'savage' or 'primitive' impulses with modern dance, and this is symptomatic of wider criticism in the 1920s of dances of African American origin. In Fitzgerald's description of Jim Powell's dancing school, the pervasive influence of African American-derived music and dance manifests itself in lazy, entranced shuffling rather than the hot-blooded and frantically sexualised 'vulgar' movements pamphleteers had warned against. In the version of 'Dice, Brassknuckles and Guitar' that appears in the *Saturday Evening Post*, Fitzgerald makes clear that the parents disapprove of his school. They accuse Jim of running 'a bar and – and *opium* den for children!' They go on to exclaim, 'you have colored men around! You have colored girls hidden!' (*TJA*, 467).[12] By the early 1920s, it was clear that Harlem was to be the centre of African American artistic innovation during this decade, which worries these wealthy WASP parents, who fear their children were practising what Basil, the protagonist of 'The Perfect Life' (1929), condemns as 'modern suggestive dances that are simply savagery' (*BJG*, 134).

It is Jim Powell's African American manservant, Hugo, who provides him with his teaching materials, which Powell then markets under his own name. The appropriation and labelling of black culture by white performers and spectators were not unique to the 1920s, but the new influence of Freud's theories, resonant in the United States during this decade, prompted a reconsideration of the primitive and the civilised. Douglas explains the dissonance inherent in white Americans' labelling of African Americans:

> It is one thing to be in search of the 'primitive,' as white artists of the 1920s were; another thing to be told, as the black New Yorkers were, that you *are* the primitive, the savage 'id' of Freud's new psychoanalytic discourse, trailing clouds of barbaric, prehistoric, preliterate 'folk' culture wherever you go.[13]

The concept of 'primitivist modernism', as established by Sieglinde Lemke, explores the racial dimensions and intercultural exchanges at the heart of European and American modernism and offers a reading of modernism and primitivism as 'accomplices'. This coexistence encourages us to interrogate racist assumptions such as those linking African Americans to the performing arts, whilst at once asking how modern trends such as ragtime dances can be considered simultaneously hyper-modern and primitive.[14]

Using Irene and Vernon Castle as an example, I first explore the appeal of the ragtime dance craze, which launched a model of self-improvement and a performative identity that have become defining features of early twentieth-century popular culture. The backlash against the modern dances from the social reform movement, and Fitzgerald's portrayal of both sides of the modern dance debate in his short fiction are considered. This raises important questions about the status of primitivist modernism in the early twentieth century. Indeed, in Josephine Baker's modern dance, Fitzgerald identifies the intersection of performative identity and primitivist modernism. I then examine the ways in which Fitzgerald deploys self-parodic currents in his characterisation of several of his memorable flapper heroines, and I argue that this can be read as a manifestation of Fitzgerald's frustration with the constraints of popular magazine short story conventions.

Irene and Vernon Castle:
'The Tall Englishman and the Girl in the Dutch Cap'

Jim Powell's dancing school in 'Dice, Brassknuckles and Guitar' was inspired by establishments such as Castle House, the dancing school opposite the Ritz-Carlton Hotel in New York City, opened in 1914 by Vernon and Irene Castle, 'the Tall Englishman and the Girl in the Dutch Cap' (*BJG*, 129). Businesses such as these were extremely profitable, cashing in on the desire of thousands of people who wanted to keep up to date with the new dances. Paula Fass has explored the shift in early 1920s youth culture from one imitative of the previous generation, to one that looked to peers for models of behaviour. This shift coincides with a younger generation who had an unprecedented amount of leisure time to fill: the telephone, the car, the cinema and the dancehall offered young adults new means of self-expression. Fass explores the emphasis on homogeneity amongst this group, with peer culture stressing the importance of conformity.[15] This ascendency of youth culture developed subsequent to what Ann Douglas has called 'the feminization of American culture' – an unprecedented increase in women's influence and representation in the public sphere at the end of the nineteenth century.[16] The flapper represented the intersection of these two phenomena. Initially seen as a radical departure from conformity, the rebellion of flappers who smoked, drank, wore short dresses and were sexually liberated quickly became widespread. Conformity was again the victor, and the popularity of the flapper can be gleaned from Fitzgerald's letters and essays. Declaring her 'over' as early as 1922, Fitzgerald none the less felt pressured into producing stories featuring flappers throughout the decade, despite complaining to his agent and his editor multiple times.[17] There were other reasons for Fitzgerald's concerns beyond fearing being typecast: he grew increasingly ambivalent towards his fêted flappers. As Rena Sanderson has established, he feared 'that the flapper embodied not freedom but moral anarchy and lack of direction'.[18] These concerns are still visible in the Basil and Josephine stories, written almost a decade after his first flapper characters appeared.

Kathleen Drowne has written about how the flapper, as a widespread stereotype, served as the scapegoat for myriad cultural anxieties of the period. Far removed from the previous ideal of beauty and sophistication, the corseted, full-skirted Gibson Girl, the flapper's irreverence was both refreshing and threatening: 'sometimes portrayed as the saviour of modern womanhood, and other times as the harbinger of cultural decline'.[19] Newly visible in the public sphere thanks to the culture of women joining their beaux at *thé dansants*, cabarets, and nightclubs, the work of the Castles and other professional dancers encouraged the transition of dancing from the private arena of the ballroom into the public eye. Fitzgerald portrayed these transitional years in 'The Perfect Life' (1929), which is set immediately prior to the First World War, when the flapper was ascendant and the Castles' fame was at its peak.

The story is seventh in the series of nine stories that follow the exploits of Basil Duke Lee, a young Minnesotan who bears a striking resemblance to Fitzgerald himself during his St Paul adolescence. In 'The Perfect Life', Fitzgerald satirises the critics of dance who wrote sensationalist articles such as 'Where is Your Daughter This Afternoon?' and 'From the Ballroom to Hell', when Basil is accosted by an alumnus of his prep school and beseeched to give up all morally imperfect activities and encourage others to live 'the perfect life' free from smoking, drinking and dancing.[20] Basil proceeds evangelically to spread this moral syllabus, alienating his friends as he preaches, but eventually he relents in order to win the affections of a love interest.

During the story, Basil and the object of his affection, Jobena, visit Castle House for an afternoon of dancing, but Basil studiously avoids the modern dances in favour of Waltzes and Tangoes: the former because of its comfortingly Victorian formality, and the Tango on the basis that it is Spanish and therefore a form of cultural exploration rather than a modern American sexualised abomination.[21] The dances popular in the Victorian era had reassuring rules to follow, and fixed patterns of social etiquette, inherited and modified from previous generations, whereas most of the modern dances had grown out of unfamiliar, African-influenced traditions, and were built around improvisation, with fragmentary rather than regimented routines. This transition from the Victorian to the modern era is metafictively on display in Fitzgerald's work. Some of his magazine fiction has been accused of being formulaic, as it was written for specific audiences (usually the readership of a popular magazine, such as the *Saturday Evening Post*), and can be read as following specific rules of structure and characterisation.[22] But Fitzgerald does employ many modernist features in his fiction, as well as incorporating several innovative literary techniques. In 'Dice, Brassknuckles and Guitar' Fitzgerald even subverts the narrative voice, breaking the fourth wall and commenting 'Now if this were a moving picture (as, of course, I hope it will someday be) I would take as many thousand feet of her as I was allowed' (*TJA*, 278). Fitzgerald knows what the magazine rules are but chooses to challenge them, just as Jobena chooses to break with the Victorian propriety of the Waltz in favour of the new dances. Even clothes followed this rebellious pattern: the 'long, cruel corsets' and restrictive hobble skirts of the Victorian period gave way to 'a girdle-like corset with elastic' and 'skirts [which] are subtly cut so that they fall freely', as Irene Castle explains in their 1914 manual, *Modern Dancing*.[23] Social critics feared that modern dances heralded sexual dangers, especially for working-class women in urban, unchaperoned dancehalls.[24] The new dancing postures of ragtime dances such as the Turkey Trot, Grizzly Bear and Bunny Hug delighted in all of the prohibited physical movements the Castles legislated against in *Modern Dancing*.

The Castles' clientele was a mixture of high society and the upper middle classes: 'Vernon and Irene's glamour drew old and young alike,' as long as they could afford the $2 ($3 on Friday or Saturday) admission charge.[25] The Castles gave their patrons a means of perpetuating the social ritual of European ballroom dances but with modern ragtime music, combined with strict codes of conduct and insistence on desexualised bodily movement. The pictorial demonstration of the Tango from *Modern Dancing* (Figure 1.2) depicts the

1.2 'The Tango of To-Day', from *Modern Dancing* (1914), 36.

Castles with poker-straight backs, Vernon's hands by his sides and Irene's low on her hips, with no contact between them whatsoever, and the only aspect of the picture which deviates from the vertical line of their bodies is their nearside legs, which are neatly deployed at a 30-degree angle, parallel to each other with no contact. The only intimacy suggested by the image is his intense gaze, which is directed at her face. Irene, haughtily as a Fitzgerald heroine, and sporting her signature 'Dutch cap', avoids Vernon's gaze, staring directly into the camera lens. This pose was carefully choreographed so as to assuage objections by social reformers who felt that the new ragtime dances amounted to a threat to social order. Ragtime dancing 'was judged as "indecent" and "vulgar" for the kind of wiggling, shaking, swaying and pivoting motions it permitted', according to Susan C. Cook.[26] The 'Castle House Suggestions for Correct Dancing' (Figure 1.3) address these concerns, advocating the strict avoidance of any such 'wriggl[ing]' and 'twist[ing]'.

CASTLE HOUSE SUGGESTIONS
FOR CORRECT DANCING

Do not wriggle the shoulders.
Do not shake the hips.
Do not twist the body.
Do not flounce the elbows.
Do not pump the arms.
Do not hop—glide instead.
Avoid low, fantastic, and acrobatic dips.
Stand far enough away from each other to allow free movement of the body in order to dance gracefully and comfortably.
The gentleman should rest his hand lightly against the lady's back, touching her with the finger-tips and wrist only, or, if preferred, with the inside of the wrist and the back of the thumb.
The gentleman's left hand and forearm should be held up in the air parallel with his body, with the hand extended, holding the lady's hand lightly on his palm. The arm should never be straightened out.
Remember you are at a social gathering, and not in a gymnasium.
Drop the Turkey Trot, the Grizzly Bear, the Bunny Hug, etc. These dances are ugly, ungraceful, and out of fashion.

1.3 Irene and Vernon Castle's 'Suggestions' for correct dancing technique, from *Modern Dancing* (1914), 177.

The Castles sought to 'uplift dancing, purify it, and place it before the public in its proper light', as they explained in the Foreword to *Modern Dancing*:

> When this has been done, we feel convinced that no objection can possibly be urged against it on the grounds of impropriety but rather that social reformers will join with the medical profession in the view that dancing is not only a rejuvenator of good health and spirits, but a means of preserving youth, prolonging life, and acquiring grace, elegance, and beauty.[27]

This promise of health, vitality and beauty significantly differs from contemporary discourse on dance which adopts a lexis of disease. The pre-war years were a dance 'craze'. Young Americans had gone 'dance mad', and the epidemic was spread through close physical contact such as that which the Castles warned against, lest it cause the dancers to become infected with dance 'fever'. Cook links social reformers' concerns with changes to the growing urban population: 'As ragtime dance was initially seen as a product of urban and largely immigrant working-class population, this discourse of dance pathology perpetuated notions of the growing "immigrant menace."'[28] Approximately 28 million immigrants arrived in the United States between 1880 and 1920, an influx that led the Harding administration to respond with the 1921 Emergency Quota Act and the Immigration Act of 1924, which severely limited European immigration, and effectively prohibited Middle Eastern and Asian immigration. The concern with foreign influence on modern dancing extended to the African American origins of most modern dances. From 1915 to 1930, around 1.5 million African Americans moved north, in what became known as the Great Migration, and in the 1920s, African Americans populated urban centres in hitherto unseen numbers, in what Douglas has called 'a seismic sociological shift'; ragtime and jazz music (and dance) spread around the country, North and South.[29]

Fitzgerald depicted the spectrum of responses felt by the critics, as well as practitioners of the modern dances, in his portrayal of dancers in his short stories. He details how they danced themselves ill, provoking predictions that they would dance themselves to death (in the 1920 story 'Bernice Bobs Her Hair'); they danced into ghostly states (in 'The Offshore Pirate', also 1920); and they danced into the semblance of being under, or even casting, a witch-doctor's spell (as seen in both 'The Offshore Pirate' and the 1928 story 'The Scandal Detectives'). It is Ardita of 'The Offshore Pirate' who exclaims how the natives of the mysterious island she has been kidnapped and taken to would not approve of her dancing: 'I'll bet the cannibal women are saying that we dance too close, and that it was immodest of me to come without my nose-ring' (*F&P*, 30). She is powerless to resist dancing, and enchantment and compulsion occupy related lexical sets in Fitzgerald's presentation of dance.

Disease and enchantment punctuate Fitzgerald's dance descriptions with the regularity of the syncopated beat which provokes the dances, and heroines from Amanthis in 'Dice, Brassknuckles and Guitar' to Imogene in the Basil story 'He Thinks He's Wonderful' (1928) all exclaim the impossibility of sitting still and resisting the urge to dance when the orchestra is playing a rag. This notion of spontaneous movement echoes Vernon Castle's own description of how the rhythm of ragtime affected him: '"When a good orchestra plays a 'rag' one has simply *got* to move" he confessed.'[30] In the early 1920s, the word 'jazz' became interchangeable with 'ragtime' when referring to the new music. Thus when Ardita hears 'the sound of weird ragtime . . . drifting softly over on the warm breath of the night', there is no contradiction when she goes on to exclaim 'I can't sit still with that perfect jazz going on' (*F&P*, 27, 29). In 'Presumption' (1926), Noel Garneau hears 'a tune they had danced to' and 'the wings of a trance folded about her' (*ASM*, 254). Although there is an 'inscrutable someone who waited always in the middle distance . . . with . . . dark romantic eyes' looming over her, Noel's reaction to the music is machine-like and she is compelled to engage with the car she is in: 'Almost mechanically, she started the engine and slipped the gear into first' (*ASM*, 254). This recalls the vogue for Tayloristic chorus lines and mechanistic dance troupes such as the precision-orientated Tiller Girls, who Zelda (presumably along with Scott Fitzgerald) saw perform in May 1921 at the Folies Bergère in Paris, pasting the programme for the show into her scrapbook. By 1915, Jayna Brown writes, 'hundreds of women danced in perfect unison, forming a corridor of mirrors, the poetic reflection of the avenues of the city, the factory assembly lines, and the military maneuvers of marching soldiers'.[31] For Fitzgerald, whether dancers were mechanistic or were enchanted, the physical compulsion provoked by ragtime and jazz music was the same. This compulsion is often related to the music's African American roots, in order to describe dancers who are enchanted, in both senses of the word. Girls like Marcia Meadows in 'Head and Shoulders' (1920) have lost control of themselves, and are seemingly being controlled by another, whether in the witch-doctor metaphors or through the African American provenance of the music; Fitzgerald conflates the two. Cook summarises the social ramifications feared by dance reformers:

> Ragtime dance – like TB – spread through touch. And its music held the potential to cause this very bodily response to take place. Thus at the heart of the matter was the ultimate fear of touch and contact – the mixing of blood, of miscegenation.[32]

This fear was reflected by the eugenicist movement's concerns with the prevention of inter-racial breeding, as well as breeding amongst those deemed unfit, and the avoidance of 'race suicide', a pseudo-scientific concept which was famously built upon by Lothrop Stoddard in his 1920 book, *The Rising Tide of Color Against White World-Supremacy*, parodied in 1925 by Fitzgerald in *The Great Gatsby*.[33]

Josephine Perry, the anti-heroine of a series of stories written just after the Basil stories, in 1930 to 1931, (unsuccessfully) pursues a man with an African American wife in 'A Nice Quiet Place' (1930). In 'A Snobbish Story' (1930), set in summer 1916, Josephine is recruited to star in a play called *Race Riot*, in which the role requires her to appear alongside African American actors, and she considers whether she would be playing the 'high yellow' lover of an African American man. Josephine has no qualms about this, but her parents do. Whilst this speaks more of her proto-flapperish desire to shock her parents and eschew social convention than of her need to assert racial equality, Fitzgerald's retrospective viewpoint, writing about Chicagoan Josephine's exploits during the 1910s from the vantage point of the 1930s, includes the knowledge of the 1919 Chicago race riots in which dozens were killed and hundreds injured, and a thousand black families had their homes set alight.

As a teenager, Fitzgerald won a Cakewalk dancing prize in his home town of St Paul, Minnesota. This dance, popular in the late 1890s, was based on imitation and parody. Originally, the Cakewalk was a dance performed by slaves on Southern plantations, imitating white dancers dancing minuets and marching arm in arm, and mocking their elaborate steps. Plantation owners enjoyed watching this parody of their 'superiority', awarding the best couple a cake as their prize, and not recognising the undermining of their power inherent in the Cakewalk. By the time Fitzgerald won his Cakewalk prize, in 1911, the dance had become a craze throughout the United States and had even spread to the ballrooms of Europe.[34] Fitzgerald's Cakewalk was a crystallised imitation of slaves (who were already imitating their masters), in the name of entertainment.

The ragtime 'barnyard' dances like the Turkey Trot, the Bunny Hug and, most famously, the Foxtrot, were also built around imitation and parody, this time of animals and animalistic movements. In contrast to the European dances such as the Waltz and the Two-step, which were usually danced in private ballrooms, the barnyard dances were danced in nightclubs, cabarets, juke joints and honky tonks, where ragtime music was played. As dancing amongst the elite social circles began to displace itself out of private ballrooms and moved into more public places such as cabarets, the Castles sought to capitalise on the coexistence of European-influenced and African American-influenced dancing styles, at this exciting historical moment.

This transition from Victorian to Modern is an overarching theme of the Basil and Josephine series of stories, which have often been considered as a cycle, not least by Fitzgerald himself.[35] Fitzgerald conjures up this transitional period with a combination of evocative period detail and grand sweeping judgements in 'The Perfect Life':

They were going dancing – for those were the great days: Maurice was tan-going in 'Over the River', the Castles were doing a swift stiff-legged walk in the third act of 'The Sunshine Girl' – a walk that gave the modern dance a social position and brought the nice girl into the café, thus beginning a profound revolution in American life. The great rich empire was feeling its oats and was out for some not too plebian, yet not too artistic, fun. (*BJG*, 128)

The Castles themselves are described as a single asexual entity, and their 'swift stiff-legged walk' is awkward in cadence and possessing of a sibilance that unsettles the ear. Fitzgerald's description of their Castle Walk could easily be applied to a military march: they bring about a 'revolution' in the 'empire' which is focused on avoiding the 'plebian', yet this radicalism is undermined by the militaristic marching cadence. Such a tension between establishment and rebellion is one that recurs in Fitzgerald's depiction of his flappers and their (eventual) domestication narratives. The First World War breaks out over the course of the Basil and Josephine stories, but it fails to register on either of their consciences beyond the appearance of Josephine's final beau, who was a military aviator (as was Vernon Castle), and the war's absence subtextually criticises Basil and Josephine's self-absorption.

In the passage on 'the great days', quoted above, Fitzgerald anonymises and universalises the changes effected by the increasing respectability of the café with the epithet 'the nice girl', while he prioritises the music, identifying the musical comedies by name, despite the fact that they were staged twenty years previously. By granting the music the esteem of being named (and thus recognised by his readership on an aural level, perhaps even provoking an emotional response), Fitzgerald allies himself with the youth, who just want to dance. He subtly satirises the perceived threat to social power posed by the ascendancy of black music and culture, focusing on the desired outcome of 'fun'.

By speaking of 'the nice girl' in a singular context, he universalises the experience, inferring that all nice girls were brought into the café. This hints at the imitative model of identity amongst the youth: all the nice girls were following suit. Though writing about Britain at the *fin de siècle*, Sally Ledger explores the shift of the modern city at the turn of the century in terms of its provision, in certain places, of a welcome public arena for the middle-class woman previously virtually confined to her domestic sphere.[36]

These welcoming spaces included 'the music halls in London and in other cities [. . . where] women featured both as performers and as members of the audience'.[37] Fitzgerald's fiction is filled with both.

In providing 'the nice girl' with a further public space in which to develop her confidence and increase her mobility (on both micro and macro scales – as a dancer and as a *flâneuse*), the Castles, for all their emphasis on propriety and self-control, offered the archetypal 'nice girl' a socially acceptable fun time, in public. In the final sentence of the passage, Fitzgerald unselfconsciously unites all Americans under the banner of the 'great rich empire', before conflating self and nation by singularising the empire, adding the pronoun 'its'. But whilst he is one of them, he employs his classic 'double vision' of separating himself from Americans and looking at the country with fresh perspective.

Fitzgerald introduces the concept of Americans seeking 'not too plebian, yet not too artistic fun', a statement that is class-loaded and wry at the same time. His description reflects the mounting interest in the mid-1920s among adventurous white Americans in being at a wild, African American dance. Lewis Erenberg argues that, despite this desire for 'authentic' experience, they largely retained a distance from the performers even after the proscenium became blurred, as dancehalls and cabarets began to encourage professional dancers to mingle with the dancing clientele.[38] One of the main aspects of this perceived 'fundamental' difference between white spectator and black performer was the racist assumption that black entertainers were 'natural, uncivilized, uninhibited performers, naturally smiling, because they had what whites lacked: joy in life'.[39] Erenberg explores how the changing format of the cabaret encouraged the impulse for self-expression which was being fostered by other areas of modern life such as advertising and the movies. Yet in the pre-war setting of 'The Perfect Life', it was important that this class of the 'great rich empire' did not traverse the barrier into the realm of the 'artistic', as this realm still connoted a lack of refinement and lower-class Bohemianism: relics from popular opinion at the turn of the century. Here, Fitzgerald can be perceived to be subtly satirising 'the great rich empire'.

The ragtime dance craze lasted for five years, from 1912 to 1916, and by the time Vernon Castle was killed in a military training exercise in 1918, popular dance culture had moved on to jazz dance proper: the Turkey Trot and 'Tango of To-Day' had given way to 'the swinging cadences of the Charleston' and the agitated hops of the Black Bottom, and the rags of Scott Joplin and James Scott were displaced in popularity by songs such as W. C. Handy's 'Beale Street Blues' (1916) and the Original Dixieland Jass Band's recording of 'Darktown Strutters' Ball' (1917).[40]

But the dance craze had been wide-ranging: in 1914, the Castles wrote that 'the gray-haired matron and the sedate man of affairs are seen dancing as often now as the younger generation'.[41] Fitzgerald more vividly captures the inclusiveness of this revolution in dancing habits, and the desire not merely to participate, but also to excel at dancing: 'sedentary stockbrokers, grandmothers of sixty, Confederate veterans, venerable statesmen and scientists, sufferers from locomotor ataxia wanted not only to dance but to dance beautifully' (*BJG*, 129). The sibilance in this quotation underscores the despondent subtext of Fitzgerald recalling the dance craze, from the 1929 perspective of writing 'The Perfect Life'. The reference to the confederacy in 1929 bears an unmistakably racial angle, whilst the reference to the illness 'locomotor ataxia', which resulted in a loss of control of one's body and which is a side-effect of tertiary syphilis, introduces a sexual strand to the dance craze discourse.

For the dancers, talent and industriousness are rewarded:

> Fantastic ambitions bloomed in hitherto sober breasts, violent exhibitionism cropped out in families modest for generations. [. . .] Because of a neat glide or an awkward stumble careers were determined and engagements were made or broken, while the tall Englishman and the girl in the Dutch cap called the tune. (*BJG*, 129)

The emphasis is on drastic change and inevitability: people are unleashing their previously suppressed potential, and the employment of floral imagery reinforces the sense of a natural, inevitable process. However, blooming is a short-lived state which gives way to decay, and this embedded negativity is repeated in the description of 'exhibitionism crop[ping] out in families' after 'generations'. This fear of cropping out is contemporary with the idea of recessive traits suddenly becoming prominent characteristics, which was a central concern of the growing popularity of eugenics in and beyond the United States in the 1920s.[42] The uncontrollable genetic element is paired with the importance of hard work and ambition, and imitative identity rears its head again when Fitzgerald tells us that the Castles are 'call[ing] the tune'.

With the perspective of writing in 1929, Fitzgerald can appraise the seismic effect of the dance craze on popular entertainment of the decade: the 'nice girl's' emergence from ballrooms and into the public sphere of cafés and cabarets was reflected by hotels and restaurants' hasty additions of dance floors in an attempt to capitalise on this new vogue. As the arenas for dance proliferated, orchestras and bands increased in number, and the dance craze even affected the music itself:

> early jazz composition and arrangement were heavily influenced by having to serve the dancers' need for respite, variety, partner change, and a fixed number of choruses for taxi dancing (where a dime would buy, say, two choruses' worth of partner).[43]

The fashionable modern dances were accessible to everyone, not just the professionals. As the popular 1911 Irving Berlin song went, 'Everybody's Doin' It Now'. Manuals such as the Castles' facilitated the imitation of professionals and fed into the increasing performativity of daily life in the 1920s.

Given such wide-ranging implications of modern dancing, it is not surprising that Basil, in 'The Perfect Life', is 'attacked' by 'sudden anxiety' on the dance floor (*BJG*, 129). The atmosphere in the room becomes tense, Basil 'trying to pretend to himself that he disapproved of it all' whilst the dancers of 'all ages and several classes of society shuffled around tensely to the nervous, disturbing beats of "Too Much Mustard"'. Basil is transfixed by watching Jobena dance, but only minutes later unwisely counsels her against 'dancing modern suggestive dances which are simply savagery' (*BJG*, 134). Basil feels torn between his true feelings and those he feels he ought to have in order to imitate the Princetonian John Danby. By the end of the story, Basil has started smoking again and has imbibed his first ever cocktails, all in an attempt to save Jobena from a hasty elopement with the wonderfully named but eminently unsuitable Skiddy De Vinci. However, we do not see him dance again in the story. His anxieties about his body persist to the stage where he even asks Jobena to leave the lights off when they finally embrace: 'Just for this once we don't need the light' (*BJG*, 144).

Basil is uncomfortable in his own body and the expectation that he would dance provokes a violent attack of anxiety. It is not the first time Basil has been uncomfortable in his own skin. In the second (but first published) Basil Duke Lee story, 'The Scandal Detectives', Basil feels sexually challenged by Hubert Blair, a new boy in town who dazzles the girls with his 'lithe, stylish, athletic torso' and his 'virtuosic athletic ability', which includes extremely advanced roller-skating, and leads Basil and his friends to hatch a plan to surprise Hubert, in disguise, and ruthlessly bundle him into a garbage can (*BJG*, 24). But when Basil hears Hubert whistling the tune to the 'Grizzly Bear' (a popular ragtime dance song drawing upon African American musical innovations with lyrics containing verbal sexual innuendoes), Basil changes his opinion of Hubert wholeheartedly, his jealousy turning to admiration, and they abandon the attack.[44] The disguises Basil and his friends choose are telling: Basil dresses with a 'confederate moustache' as a 'Southern planter of the old persuasion', his friend Bill 'with a long Balkan mustache', and the third in their party, Riply, 'in a full rabbinical beard'. In recounting his tale to their parents, Hubert gains more sympathy because of the ethnic 'otherness' of his would-be 'assailants' (*BJG*, 28). Anthony Berret explains that 'in the story, both parents and children see the "foreigners" as a threat, but the children also imitate and disguise themselves as them. They do the same thing on the dance floor.'[45] For Basil, this leads to a state of profound anxiety.

The dance-floor anxiety which Basil experiences in 'The Perfect Life' is made up of three parts: a racial dimension of fearing that which is other, an anxiety about the sexual dimension of the new popular dances, and a resulting sense of identity confusion. Basil and his peers try on different masks to sample each identity. Basil tries out being a prudish critic of all things modern, but this only serves to highlight his innate adolescent anxieties about his body and sexuality. The boys dress up as ethnic others to intimidate

Hubert but literally take off their masks before they carry out the deed. Hubert Blair is described in racialised terms throughout the story. Whistling the 'Grizzly Bear', with its lyrics supposedly written in African American 'dialect', and showing extraordinary physical prowess and showmanship stereotypically associated with the African American entertainer in the 1920s, Hubert is eventually described as 'making little rhythmic jumps and twirls on his toes, like a witch doctor throwing a slow hypnosis over an African tribe' (*BJG*, 25). Basil dislikes him but admires him, almost in spite of himself.

In his influential 2007 study exploring Fitzgerald's 'racial angles', Nowlin is particularly interested in Fitzgerald's portrayal of African American characters as simultaneously highly desirable and ominous. Writing about 'Head and Shoulders', the story of a chorus girl who becomes a successful author, and an academic who becomes a popular entertainer, Nowlin explains that the narrative

> reveals, in effect, that the story of the Fitzgerald hero's ambivalent relation to American popular culture and to contemporaneity is inseparable from the story of his anxious relation to his own body, for it is precisely that body that heeds the call of the pleasure principle to which American popular culture gives voice.[46]

The story of Horace and Basil's anxious relation to their own bodies is not just sexual, then, but also a racially coded one that Fitzgerald explores through the personally poignant medium of dance.

Fitzgerald's Syncopated Flappers

A contemporary of Basil, although they never meet, Josephine Perry is the product of her time, the ragtime era when young women were forced to compete socially for male validation that was finally conferred by marriage. This social competition was often facilitated by organised dances in clubs and ballrooms. This began to change by the 1920s, but not soon enough for Josephine, who wears herself out in the pursuit of admirers and is rendered old before her time by the end of the final Josephine story, in which she is declared 'emotionally bankrupt'. In crafting and projecting her proto-flapper identity, Josephine Perry comes to the realisation that she would rather choose than be chosen. Unfortunately, her serial seductions leave her without any emotional reserves to call upon when she finally does meet the man who she chooses as her true love.

Mary McAleer Balkun provides a gendered reading of the emotional bankruptcy the story depicts: Josephine 'poses a threat to the social order because she attempts to move from the position of product to that of conspicuous consumer in the marriage market'.[47] Fitzgerald makes clear that for all the liberation afforded to the New Woman of the ragtime era, she was still fundamentally dependent on the patriarchy from which she tried to assert independence. He goes further, by identifying Josephine's generation as at the heart of the 'Era of the Flapper', which began in 1912, when 'the Castles, by making modern dancing respectable, brought the nice girl into the cabaret and sat her down next to the distinctly not-nice girl', and was over 'by about 1922' when it became too widespread a counterculture. Fitzgerald explains in his 1930 essay 'Girls Believe in Girls':

> roughly speaking the girls who were or would have been debutantes in 1917–1919 were the nucleus of the wild generation – their numbers were swollen by older and younger girls who were determined not to miss anything, for the wild ones seemed to be having a good time. (*MLC*, 100–1)

Wild as she may be, Josephine is unfulfilled by her relentless mission to find a partner ('I don't care about anything in the world except men,' she tells us) and the sheer number of men she has targeted ultimately negates her capacity to emote (*BJG*, 275).

Another environmental cause of her emotional bankruptcy can be read as a side-effect of the post-war society in which the emerging fields of advertising, movies and efficiency experts encouraged women to reinvent themselves through leisure activities. In 1914's *Modern Dancing*, Irene and Vernon Castle had promised that dancing would make women more beautiful, more graceful and healthier, and would stop them (and their beaux) from drinking.[48] A dance manual with self-help undertones, the book became a bestseller. By moving beyond the Victorian sensibility of settling for the first good match she encounters, and instead entering the marketplace as a consumer whose choice of acquisition speaks of her own authentic self and style, Josephine fares much worse than other Fitzgerald heroines who conflate the material and the emotional, such as the bored heiress Rags in 'Rags Martin-Jones and the Pr-nce of W-les'. Rags ends up figuratively patronising the 'best bazaar in the world' to buy '"some perfectly be-*oo*-tiful love"' (*ASM*, 99). Josephine's unhappy ending stems from her failure to budget: she is not a discerning shopper.

Fitzgerald had a unique insight into consumerism as he anxiously toed the line between the roles of literary craftsman and of *Post* writer courting mass appeal. As a celebrity, he consciously manipulated his own public image – despite his faux-innocent protestations in 1932's essay 'My Lost City' that he was shocked at the attention: 'to my bewilderment, I was adopted . . . as the very archetype of what New York wanted' (*MLC*, 109). Fitzgerald knew about the imitative tendencies consumer culture heralded and he recognised the inherent dangers for the authentic expression of identity the advertisers promised they would enable. Thorstein Veblen's concept of the pecuniary emulator, whose main objective is to keep up with the wealth of others, fascinated Fitzgerald (partly because he feared being one himself).[49] Jay Gatsby is Fitzgerald's fullest exploration of the *nouveau riche* who mistakenly conflate the material and emotional pre-crash, but in 'Babylon Revisited' (1931), Charlie Wales, post-Crash, shows how the blinkered pursuit of prosperity is just as dangerous a concept as the relentless pursuit of hedonism.

Disposability, as demonstrated by both Josephine's carousel of suitors and Charlie's outrageously extravagant tips, led to increased consumption, but also to decreased resources. Curnutt summarises the notion, propagated by the advertising industry, that 'without the satisfaction of "using up" an item [. . .] consumers would have little motivation to spend their disposable income on a continuous basis'.[50] Josephine is still attractive to her ideal man, though she is used up emotionally. She has already begun the process of substituting her authentic feelings and thoughts for other market products, such as song lyrics. Curnutt continues:

> As Fitzgerald implies, if consumerism encourages individuals to view themselves as commodities, it only stands to reason that the same

satisfaction to be had in using up and throwing away a marketplace good
can be derived by wasting one's own assets.

From this perspective, it is a class issue, and Veblen gives a name
to the impulse to show 'conspicuous waste' as a mark of wealth
and prosperity.[51]

Josephine tries to become a consumer too soon: she is a commodity and is driven to use herself up in a perverse fulfilment of the
hedonism Fitzgerald condemned on the dance floor. Her gender
disadvantages her, for though Zelda Fitzgerald recognises herself,
and the flapper in general, 'as an artist in her objective field, the art
of being – being young, being lovely, being an object', it is Scott
Fitzgerald who complains of being 'not only . . . spokesman for
the time but . . . the typical product of that same moment' (MLC,
110).[52] The men are permitted to sell and market themselves, but
women, navigating their way from Victorian to modern sensibilities, are there to be chosen, not to choose. After all, Zelda writes
this piece in 1922, the year after the first Miss America competition
crystallised the old social ritual of choosing partners that used to
take place in ballrooms in bustles, and now took place in hotels,
wearing swimsuits. Zelda's piece, which playfully recommends a
dabble in flapperdom as good preparation for settling down to
marriage and motherhood, was published in McCall's under a joint
byline with her husband's name.[53]

In the transition from the ragtime dances (presided over by
the Castles and practised by Basil) to the jazz and blues dances
(engaged in by the students of Jim Powell's dance school and later
reimagined by Josephine Baker), it is possible to trace Fitzgerald's
portrayal of dance as a racially and sexually coded response to
modernity. However, Fitzgerald is unable to disguise his fundamentally moralistic stance which criticises empty hedonism, and
sends his dance teacher, Powell, dejectedly back to the South with
no plans to continue with dance instruction. He has Basil ultimately
reject modern dancing, leaving him standing on a veranda outside
a dance in the final story in the series, 'Basil and Cleopatra' (1929),
pensively looking up at his stars: 'symbols of ambition, struggle
and glory'. In the original ending of the story (Fitzgerald having
sent the new ending directly to the Saturday Evening Post as they

considered the purchase), Basil 'replaced his pride in his pocket for safe keeping and hurried back to the dance' (*BJG*, 373–4). By having Basil reject the dance, Fitzgerald is able to suggest the nobler purposes to which Basil can aspire. Fitzgerald offers Josephine Perry no such option.

Ultimately, it seems that though Fitzgerald shows the modern dances to be both 'suggestive' and 'savage', what irks him is not the sexual or racial content of the dances, but rather the hedonistic 'not too plebeian, yet not too artistic, fun' (*BJG*, 128) that he resents at this emotionally turbulent time in his career, and the practition- ers of self-indulgence, who fail either to reform themselves or to make a truly authentic artistic contribution to the form, are pun- ished with the 'emotional bankruptcy' that Josephine eventually suffers, and with which Fitzgerald diagnosed himself in the 1936 'Crack-Up' essays.

Fitzgerald's treatment of Josephine Perry is rather unforgiving, but although she possesses all the qualities West lists as embodying Fitzgerald's early 'famous heroine', who was 'strong, willful, selfish, beautiful, alluring, independent, [. . .] ruthless [and] young', these traits somehow fail to translate into the captivating heroine of his early love stories.[54] Rather, she is something of an anti-heroine, rep- resenting the transition between Fitzgerald attempting to produce more stories of young love, and giving up on 'rework[ing] his old romance formula'.[55]

By bestowing on Josephine the epiphany of self-knowledge, Fitzgerald 'de-romanticized the girl and de-emphasized the glory of the quest': for Josephine, love is no longer romantic nor is the quest for love glorious.[56] This gradual de-romanticisation is epitomised by Fitzgerald's portrayal of the flapper figure. He treats certain of his flapper heroines in a parodic way. Parody involves restating the status quo but repeating it with a difference, and by tracing something of a brief genealogy of Fitzgerald's parodic portrayals of three heroines that precede Josephine Perry, it is possible to show not only how Fitzgerald was parodying the flapper as a popular cultural mainstay, but also how he was specifically parodying his own inventions.

'Rags Martin-Jones and the Pr-nce of W-les' was published in July 1924, and relates the colourful romance between Rags, a bored heiress, and John M. Chestnut, who concocts a scheme in which he fakes being a fugitive murderer to elicit excitement from Rags, who marries him on discovering the truth (after having 'fainted from excitement' [*ASM*, 110]). The characterisation and plot parallels with 'The Offshore Pirate' are clear, and John Higgins has also identified the thematic 'parody, probably unconscious' of *The Great Gatsby* (1925) in the portrayal of Chestnut, who longs for Rags for five years before making a fortune and putting on an ostentatious display (in which he poses as a criminal) to attract her attention and secure her affections.[57] Arguably, Rags herself also serves as a parody of Fitzgerald's dancing, singing, movie-infused flapper heroine. Her nonchalant unconventionality surpasses quirkiness and becomes ridiculous, symbolised by her purple dogs and errant monocle.

In 'Rags', Fitzgerald parodies Ardita's boredom and willingness to love a proven liar in 'The Offshore Pirate'. The opening of 'Rags' takes places at a New York City port as Rags's transatlantic liner is docking. This echoes the memorable opening of 'The Offshore Pirate': 'This unlikely story begins on a sea that was a blue dream' (*F&P*, 5). Rags is identified as being the personification of the sea, wearing 'a dress made in great splashy checks of sea-blue and grey' (*ASM*, 96). When she pushes John off the disembarkation gangway into the Hudson river, she is symbolically pushing John into herself. Rags, then, in the subtext of her story, is in fact far more in control of her fate than John would acknowledge. Ardita is described contemplating how the people 'she had known were but driftwood on the ripples of her temperament' (*F&P*, 14). The 'blue dream' of 'The Offshore Pirate' is also echoed in 'Rags' when 'the music seemed to come from far away [. . .] with the added remoteness of a dream' (*ASM*, 102). Not only did the original ending of 'Pirate' involve Ardita realising the whole story was a dream, but also this faraway music trope directly mirrors how 'the sound of weird ragtime was drifting softly over on the warm breath of the night' in 'Pirate' (*F&P*, 27). In 'Rags', they enjoy entertainment in a heated roof garden in Manhattan that is open to the sky. In 'Pirate', Curtis Carlyle claims to have recently been engaged to perform at the Midnight Frolic, Florenz Ziegfeld's 'sumptuous cabaret, serving superb food, dancing, and elaborate chorus girl productions' on the roof of the New Amsterdam Theater on 42nd Street.[58] Such close echoes ensure that we read Rags in comparison to Ardita, and find Rags to be somewhat more enfranchised than Ardita. There is repetition, but the 'repetition with a difference' that makes the portrayal parodic is found in Rags's increased agency and independence: she satirises the empty-headed, amoral flapper figure at large, as well as Fitzgerald's previous individual flappers like Ardita. True to her name, Rags is being used by Fitzgerald to 'rag' Ardita, 'ragging' being the musical practice of taking a tune and performing it in 'an unpredictable and percussive manner'.[59] In his book, *Jazz* (1926), the bandleader and dubiously self-appointed 'King of Jazz', Paul Whiteman, describes how, 'to rag a melody, one threw the rhythm out of joint making syncopation'.[60] These heroines, who share certain traits and situations without outright duplication, can be read as syncopated flappers. In one of Fitzgerald's earliest stories, 'Head and Shoulders' (1920), Marcia Meadows Tarbox breaks out of the flapper stereotype to author a bestselling book, which she calls 'Sandra Pepys, Syncopated' (*F&P*, 82).

Of course, since Fitzgerald's stories originally appeared in ephemeral magazine contexts, the comparisons made here could have been difficult for Fitzgerald's original audience, but significantly he chose to include 'Pirate' and 'Rags' in *Flappers and Philosophers* and *All the Sad Young Men*, respectively, allowing for readers to make these comparisons easily. Alongside this comparison of Rags and Ardita, we could read this intertextual teasing as Fitzgerald subtly criticising the public's voracious demand for flapper stories.

Another of Fitzgerald's stories that has been identified as relying on a 'gimmick', accused of being a 'pot-boiler' and foreshadowing elements of *Gatsby*, is 'Diamond Dick and the First Law of Woman', published in April 1924.[61] In this story, a World War One veteran is restored from his amnesic state by Diana 'Diamond Dick' Dickey in order for him to remember that she is in fact his wife. As in 'The Offshore Pirate', Diana and Rags are chronically bored, Diana feeling that the war was the pinnacle of excitement, and Rags also missing Europe. Recalling how Ardita effectively became an accomplice to a criminal gang, both Rags and Diana are associated with the criminal world to stoke their excitement: while Rags's bob is twice described as being of convict's length, Diana imagines herself to be a gangster as a child, and in the story's climax she engineers a scene in which she holds her husband and his lover hostage at gunpoint.

Additionally, all three stories employ scenes in which jazz music is depicted as 'melancholy', primitive and intoxicating. In 'Diamond Dick', the 'sad, dissonant horns were telling a melancholy story' and the voices had a 'barbaric urgency' (*TJA*, 309–10), Rags witnesses a singer in a 'barbaric light' singing in a 'wild minor' (*ASM*, 103), and Ardita hears a melody 'haunting and plaintive as a death dance from the Congo's heart' (*F&P*, 29). The cumulative effect is for us to read Diana in the context of Rags and Ardita, and in doing so we discover that Diana is in fact a different breed of flapper. She seeks, rather than being sought, and masterminds the climactic gunpoint hostage scene herself. Echoing Rags's fainting spell at discovering the ruse, in 'Diamond Dick' it is Diana's husband Charley who faints, in a swoon described in floral terms: 'his whole body seemed to wilt under him' (*TJA*, 316). The eventual happy ending of 'Diamond Dick' has been derided as a potboiler. Higgins suggests that 'This is a quick-money story for a popular magazine, and undoubtedly for that reason Fitzgerald tacks on the happy ending ostensibly showing that if one perseveres and packs a .44, one can repeat the past after all.'[62] Having put 'Diamond Dick' in the context of these other stories, whether or not his primary concern is a marketable story, Fitzgerald is undoubtedly stretching his literary muscle by indulging in some subtle self-parody.

There is a critical precedent for interpreting this self-parody. Both Ruth Prigozy and Brian Harding have analysed tendencies in the plots of Fitzgerald's stories focusing on young love and have found evidence of self-parody. In an essay published in 1982, Prigozy identifies a transitional period in Fitzgerald's story-writing between 1930 and 1936, when his plots became 'outworn, stale, mechanical – unintentional parodies of the exuberant accounts of young love and romantic longing that so captivated audiences during the boom years', going on to concede that some of the self-parody may actually be deliberate.[63] If we compare Rags, Ardita and Diamond Dick, this deliberate self-parody becomes apparent. Fitzgerald's self-parody is not limited to the period in which he struggled to recapture his 'old romance formula' for the 'slicks': self-parodic currents also run between his successful stories. Higgins himself has suggested that the dream sequence that opens the Basil story 'The Freshest Boy' (1928) echoes the climaxes of 'Rags' and 'Diamond', showing Fitzgerald 'ridiculing his own earlier stories'.[64]

In a 1989 essay, Harding suggests that Fitzgerald uses several tactics to subvert and undermine the formulaic expectations placed upon him by being a *Post* writer: the use of the unhappy (or 'modif[ied]' happy) ending, 'ironies of characterisation and plot' to undermine 'the gestures towards romance that were made "for the trade"', and implausible plot resolutions that 'create instant fortunes and remove class barriers that would otherwise block the way to 'happy' marriages'. He argues that certain of the features for which Fitzgerald's commercial fiction has been criticised are actually examples of Fitzgerald subtly subverting the expectation of his magazines' readers in order to expose 'the conventions on which that story depended'.[65] Josephine's epiphany is a modernist feature that bridges the transition between Fitzgerald's 'old romance formula' conventions and his more obviously modernist work of the 1930s, such as the Pat Hobby stories. His self-parodic undertones are a key strand of his modernist technique, as well as a central facet of American (and especially African American) culture of the 1920s and 1930s. Fitzgerald's dancing flappers are at the epicentre of his ambivalence towards modern culture: glamour and moral vacancy form a heady mixture to which Fitzgerald is drawn and then recoils from, repeatedly.

CHAPTER 2

The 'Chocolate Arabesques' of Josephine Baker: Fitzgerald and Jazz Dance

In 'First Blood' (1930), Fitzgerald's rebellious teenage protagonist, Josephine Perry, gives her parents grave cause for concern and begins to show signs of the 'Emotional Bankruptcy' (1931) with which she will end the cycle of short stories. Emotional bankruptcy, closely linked to the concept of dissipation that is central to 'Babylon Revisited' (1931), is the act of calling upon emotional resources that have already been spent and finding oneself devoid of any capacity for experiencing emotion. It is a condition Fitzgerald self-diagnosed in the 'Crack-Up' essays of 1936, as well as a state he attributed more widely to certain flappers of the late 1910s and early 1920s, such as Josephine. 'One cannot both spend and have,' realises Josephine, after being kissed by her true love (*BJG*, 286). She is devastated to perceive that she feels nothing.

Fitzgerald's first use of the term 'emotional bankruptcy' is in the title of the 1931 story, the fifth and final one in the Josephine sequence, which in turn are linked by socio-historical context and theme to the nine Basil stories, published between 1928 and 1929. Josephine is a product of her time – her rebelliousness and flirtation are ultimately quashed by her lack of skills and education.[1] By the end of the 'quietly terrifying little morality "play"', she still has no visible prospect of future emotional fulfilment, despite her epiphanic self-knowledge.[2] Reader sympathy for her is limited, especially in comparison to Basil, who repents his selfish behaviour and matures, but Josephine (who ages only two years in the sequence of stories, compared with Basil's six) remains vain, shallow and often spiteful right up until her dramatic realisation with which the sequence ends.

Josephine considers dances, and the music that accompanies them, to be of paramount importance in her life. The social whirl in which she operates gives rise to several instances of her theorising on the gender relations of her society. When attending a dance at Yale, she becomes 'abruptly aware' that 'a girl took on the importance of the man who had brought her' and realises that 'the more beautiful and charming she was, the more she could afford to disregard public opinion' (*BJG*, 230). Her sexuality becomes her bartering power, she realises, in a society in which she is dependent on who chooses her: in other words, she is limited by how desirable a product she renders herself. It is hardly surprising that she too, echoing Basil, imbues the dance floor with danger. Josephine views the dance floor as a scene of battle or sporting clash: 'the field of feminine glory [was] the ballroom floor', she muses, in free indirect discourse. Paradoxically, the objective in such a battle was actually to leave the 'field' of combat: '[it] was something you slipped away from – with a man' (*BJG*, 191). It was Josephine's fluid sense of self and embrace of imitative identity shifts that enabled her to become so successful with the opposite sex, leading her to expend all her emotional capital so early in life. Demonstrating the centrality of imitation to interwar culture, Josephine repeatedly mimics her love interests to make herself more attractive to them, taking up various political stances or even copying body language, as Quentin E. Martin has identified: she affects 'continual submersion of her identity in order to attract the man she wants. The values, thoughts and even words of her current love interest become her own.'[3] Josephine is clever and wilful, but as Balkun has noted, she is 'brought to the realization that it is only through men that she has any power or authority, and she must agree to lose herself in a man'.[4]

She is, however, a teenager, and does not fully articulate what she has discovered, instead delivering gems like 'Nobody thinks of anything but boys and dances from morning till night' (*BJG*, 222). Josephine's blinkered pursuit of 'feminine glory' has caused her to become disconnected from her mind: she becomes lazy in articulation of her thoughts, choosing instead to indulge in 'much quoting of lines from current popular songs, as if they expressed the writer's state of mind more fully than verbal struggles of her own' (*BJG*, 198). Going from dance, to party, to luncheon, she heeds Nowlin's call 'of the pleasure principle to which American popular culture gives voice'.[5] By the mid-1920s, good English translations of Freud were available, although his writings became most resonant for his American audience in the 1940s and 1950s. The drive to seek pleasure and avoid pain is central to the concept of the id, although Josephine would not have the vocabulary to describe it as such. Certain artists of the 1910s perceived non-Western (especially African and South Pacific) visual art to represent social and sexual freedoms that contrasted with the apparently repressed state of Western civilisation. Yet in Josephine's pursuit of hedonism, this *enfant terrible* ends up disconnected from her body, incapable of feeling emotion when she is kissed. This puts her in a great state of anxiety, like Basil, and like Zelda Fitzgerald.

In January 1927, partly prompted by Fitzgerald's admiration for a hard-working and ambitious young actress he had recently met, Zelda Fitzgerald decided that she would try to become a professional ballet dancer at the age of 26. By the summer of 1927, she was practising for ten hours a day, and was treated for exhaustion. Understandably, dance features heavily in Fitzgerald's fiction produced during the period of Zelda's obsession, from 1927 to 1931. In this period, dance was very much imprinted upon the public consciousness, as in these five short years the dance world mourned the premature loss of Rudolph Valentino (1926), Isadora Duncan (1927) and Anna Pavlova (1931).

In letters written during Zelda's first breakdown, Fitzgerald clearly perceives himself to be Zelda's parent figure, and as part of her treatment he writes to her dancing teacher, Madame Egrova, seeking a 'report' on her progress and potential in the summer of 1930.[6] It is not surprising that the parent–child relationship is central to a story of 1931 that links these themes of dancing, dead or unresponsive romantic partners, and the conflation of the fiscal and the emotional: 'Babylon Revisited'. Written in December 1930 while Fitzgerald was staying in Switzerland, near Zelda's hospital, 'Babylon Revisited' is a story that opens with absence and stillness. Charlie Wales makes enquiries in the Ritz bar in Paris, finding all his friends of eighteen months prior to be absent. The subject of the enquiry that opens the story, Mr Campbell, is recuperating in Switzerland, where Fitzgerald was writing the story. The lack of movement in the bar unsettles Charlie and assaults his national identity: 'the stillness in the Ritz bar was strange and portentous. It was not an American bar any more' (*TAR*, 157). Wandering through Montmartre, Charlie comes across a nightclub which is static until the *maître d'hôtel* notices him and 'Immediately an eager orchestra burst into sound, a pair of professional dancers leaped to their feet' (*TAR*, 161). He rejects this inauthentic display, alluding to the Parisian cabaret tradition drawn upon by the Castles for their Manhattan cabaret *Sans Souci*, and moves on.

When he visits his daughter, who is being cared for by his sister-in-law, he begins to assert his own corporeality: he 'grip[s] the sides of the chair' to disperse his frustration physically rather than verbally, and his sister-in-law sees that 'Charlie's feet were planted on the earth now' (*TAR*, 168–9). He is reconnected to his body after the period of wild partying which was the successor to Josephine Perry's tea dances. Yet significantly, Charlie's pain at his past behaviour manifests itself in the form of dancing and movement. He dreams of his dead wife, whom he neglected, 'in a swing in a white dress and swinging faster and faster all the time' until she is unintelligible to him (*TAR*, 171).

The effect of such manic dance practice on Zelda permeates her letters of this period. For example, writing to Scott in autumn 1930, she laments: 'Dancing has gone and I'm weak and feeble and I can't understand why I should be the one, amongst all others, to have to bear all this – for what?'[7] These biographical details help to explain the centrality of bodily movement to 'Babylon Revisited'. At the story's close, when Charlie is denied custody of his daughter due to drunken friends from his past ruining his reformed image, his brother-in-law 'swing[s] Honoria back and forth like a pendulum from side to side' (*TAR*, 175). The child is swinging to mark the time, as a record of its relentless passage and Charlie's helplessness. Time, for Charlie, has lost its linearity: his past mistakes haunt and infect his present, and the future he longs for is constantly held just outside of his grasp. The child, Honoria, is oblivious to this, feeling no anxiety about her body being used to symbolise such past, present and future despair: 'They couldn't make him pay forever,' Charlie thinks, at the story's close (*TAR*, 177). The mirroring of Honoria and her mother Helen's repetitive physical movements suggests a reiteration of the past. Helen's swinging is of her own volition, although she seems to lose control of herself, 'swinging faster and faster', which contrasts with Honoria's steady pendular oscillation, the very purpose of which is to regulate and measure time. Honoria's swing, whilst alluding to the out-of-control past of her parents, simultaneously establishes a symbol of safety, or even entrapment, as she is not moving of her own free will, but rather is being swung by her surrogate father. Her lack of agency in her living arrangements is symbolised in her corporeal compliance.

The story offers other visions of dancers. In fact, performative identity is a pervasive presence throughout, not least when Charlie attends a Josephine Baker performance:

> He bought a strapontin for the Casino and watched Josephine Baker go through her chocolate arabesques [but he felt that her stuff was poor – she followed the same contorted patterns but they lacked something. She needed America, she needed refreshment – the bloom was going because the roots were dry]. (*TAR*, 161)[8]

Although Fitzgerald's final version of the story cuts the encounter down to Charlie watching Josephine 'go through her chocolate arabesques' and leaving after an hour without comment, in the earlier working typescript of the story, given in square brackets above, Charlie feels that her performance is inauthentic: she is literally just going through the motions.

Fitzgerald deploys performers like singers, dancers and actors as a means of exploring his own role as a literary craftsman who sought both popular success and critical acclaim. Fitzgerald criticises these performers for perceived bouts of inauthenticity, whilst appreciating the nuances of their consciously performed artistic endeavours. In an entertainment system that was so deeply indebted to black culture, yet so resolutely resistant to acknowledging that debt, layered identity and imitations were rife, amongst both professional performers and regular citizens. This is reflected by the thematic potency of performance in Fitzgerald's stories, from

Baker's 'chocolate arabesques' to Irving Berlin's 'Cheek to Cheek'. Performance also functions at a formal level in Fitzgerald's stories: just as Baker's routine is delivered with subtle customisations and variations (though they may be overlooked by some), Fitzgerald too sees himself as performing a given role, as an author of popular magazine stories, which comes with its own set of expectations and formulae, delivered with a selection of individuating strategies that mark the stories as his own. Performers, like Josephine Baker, can thus be read as explorations of Fitzgerald's own self-conception as an artist.

Fitzgerald and Josephine Baker: Americans in Paris

Josephine Baker had a fascinating life spanning the roles of dancer, actress, singer, humanitarian, civil rights activist and Resistance spy, but it was her first role, as dancer, for which she is most famous. Baker's semi-nude performances on Paris stages grew out of her training in New York as a chorus-line dancer. Dancing at the end of the line, Baker followed the tradition, said to originate with Ethel Williams, of incorporating humorous nuances into the routines, using slapstick physical comedy as well as comic facial expressions to draw attention to herself. Her mix of eroticism and comedy proved irresistible to French audiences, and Baker went on to claim French citizenship in 1937. In the 1920s, she became a muse to modernist figures across the arts, including, according to Anne Anlin Cheng, Le Corbusier, who wrote a ballet for her; Henri Matisse, who made a life-size cut-out of her that he kept in his bedroom; and Alice B. Toklas, who invented a pudding named after her, completing the assimilation of her public persona into popular culture.[9]

As Christa Daugherty and West have explored, Charlie is insinuating that Baker needs to reinvent herself and refresh her identity, just as Charlie himself seeks to do.[10] Ironically, that was the exact function of the Casino de Paris show, which Terri J. Gordon and others have identified as a turning point in Baker's career in which she began to cultivate her multiple talents and diva persona, from adopting elaborately bejewelled and feathered costumes, to developing her bilingual singing voice, and acting in comedic sketches.[11]

A solo show, Baker's *Paris qui Remue* opened in October 1930, just three months before Fitzgerald wrote 'Babylon Revisited'. The name of the show translates literally as 'Paris that moves', or, more elegantly, 'bustling Paris'. As we have seen, Parisian movement and stasis are also important themes in 'Babylon Revisited'.

In deleting the latter half of his description, Fitzgerald leaves us only with the distilled gesture of 'chocolate arabesques', a deceptively simple phrase. Within the story, dance figures as a shorthand for the painful past, and Baker's arabesques in part serve as a bridge between the past and present. Like Jim Powell's production line jazz academy, the distilled gesture of 'chocolate arabesques' recalls Taylorist philosophies and constitutes an important motif in the story: Honoria swings like a pendulum, and her mother swings with increasing speed that obscures her speech. Both have been severed from Charlie, who feels increasingly disembodied, at one point attempting to reassert his corporeality by firmly gripping the chair in Marion's house, and 'plant[ing]' his feet 'on the earth' as he fights to regain custody of Honoria (*TAR*, 169). When Fitzgerald judges that Baker needs to return to America to affirm her sense of self and reignite her authenticity, it is possible to read that as Charlie's self-diagnosis, and tempting to read it as Fitzgerald's own desires, as expressed from Switzerland, where he anxiously awaited news of Zelda's psychiatric treatment.

Zelda herself was familiar with the technicalities of the arabesque position, whether performed *en pointe*, *demi pointe* or with flat feet. In fact, Bruccoli reports that in early 1930, a scout attended one of Zelda's ballet recitals. Zelda thought he was from Diaghilev's Ballets Russes (despite the company closing in August 1929 after his death) but in fact he was from the Folies Bergère, Baker's old employers, and was apparently 'interested in making [Zelda] a shimmy dancer'.[12] Baker also studied ballet in the early 1930s, fusing what she learned of classical ballet with the modern dance traditions of vaudeville, the ragtime dances that the Castles adapted, and jazz dance.[13] It was Baker, not Zelda, who went on to receive private ballet lessons from George Balanchine of Ballets Russes fame, in the early 1930s.[14]

The arabesque, as a ballet position, requires the dancer to balance on one leg and extend the other behind their body, usually

2.1 Zelda Fitzgerald performing an arabesque whilst a patient at Prangins Hospital,
Switzerland, c. 1930–1.

at a 45- or 90-degree angle (Figure 2.1). It is a controlled, almost
static movement, with emphasis on straightened knees and controlled poise. In essence, it is the very opposite of the Charleston for
which Baker was famous, with its swinging limbs and soft, flexed
knees. Regardless of the shared balletic interests of Zelda and Baker,
given that the peak of Zelda's ballet obsession and Baker's solo
show occurred in the months directly preceding the composition
of 'Babylon Revisited', Fitzgerald's choice of phrase demonstrates a
nuanced engagement with popular culture.

Aside from referring to Baker's skin colour, the use of the word
'chocolate' in 'chocolate arabesques' may seek to recall the series of
all-black revues such as the *Chocolate Dandies*, which built on the
success of the 1921 show *Shuffle Along*, which had launched Baker's
career and brought jazz dance into the international spotlight.
Josephine Baker's fame arose from a complex mix of admiration
and objectification that was racially coded, complex and inconsistent. In Baker's autobiography, she recalls being rejected at audi-
tions in the United States for being both too light-skinned and too
dark-skinned: 'To the whites I looked chocolate, to the blacks like
a "pinky"; there was no place I belonged.'[15] After another chorus

girl was injured and Baker replaced her, she soon found out that there was a place she belonged: the City of Light. As the British novelist Angela Carter has observed, Baker's reception in Paris was distinctly different from her American reception: 'She left behind nascent Broadway stardom as a comic dancer, an elastic-limbed, rubber-faced clown, grimacing, grinning, crossing her eyes, to find herself freshly incarnated as a sex-goddess without, it would seem, changing her act very much at all.'[16] She succeeded in Paris with the same skills she displayed in New York City because Paris was fascinated with the concept of defining the modern condition through that which is ancient, or 'primitive'.

The transatlantic differences in the reception of Baker's performance convey differing reactions to African American culture, as well as America's reaction to its own 'native' medium of vaudeville. In stories such as 'Dice, Brassknuckles and Guitar', Fitzgerald shows how white Americans' appreciation and enjoyment of African American cultural traditions is complex, and he situates his story in a context that also elicits tensions between the social classes. The compliment paid by the imitation of African American dances and music of the time is revealed to be a double-edged sword, as not only does Jim profit from this appropriation, but also Fitzgerald's characterisation of the story's only African American character is woefully inadequate. Jim's 'manservant' Hugo, to whom he owes his knowledge of African American culture, remains virtually mute throughout the story – professionally and narratively subservient to Jim. The story's dénouement confirms that there are inherent dangers in appropriating African American culture for a living as Jim does, as a dance teacher. Powell loses his livelihood, and in a twist reminiscent of the 'secret identity' strand in the earliest Fitzgerald story which explicitly confronts the issue of race, 'The Offshore Pirate', Powell discovers that his love interest Amanthis, whom he had hoped to integrate into high society, already numbers amongst them, having tricked Jim into believing them to be peers. Having taught the youths of Southampton what he knows about the culture he appropriates, he cannot prevent them from using this knowledge once he and his services have been unceremoniously rejected from the community, and this anxiety of reception can be related to Fitzgerald's self-conception as an artist. Nowlin concisely summarises this anxiety: 'For a white artist such as Fitzgerald, able to conceive of himself as an outsider seeking the cultural recognition of the powerful, affiliation with black culture carries with it the risk of either cultural ephemerality or cultural illegitimacy.'[17] In the United States, at least, this may have been the case.

In Europe, and specifically in Paris, affiliation with black culture did not carry such strong risks of cultural ephemerality or illegitimacy, which is why Josephine Baker could take the same skill set to Paris and elicit much more of a sense of artistic legitimacy than she found in the United States. The reasons for this warm reception lie in the complex cultural atmosphere described by Petrine Archer-Straw as 'Negrophilia' (from the French *'négrophilie'*). Literally denoting a love for black culture, the word describes the Parisian desire to embrace all things African and the avant-garde's intentions to 'co-opt black culture to promote their ideas about modernity'.[18]

There are, of course, inherently racist assumptions involved in attempting to understand some kind of universalised African experience of identity. Stereotypes of Africans as 'pure', 'uncivilised', highly sexual and instinctively musical invaded popular culture of the 1910s and 1920s, and in France, these racist assumptions were making their way into popular culture via such revue sketches as *La Folie du Jour* (1926–7). In this revue, Baker appeared as 'Fatou, a native girl, bare-breasted and clad in a skirt of rubber bananas [. . .] [who] encounters a white explorer'.[19] Remembered for the presence of Baker's signature comically phallic banana skirt, the role spoke to a French audience at a time when their country's colonial empire was at its height, including territories in North and West Africa.

Debate continues over the degree to which Baker was complicit in creating (as well as performing) French colonial imagery in her stage and film roles, as well as the degree to which her performances were parodic. Mae Gwendolyn Henderson argues that, read incorrectly, Baker's work can be interpreted as 'reproducing gender and race clichés, caricatures, and stereotypes as they are produced by the dominant and hegemonic discourse'.[20] Take, for example, Baker's own description of her 1925 debut in *La Revue Nègre*: 'Driven by dark forces I didn't recognize, I improvised, crazed by the music [. . .]. My teeth and eyes burned with fever [. . .]. I felt [. . .] intoxicated.'[21] This recalls the lexis of disease that Fitzgerald and others used to describe ragtime dance and can be read as reinforcing racist stereotypes of 'the savage'.

Though Baker often worked within the confines of expected racial stereotypes and clichés of this period in her performances, she also asserted herself through subtle choreographic means that became her trademark: from her crossed eyes and clowning, to parading her pet cheetah around Paris, she mocked the roles she played at the same time as redefining them. Daphne Ann Brooks finds that Baker even transforms iconic minstrel caricatures into tools of farce that could dissolve authority.[22] Such subversive reimaginings of the roles assigned to her run the risk of misinterpretation, and in his reference to Baker performing a classically balletic move, rather than a peppy jazz manœuvre, Fitzgerald hints that he may have been aware of Baker's work to redefine the role of the jazz dancer through parodying caricatures.

Although Fitzgerald's ambivalent portrayals of popular culture are vulnerable to misreadings, Fitzgerald is often actually using these references to engage critically with ideas about leisure. In 'Dice, Brassknuckles and Guitar', the 'Slow Chicago with the Memphis Sideswoop' sounds exciting – Fitzgerald reminds us in 'The Perfect Life' that 'because of a neat glide or an awkward stumble, careers were determined and engagements were made or broken' – but Jim's elite clientele make their ennui apparent through their near-somnambulance (*BJG*, 129). The dancers in Jim's academy are merely 'going through the motions': it is this same assessment that causes Charlie to regard Baker's performance as inauthentic.

Elsewhere, we see Fitzgerald using dance as a measure of authenticity and punishing his characters for falling short and displaying inauthentic feelings on the dance floor: Marcia Meadows, as mentioned earlier, has a mid-Shimmy epiphany and leaves the stage for good. Basil Duke Lee, in 'The Perfect Life', is 'attacked' by 'sudden anxiety' on the dance floor (*BJG*, 129). In 'The Dance' (1926), the Charleston is even used as a false alibi by a murderess, who performs the Charleston to attract attention and prevent anyone from discovering the murder she has committed upstairs. Fitzgerald describes her gingham 'country girl's dress' with a 'wide sunbonnet' and her face 'stained yellow with powder [. . .] with rolling eyes and a vacant negroid leer' (*ASM*, 303). He seems to be referencing Topsy, the child slave from Harriet Beecher Stowe's novel *Uncle Tom's Cabin* (1852), a mischievous character (who is later converted to Christianity) featuring in numerous play adaptations and often played by white actors in blackface. Described by Jayna Brown as constituting 'a lesson in physical contact with "primitives"', she argues that 'the project of civilising Topsy was a metaphor for colonial missionary programs and their paternalist agendas'.[23] It is a curious allusion for Fitzgerald to make in a story set in a country club in a small Southern town, but interestingly, Baker had played a Topsy role in the 1924 revue *Chocolate Dandies*, in which she appeared, in gingham and giant clown shoes, as a cross-eyed Topsy Anna (Figure 2.2).

In her breakthrough role in the chorus of *Shuffle Along* (1921), Baker's dancing played with notions of authenticity. She imitated Ethel Williams's disruptive practice of seeming unable to perform the correct steps, before dazzling the audience in the encore by surpassing the skills of the other dancers.[24] Her dancing combined graceful, controlled movements with madcap 'mugging', wild limbs and crossed eyes. The surprise element in Baker's routines destabilised expectations of identity, to the delight of her audiences. Baker's apparent unpredictability was part of her performances, whereas when Zelda's dance mania revealed itself, this was not a controlled manipulation of expectation, but something more dangerous and uncomfortable.

In 'Babylon Revisited', dance figures as a shorthand for the painful past, and Baker's arabesques also serve as a bridge between the past and present. Fitzgerald implies that Baker is going through the motions of a set routine, 'the same patterns' yielding a different reaction in Charlie from his previous response to Baker's dancing, creating an unspoken 'then' to contrast against the present. Similarly, in the 'novelette', 'May Day', published at the outset of Fitzgerald's literary career in 1920, the word 'arabesque' has again been used as a temporal bridge, recollecting a dead love:

> The affair had died, drowned in the turmoil of the war and quite forgotten in the arabesque of these three months, but a picture of her, poignant, debonnaire, immersed in her own inconsequential chatter, recurred to him unexpectedly and brought a hundred memories with it. (*TJA*, 70)

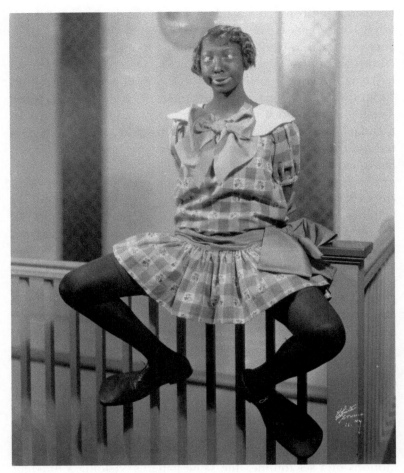

2.2 Josephine Baker as 'Topsy Anna' in *Chocolate Dandies* (1924).

It is telling that Fitzgerald chooses to use dance to represent temporal trauma in two stories a decade apart. It seems that he sees potential in dance gestures to convey temporal markers beyond those available in the vocabulary of language. By importing dance techniques such as the arabesque into his fiction, and utilising them both thematically and formally, Fitzgerald displays his interest in other art forms' abilities to represent experience.

In 1924's '"The Sensible Thing"', he envisages dancers as a literal bridge, pre-empting the architect Le Corbusier's fascination with Baker as a representative of modernist aesthetics of display and the cityscape:

> All his life he had thought in terms of tunnels and skyscrapers and great squat dams and tall, three-towered bridges, that were like dancers holding hands in a row with heads as tall as cities and skirts of cable strand. (*ASM*, 152)

The image is an arresting one, and the story proceeds to hinge around the impenetrable chasm between the past and the present, and the failure of the hero to reignite his past love. It also associates the figure of the dancer with the new vertical aesthetic of city skyscrapers and grand-scale bridges. Dancers, here, are a fundamentally modern feature of the cultural and literal landscape; architects and choreographers are conflated.

In this way, Fitzgerald is positioning Baker's artistic expression as a bridge: her arched body links the 'high' artistic impulses of ballet with the popular treat embodied by both chocolate and a cabaret show. As well as referencing confectionary, the word 'chocolate' is used to describe Baker's skin colour, which was itself the subject of much discussion in the 1920s, with rumours of her use of natural (lemon juice and milk) and chemical (creams and treatments) skin-lightening techniques, complemented by her strategic use of cosmetics.[25] Coming from an entertainment background steeped in the traditions of minstrelsy, and having appeared in *Shuffle Along*, which specifically recruited lighter-skinned African American women to appear in their chorus line, Baker frequently mentions an early dissatisfaction with her skin colour in her memoirs, and though the subject of her skin tone is too broad in scope to explore here (and has been examined in depth by Cheng, amongst others), one aspect in particular is relevant to this discussion.[26]

Baker appeared in the musical revue *Chocolate Dandies* (which itself had grown out of a Broadway show called *Chocolate Kiddies*) from September 1924, leaving the United States in September 1925 to star in *La Revue Nègre* in Paris. In Fitzgerald's September 1924 piece, 'How to Live on Practically Nothing a Year', he satirises the public's impressions of Americans in Europe, describing himself and Zelda on a Riviera beach thus: 'Both of them were burned to a deep chocolate brown so that at first they seemed to be of Egyptian origin' (*MLC*, 53). Accompanied by their 'small black child with cotton-white hair', Fitzgerald tells us that 'closer inspection showed that their faces had an Aryan cast' (*MLC*, 53). Mistaken identity is a favoured device in Fitzgerald's magazine fiction, often enabling characters to express their true desires and traits before returning to more socially acceptable personas, as in 'The Offshore Pirate', 'Dice, Brassknuckles and Guitar' and 'Rags Martin-Jones and the Pr-nce of W-les' (1924). Nowlin has shown how Fitzgerald's complex identification with the African American entertainer as a fellow artistic outsider permeated his fiction deeply, and here this identification is role-played.[27] The identification of themselves as seemingly 'Egyptian' before clarifying their 'Aryan cast' has been preceded by the description of the Fitzgerald figure as a 'distinguished-looking young man' with 'deep chocolate brown' skin. Just a few months earlier, Fitzgerald felt the need for racist clarification of George's skin tone in '"The Sensible Thing"' (1924) when he returns from Peru 'almost black with tan, but it was a romantic black' (*ASM*, 160). In 'How to Live', this section of the essay serves as a satire on Americans abroad embracing 'becom[ing] absolutely French' while enjoying a kaleidoscope of home comforts, from the *New York Times* to baked beans from Akron, Ohio (*MLC*, 54). They are in denial about the obviousness of their true identities, kidding themselves that they have seamlessly assimilated with the locals, both culturally and physically. Fitzgerald uses 'deep chocolate brown' skin colour as a conspicuous marker of their self-delusion.

The fact that Fitzgerald is happy to be mistaken for an African, whilst in France, bisects with the vogue for 'Negrophilia' and Fitzgerald's own creative identification with the African American entertainer, but the Riviera setting also invokes contemporary debates around tanning, explored by Susan L. Keller, who states that 'Suntanning constituted an unprecedented change in how the body was conceptualized, a new form of self-construction wherein white skin as a symbol of prestige was replaced with dark skin as an index of one's wealth and leisure.'[28] Fitzgerald's description of his suntanned family situates this wealth and leisure in the foreground of a scene in which 'Out of the casino nearby drifted weird rococo music – a song dealing with the non-possession of a specific yellow fruit in a certain otherwise well-stocked store' (*MLC*, 53). Pre-dating Baker's famous banana skirt in her 'Danse Sauvage' by a year, Fitzgerald's reference to the novelty song 'Yes, We Have No Bananas' highlights their exotic setting, counterpointing it with this popular musical revue number from 1922. Fitzgerald's facetious treatment of race here sits in tension with his serious, creative identification with the African American entertainer elsewhere.

Baker's alleged desire to bleach her 'chocolate' skin and the tanning of the Fitzgeralds' to a 'deep chocolate brown' were concurrent: a photo of Baker from 1926 (a year that the Fitzgeralds spent on the Riviera) reveals an elegantly dressed and beaming Baker to be caked in light-toned make-up, and looking ghostly.[29] Baker, it seems, tries to lighten herself whilst simultaneously having achieved phenomenal success in the same black body which she tries to lighten. Fitzgerald, on the other hand, identifies with the black outsider as a means of validating his artistic mission, whilst enjoying the privileges attendant on being a white male. Archer-Straw recognises that whilst 'many blacks in Paris bleached their skin [. . .] in order to assimilate better', the white 'Negrophiles' of Paris 'compromised their racial purity for the sake of contact with blacks. Parisian women even used Bakerfix, the hair product named after Josephine Baker, to give their hair the same short, shiny lacquered look.' Archer-Straw finds that this black mimicry was born of necessity (and the memory of slavery, when lighter-skinned slaves could qualify as house slaves rather than field slaves), whereas white mimicry 'resulted, at best, from spiritual deprivation, and at worst, from whim'.[30]

The politics inherent in this 'mimicry' and 'assimilation' are incredibly complex and permeated multiple strata of social experience but were particularly prevalent (and visible) in the entertainment industry. Linda Mizejewski describes how, in the United States, 'café au lait – that is, light-skin or mulatto-effect blackface . . . became a standard sexual mask for the more daring Ziegfeld Girls' performances, a way to appropriate but also distance a racially structured, forbidden sexuality'.[31] In examining the Castles' project to 'elevate' modern dancing, we have encountered the efforts of the white social elite to 'civilise' what was perceived as an expression of 'primitive', raw, African American sexuality. In the 1910s, the Castles sought to 'sanitise' black art to make it fit for white consumption, whilst reaping the commercial benefits. This coexisted with an emerging tendency amongst some modernists to use African art as an example of 'primitive' and therefore 'pure' art. Previously rigid categories of race and class were being eroded.

The curious image cluster above bears this out: Baker's attempts to lighten her skin resulting in chalky dryness, Charlie Wales remarking that her roots were dry when he saw her perform at the Casino de Paris theatre, and the Fitzgeralds taking pleasure in bronzing themselves to 'a deep chocolate brown', listening to music about bananas emanate from a casino. The purposefully discordant combination of the balletic, historically white-dominated, 'arabesques' with the description 'chocolate', which recalls the European vogue for all-black revues (*Chocolate Dandies*, *The Blackbirds*, *Tan Town Topics*, amongst others) situates Josephine in a liminal space. She is performing at the Casino de Paris music hall: a famous and historic venue, hosting many mainstream stars in its time. The cheap, foldable 'strapontin' seat Charlie Wales purchases either could suggest a seediness which the *Saturday Evening Post* editors may have picked up on, or conversely, could indicate a sell-out performance necessitating the adding in of extra chairs to meet the demand. Fitzgerald is ambiguous about this, indicating only that Charlie remains for an hour of the performance, which would have been likely to constitute about half of the act.

Fitzgerald counterpoints the familiar and desirable, but racially loaded 'chocolate' with the white-dominated and socially elevated 'arabesques', both words appropriately coming to English via the French: *les arabesques au chocolat*. Charlie then imagines the restorative effect that America would have on Baker, uprooting her from her Parisian success and returning her to her origins (to which she was not to return until a brief and disastrous 1936 visit in the wake of the continued enforcement of segregation in the United States). Charlie renders her an outsider on her own stage by judging that she 'lacks America'.

The reasoning for this is complex: Fitzgerald was, firstly, angry at dance in general at this time, especially ballet, given Zelda's condition. He identified, as Nowlin has shown, with black entertainers because of his own anxieties about his social status, as well as because of the great artistic potential which he saw in himself. Charlie Wales is displaced from America just as Josephine Baker is. Though Charlie's business success is back on track after his lost Babylonian years, his life is not complete: it is Lincoln and Marion's home that is 'warm and comfortably American', while Charlie spends time in the Ritz bar, which 'was not an American bar any more' (*TAR*, 159, 157). As Wales judges Baker's act to be tired, Fitzgerald's 'act', his writing, was becoming more of a struggle. It is possible that in his identification with Baker, Fitzgerald transfers some of his own feelings of inadequacy and anxiety on to her, through his loaded allusions to popular culture.

'The Realest Part of Her Life': The Authentic Artist

Fitzgerald is clear to point out, in 'Babylon Revisited' and elsewhere, that too much dancing, or the wrong kind of dancing, can cause a splintering between the cognitive and corporeal functions of dancers – a split that Zelda, ever representative of the age, experienced at first hand. Dancers who feel disconnected from their bodies form a motif that conveys Fitzgerald's ambivalence towards dance. It is fun, expressive and artistic; it is also hedonistic, immoral and dangerous. These same conflicting traits can be applied to Fitzgerald's commercial fiction-writing enterprise. The bodily disconnected dancer can be read as a representation of Fitzgerald the *Post* writer. Jim's production-line dance academy could stand as a metaphor for the strictures and conventions of popular short stories, within which Fitzgerald worked. In this vein, Baker's arabesques can be read as representing inauthentic artistry: rather than using her creative talents to fashion something innovative, Baker is described as merely going through the motions – Charlie perceives her as being uninspired.

It is in Emmy Pinkard McChesney in 'Two Wrongs' (1930) that we find the best example of an authentic dancer who is connected to her body: we are told that 'she wanted to use herself on something she could believe in and it seemed to her that dance was woman's interpretation of music' (*TAR*, 39). This combination of belief and interpretation secures her agency in the choreography (or authorship) of her work, and she is described in terms of good character and excellent work ethic. 'She was a fine girl – one of the best' (*TAR*, 44), who spent 'four hours a day at bar exercises, attitudes, *sauts*, arabesques and pirouettes' (*TAR*, 39). She is rewarded for her efforts by the chance for professional and personal success, her neglectful husband being banished to the mountains with tuberculosis. The story is an emotionally charged imagining of the Fitzgeralds' future in the wake of their changed dynamic: in 1930, Zelda was industriously pursuing her newly discovered vocation for dance, while Scott's novel production stalled. It is pertinent that Emmy is a classical ballerina rather than a jazz dancer – in contrast to Baker, she is not trying to mix popular and high culture. Without wanting to overstretch the metaphor, it may be relevant to consider the extended narrative of a ballet compared to that of the novel, as opposed to dance numbers lasting the length of a popular song, and revue sketches that could be read as more closely aligned with the short story form.

Emmy's focus on authenticity (dance 'became the realest part of her life') is complemented by a small detail Fitzgerald gives us that redeems her from a saintly long-suffering wife stereotype (*TAR*, 39). At the story's close, when Emmy has chosen to focus on her career, she realises 'for one last honest moment how quickly she would forget' her feelings of indecision and guilt (*TAR*, 43). Without completely undermining the good character Fitzgerald has taken pains to portray, he allows her to add colour and resist the obedient wife formula just a little, revealing also her physical attraction to one of the men she will be working with. By allowing these character flaws to coexist with the depiction of her as being a saintly and patient wife who becomes absorbed in her work, Fitzgerald complicates the stereotypes that might be expected from a popular magazine short story. Furthermore, in his typescript version of the story, which was adjusted by the *Post*'s editors before publication (as Baker's arabesques had been), Fitzgerald portrays Bill as anti-Semitic. Despite knowing that his descriptions would be edited, it was important to Fitzgerald to create characters that felt 'real' and 'honest' to him, rather than simply adequate for conveying the couple's reversal of fortunes. Fitzgerald prized authenticity above all, but whilst Emmy's authenticity and industriousness are rewarded with the chance for professional success, Fitzgerald himself was beginning to struggle to maintain his own professional success during this period.

In 1935, Fitzgerald clear-sightedly assessed his story output in a letter to Maxwell Perkins, remarking that of those which had not been republished in book form,

> This is in some measure because the best of these stories have been stripped of their high spots which were woven into novels – but it is also because each story contains some special fault – sentimentality, faulty construction, confusing change of pace – or else was too obviously made for the trade.[32]

This assessment is pertinent: Fitzgerald's stories are insistent that dance must come from a genuine place that is expressive of authentic and true selfhood, in order to avoid the risk of psychic and corporeal schism. When dancers are just 'going through the motions' with 'dry roots', and fall short of this ideal, they are punished. The problem for readers of Fitzgerald – and Baker – is how far we are supposed to read their stances as literal or satirical. In other words, does Fitzgerald really want to punish his dancers for falling short of the ideal of perfect synchronicity between intent and gesture? What, in fact, does this perfection look like? To approach this question from another angle, we might ask whether you can create brilliant artistic expression whilst working within rules and guidance for dancing – or, indeed, writing.

On multiple occasions, Fitzgerald sets up ragtime and jazz dance as being formulaic by establishing set expectations (as taught in dance schools and in manuals) and then presents dancers who blindly follow these precepts as being out of touch with their authentic selves, as 'lacking something, in need of refreshment'. Those who follow the rules unquestioningly are criticised by Fitzgerald for not being true to themselves and thus producing inferior creative work. On the other hand, those who have agency in their creative pursuits, interpreting the existing formulae without blind allegiance to the rules, are rewarded. We can interpret this contradiction between practitioners and interpreters as an articulation of Fitzgerald's own efforts to create authentic self-expression under the formulaic constraints imposed upon him by the commercial magazines. This interpretation gives Fitzgerald's ambiguous portrayal of modern dance new resonance.

However, deviation from dance formulae was a cultural practice that was most common amongst black practitioners, whose innovations in dance drove the dance craze of the 1910s and continued as a dominant influence on mainstream dance culture of the 1920s. In black dance, improvisation and mimicry have central roles: Baker (drawing on the work of Ethel Williams and others before her) uses her comedic brand of dance to 'satirically comment' on the absurdity of racism, even whilst simultaneously enacting colonial fantasies. Mimicry was a way of learning from other practitioners and incorporating a variety of influences into one's work. But improvisation also served as a powerful means of protest: when assigned steps, Baker pretended to forget the steps and segued into a virtuosic display of her own. This assertion of independence from (almost exclusively male) choreographers served her well and got her noticed, aiding her ascendancy from chorus girl to international superstar.

Mimicry and improvisation serve as vital choreographic tools of composition. By reclaiming ownership of these, Baker asserted her agency and authorship of her own creative processes. And by importing influences from multiple cultural arenas, from the French music hall to traditional African music and dance, Baker embodied a dance philosophy in which quotation and innovation coexisted. Mae Gwendolyn Henderson recognises that Baker used 'compositional strategies marked by the interpolation of *non*-scripted improvisation into the *pre*-scripted vocabulary of black social and vernacular dance'.[33]

This finds an analogue in Fitzgerald's attempts to work simultaneously within the strictures imposed upon him by publications such as the *Saturday Evening Post* (the 'pre-scripted vocabulary' of short story convention) and beyond them, with 'improvisation'. Fitzgerald was very proud of his ability to add an authentic personal touch to stories that might read as formulaic in less capable hands. In writing about his commercial short fiction, Fitzgerald often frames his comments in terms of authenticity, writing in his notebooks 'The price was high, right up with Kipling, because there was one little drop of something, not blood, not a tear, not my seed, but me more intimately than these, in every story, it was the extra I had.'[34] Of course, it was a lot easier for Fitzgerald to assert his authenticity as an upper middle-class white male. For Baker to assert 'the extra [she] had', there were risks inherent in seeming to endorse existing racial stereotypes. Henderson has addressed the tightrope walked by such artists:

> in translating black vernacular and diasporic performance into a rhetoric of parodized pastiche, Baker's performances inevitably risk reproducing gender and race clichés, caricatures, and stereotypes as they are produced by the dominant and hegemonic discourse. In a performance vocabulary based on repetition with a difference – that is, repeating the dominant structures of signification, but with an articulation of transgressive difference – the repetition runs the risk (depending on the reader, the reading position, and the scene of reading) of reinforcing dominant codes, while the difference often gets diminished or overshadowed.[35]

In *Shuffle Along*, as well as in her Parisian revues, Baker reproduces such racial caricatures when she 'rolled her eyes, contorted her face, and swiveled her body in a deliberate parody of the blackface vaudeville routines and the conventions of the Negro minstrel show'.[36] Her 'natural vitality and lack of inhibition' were celebrated, as markers of the savage or primitive, despite the careful construction of Baker's image and crystallised performance, which purposefully played into these expectations.[37] Baker's performance as Fatou, the banana skirt-wearing native girl who meets a white explorer in *La Folie du Jour* (1926–7), tapped into the vogue for Primitivism and was set against the backdrop of France's colonial empire, and yet it was Baker's comically phallic banana skirt that stole the show.

Baker ridicules racist assumptions that, as an African American, she is animalistic by performing a chicken dance while cross-eyed. She reproduces the images of colonial explorer fantasies, whilst pairing her role as a bare-breasted native with a public persona of royalty, wearing fine gowns and adorning herself in diamonds. In one of her autobiographies, she explained, 'Since I personified the savage on the stage, I tried to be as civilized as possible in daily life.'[38] When contemporary reviewers repeatedly described her in animalistic terms, she diffused the racism by declaring this to be a compliment, then literally demonstrated her mastery over animals by parading around Paris with her pet cheetah Chiquita on a lead. Despite these 'articulation[s] of transgressive difference', many critics continued to read her performances as the ultimate symbol of exotic primitivism, and her reputation as 'the Black Venus' was cemented.

In the United States, at least as far back as the Cakewalk, parodic dance had been used as a mode of black resistance to colonisation and subjugation, the targets of the satire recognising themselves only some of the time. But it was also a very contemporary phenomenon for Fitzgerald. As he wrote in 'Echoes of the Jazz Age', 'it was an age of miracles, it was an age of art, it was an age of excess, and it was an age of satire' (*MLC*, 131). But this satire was not always detected. The tendency towards misreading parodic intent was visible in Paul Whiteman's famous Aeolian Hall concert in 1924, when the audience failed to perceive the performance of the 'Livery Stables Blues' as a demonstration of 'the crude jazz of the past' that was meant to serve as a counterpoint to the rest of the programme, 'designed to exhibit legitimate scoring as contrasted with the former hit and miss effects which were also called jazz'. Whiteman himself reflects that upon hearing the delighted audience's reaction to the 'Livery Stable Blues', he 'had for a moment the panicky feeling that they hadn't realized the attempt at burlesque'.[39]

In Paris, Baker's parody drew upon minstrelsy and vaudeville in its conspicuousness of performativity:

> the exaggeration of her monkey's walk and savage dance were overwrought dramatizations of how blacks were believed to behave. Her animal-like movements exposed the necessary performance that blacks had assumed, revealing the Negro's supposed animalism as an ongoing act that had been proscribed by whites. Baker performed performance.[40]

Yet only some of the audience would have read her performances in this way. Just as blackface minstrelsy was often misconstrued as 'the exhibition of black cultural practice rather than the performance of racialized exaggerations', Baker's performances could easily be misread as endorsements of racist primitivist and colonial narratives constructed by white people.[41]

Baker's attempts to counter these misreadings through the careful construction of her glamorous offstage image were usually misread as evidence of the civilising effect of Europe on Baker's savage 'natural' tendencies. Baker's interrogation of dominant cultural practices through parodic representations of them meets the criteria for what Linda Hutcheon coined 'complicitous critique', running the risk of being seen to endorse their parodied targets.[42] Despite Fitzgerald's obviously privileged position as a wealthy white male, both Baker and Fitzgerald renegotiate stereotypes, from jungle natives to flappers. However, Fitzgerald actually helped to establish, at least in the popular cultural consciousness, the stereotypes he is seeking to reconfigure, and he was well aware of his role as an iconic chronicler of the Jazz Age.

Both Baker and Fitzgerald find themselves working within formulae and managing audience expectations. Adopting a satirical tone leads each of them to find a commercially viable creative position that can deliver financial returns and satisfy the majority of the audience who do not notice the parody, as well as connect with those who do. In his use of the parodic mode to depict various aspects of popular culture, Fitzgerald shows himself to be heavily influenced by African American culture, fusing the concepts of interpreting set formulae and artistic authenticity. In 1930, he wrote to Harold Ober, 'these *Post* stories [. . .] they're honest and if their *form* is stereotyped people know what to expect when they pick up the *Post*'.[43] This 'stereotyped' form had imprinted itself upon the public consciousness, and the 'Fitzgerald brand' of story became well known.

The film critic and genre theorist Robert Warshow, writing about the conventions of gangster movies, aptly summarises the situation Fitzgerald's short stories found themselves in:

> For such a type to be successful means that its conventions have imposed themselves upon the general consciousness and become the accepted vehicles of a particular set of attitudes and a particular aesthetic effect. One goes to any individual example of the type with very definite expectations, and originality is to be welcomed only in the degree that

it intensifies the expected experience without fundamentally altering it. Moreover, the relationship between the conventions which go to make up such a type and the real experience of its audience or the real facts of whatever situation it pretends to describe is of only secondary importance and does not determine its aesthetic force. It is only in an ultimate sense that the type appeals to its audience's experience of reality; much more immediately, it appeals to previous experience of the type itself: it creates its own field of reference.[44]

These 'conventions' and the associated 'aesthetic effect' manifest themselves in Fitzgerald's portrayal of the flapper. In his early career, Fitzgerald created a brand with his 'flapper confections'. Fitzgerald capitalised on this by declaring, in a January 1921 interview, 'I married the heroine of my stories.'[45] He lists the traits of the flapper as he sees her: 'we find the young woman of 1920 flirting, kissing, viewing life lightly, saying damn without a blush, playing along the danger line in an immature way – a sort of mental baby vamp'.[46]

Readers knew what to expect when picking up a Fitzgerald story: a 1920 review entitled 'Mostly Flappers' conceded that some stories in Fitzgerald's first collection, *Flappers and Philosophers* (1920), were 'good. Others are merely brightly coloured flub-dub about surpassingly beautiful 19-year-old debutantes.'[47] But Fitzgerald enjoyed playing with his audience's expectations of these flapper tales: he knew that his flapper had created her 'own field of reference'. His narratorial interjections address the reader directly, forming a shared interpretative space that often adopts a knowing, near-conspiratorial tone. Fitzgerald also invokes other metafictive devices to interfere with his readers' suspension of disbelief, such as when Ardita kisses Toby (also known as Curtis) 'in the illustration' of 'The Offshore Pirate'.[48] He also creates parodic undercurrents in his plots and characterisation to rework subtly the formulae he was working with.

By turns expressing tantalising glamour and dangerous moral consequences, Fitzgerald's exploration of the jazz dances of the 1910s and 1920s, and his evaluation of Baker's 'chocolate arabesques' show a writer who is exploring his own critical and commercial resonance, by way of interrogating the concept of an authentic, inspired creative self. Jim Powell's dancing school teaches students how to perform an assumed identity but Baker gives a masterclass in subversive performed identity, and through his descriptions of both, Fitzgerald demonstrates that, although he is working within the generic expectations of the commercial short story in which he describes stories as being 'built' rather than 'written', he sees authenticity as being of paramount, redeeming importance.[49]

Contrary to their efforts to obscure their true selves (through lightening creams or suntanning and disguise motifs), both Fitzgerald and Baker used their authentic identities in their art. Fitzgerald famously used his own life as material for his writing, whilst Josephine played versions of herself on stage and in the motion pictures she starred in. Developing a performative persona served Baker well as she built her brand through the 1920s, and performative identity itself was something of a phenomenon in that decade, as Kirk Curnutt asserts: 'Identity in the 1920s assumed an unprecedented performative dimension with the traits one *possessed* suddenly less important than how (and how well) they were *presented*. [. . .] The presentational self did not manufacture personality but externalized innate but untapped traits.'[50] In other words, the theatrical self was a means of presenting innate talents to the world, purposely performing them. In expressing their theatrical selves, both Baker and Fitzgerald are producing products to be consumed for leisure.

Fitzgerald was not the only one to criticise Baker's Parisian incarnation, and three years after 'Babylon Revisited' was published, Ethel Waters performed a parody of Baker in Irving Berlin's 1933 'topical revue', *As Thousands Cheer*. Waters played Baker, 'still the Rage of Paris', singing a song that referenced the drive to 'sanitise' and elevate music and dance cultures, that the Castles had engaged in twenty years before:

I've got Harlem on my mind,
And I'm longing to be low-down;
And my parlez-vous will not ring true
With Harlem on my mind.
I've been dined and I've been wined,
But I'm headin' for a showdown,
'Cause I can't go on from night till dawn

With Harlem on my mind.
I go to dinner with a French marquis
Each evening after the show;
My lips begin to whisper 'mon chéri',
But my heart keeps singing hi-de-ho.
I've become too damned refined,
And at night I hate to go down
To that highfalutin flat
That Lady Mendl designed
With Harlem on my mind.[51]

Berlin's parody of Baker has her 'longing to be lowdown' because she has 'become too damned refined'. The centrality of parody, and the provocative interactions between high and popular culture, endured across the spheres of both dance and popular music from the 1910s until well into the 1930s. Both Baker and Fitzgerald serve as reminders of the paramount importance of authenticity to the artist who seeks both commercial and critical success.

CHAPTER 3

'Satyre upon a Saxaphone': Fitzgerald and Music

Tales of the Jazz Age, F. Scott Fitzgerald's second collection of short stories, was published in September 1922, six months after his second novel, *The Beautiful and Damned* came out.[1] Fitzgerald's editor Maxwell Perkins was critical of Fitzgerald's chosen title for the collection, explaining in a May 1922 letter to Fitzgerald that Scribner's book salesmen 'feel that there is an intense reaction against all jazz and that the word whatever implication it actually has, will itself injure the book'.[2] Fitzgerald replied, defending his choice of title, and assuring Perkins that the book

> will be bought by *my own personal public*, that is by the countless flappers and college kids who think I am a sort of oracle. . . . If I could think of a wonderful selling title unconnected with Jazz I'd use it but I can't so we better use a safe one that has a certain appeal.[3]

Almost a decade later, Fitzgerald himself would go on to explain, in *Scribner's Magazine*, that 'The word jazz in its progress towards respectability has meant first sex, then dancing, then music' (*MLC*, 132). What Fitzgerald's brief survey seeks to demonstrate is the variety of meaning denoted by the word 'jazz', and thus there are difficulties in associating the mantel 'chronicler of the Jazz Age' solely with the musical definition of 'jazz'. That being said, musical jazz forms an important part of Fitzgerald's literary enterprise, as critics such as Ruth Prigozy, T. Austin Graham and Anthony Berret have shown in their respective studies.[4] Allegedly originating from the word 'jass', one theory posits that the orthographic change was prompted by the 'Original Dixieland Jass Band', who had their posters defaced in 1916 (vandals obfuscated the 'J').[5] Legend has it that the bandleader Nick LaRocca decided to change the spelling. There are countless theories on where the word 'jass' itself came from but most agree that the word probably originated in African American slang. The first appearance in print was in San Francisco, as Krin Gabbard has identified: 'In 1913, Ernest J. Hopkins offered this definition [in a San Francisco newspaper]: "something like life, vigor, energy, effervescence of spirit, joy, pep, magnetism, verve, virility, ebulliency, courage, happiness – oh, what's the use? – JAZZ"'.[6]

Theories of origin focus on the French linguistic influence upon New Orleans, as well as the various surviving African dialects spoken there, finding possible etymology along both branches, as well as the possibility that 'jass' was an abbreviation denoting jasmine-scented perfumes, which were apparently popular in the bordellos of New Orleans, where jazz in both sexual and musical senses was to be found. As with the music, the word eventually acquired more respectability, and could be used in polite society to refer to energetic dancing and its attendant music. By the time Fitzgerald was deciding whether to call his second collection of stories 'In One Reel', 'Youth and Death', 'Sideshow' or 'Tales of the Jazz Age', in 1922, 'jazz' hovered between connotations, simultaneously evoking the salacious and the innocent, as Perkins's trepidation attests.

Fitzgerald's novels are peppered with jazz in all of the senses he identified: sex, dance and music. Prigozy counts seventy-one song titles and 'innumerable lyrics' in his novels and stories, remarking that Fitzgerald was a 'keen analyst of the effects of popular culture on American lives' who 'acknowledged his debt to popular culture' and 'used it with meticulous care'.[7] Prigozy's groundbreaking 1977 essay was the first serious attempt to investigate Fitzgerald's relationship with music, cataloguing his use of song titles and tracing their composers, publication date and source (whether musical comedy, film or neither), though the same has yet to be done for the lyrics Fitzgerald was so fond of quoting. Prigozy identifies the key ways in which Fitzgerald uses music: to help his characters articulate their feelings, to act as an analogue for characters' moods and relationships, and to provide background music and intensify setting; in his later novels, *Tender is the Night* (1934) and the unfinished *The Last Tycoon* (1941), Prigozy finds Fitzgerald's use of music to be markedly more sophisticated. He uses music to develop themes and to comment on the action, while specific songs serve as leitmotifs for relationships (especially in *Tender is the Night*).

Prigozy's scholarship was complemented in 2013 by Graham's study, *The Great American Songbooks: Musical Texts, Modernism, and the Value of Popular Culture*. In this, Graham devotes a chapter to Fitzgerald and persuasively argues in favour of recognising Fitzgerald's use of a 'literary soundtrack' whereby extra-literary responses are evoked through Fitzgerald's invocation of songs from a communal bank of material which his initial reading public knew well, commonly known as 'The Great American Songbook'. This approach relinquishes a certain degree of authorial control, relying on the reader to make the right connections between lyric and aural experience. Furthermore, this extra-literary device deteriorates in effectiveness as the fictions, and the pool of music to which they allude, age. Graham finds that this mixture of immediacy and ambiguity reaches its apex in *The Great Gatsby*, in which the erosion of contemporaneity and the half-life of recognition actually propels the literary technique, creating a haunting sense of the half-remembered that chimes with Gatsby's selective memory and persistent tendencies to conflate the past and the present.[8]

Fitzgerald's trust in his readership to interpret his references to songs and lyrics shows his awareness of the role audience reception plays in determining the relative value of popular culture. In Warshow's phrase, Fitzgerald has created a shared interpretative space with his readers. As Prigozy reminds us, Fitzgerald had the utmost respect for popular culture, but it is difficult, especially for a modern reader, to untangle the occasions when we are meant to draw serious inferences from those times when Fitzgerald is burlesquing the very idea of seeking serious meaning from popular entertainment. Songs can provide comic relief, such as when Basil is eagerly trying to woo a girl who is distractedly humming 'My little lovin' - honey man' (*BJG*, 90), and they can also incite life-altering epiphanies, like Sally Carrol's soundtracked revelation in 'The Ice

Palace' (1920). However, in stories like 'One Interne' (1932), the use of a vaudeville-style song with the chorus of 'Bum-tiddy-bum-bum, / Tiddy-bum-bum' is more problematic and destabilises the tone of the story (*TAR*, 130). Prigozy sees a general diachronic development in the sophistication of Fitzgerald's musical allusions, suggesting his use of music was problematised as his career progressed. Graham, with space only to analyse the novels, finds that Fitzgerald's use of music is playful and varied, except in the final two novels, in which it becomes depressing and even absurd, creating dramatic irony by pairing light love songs with Dick Diver's 'torturous memories' in *Tender is the Night*, and counterpointing a soprano repeatedly recording a line of a song in *The Last Tycoon* during the midst of an earthquake.[9]

Fitzgerald's understanding of popular music was extensive – ever since his youth he had been fascinated by musical theatre, appearing in several productions in his native St Paul, Minnesota as a teenager, and going on to write the libretti for three Triangle Club productions at Princeton.[10] His passion for music was not restricted to musical comedies, however, as his musical allusions are by no means limited to the stage. Some twenty years after Fitzgerald's Princeton exploits, Andrew Turnbull recounts Fitzgerald's rendition of 'Goodnight, Sweetheart' one evening as he bade his future biographer good night (though, admittedly, Turnbull notes his voice was 'weak [and] rather tuneless').[11] Fitzgerald took an interest in the public's changing musical tastes throughout his life. In his posthumously published novel, *The Last Tycoon*, set in 1936, Fitzgerald's protagonist, Monroe Stahr, reflects:

> I turned the dial and got either *Gone* or *Lost* – there were good songs that year. The music was getting better again. When I was young during the depression, it wasn't so hot, and the best numbers were from the twenties.[12]

We should be wary of identifying Stahr's voice too closely with Fitzgerald's, but it is clear from Fitzgerald's œuvre that the two shared similar feelings. Attuned to the exports of Tin Pan Alley, New York's West 28th Street that formed the epicentre of the songwriting and music publishing industries in this period, Fitzgerald's notebooks contained lists of his favourite songs and lyrics, as well as his own creations.[13]

Music critics have suggested that Tin Pan Alley's relentless marketing strategies reached saturation point around the time Fitzgerald was writing the Basil and Josephine stories, which could have been a factor in Fitzgerald's decision to feature the music of the 1910s so prominently in the stories. Of course, the changed outlook of a nation plunged into the Great Depression affected its appetite for diverting music, a development identified by Hughson F. Mooney in 1954:

> In the late 1920s, on the heels of the smartly daring generation whose naïve faith in rebellion and thrills had been stamped since 1895 on popular music, came satiation and disillusion. Relaxation rather than rebellion, indifference rather than enthusiasm, introspection rather than activity, became the order of the day.[14]

This shift reflects an introspective period for Fitzgerald and his creative practices, in which he was feeling confused and uninspired, and financially obligated to focus on the commercial certainties of short stories for the slicks in place of the long-gestating novel he was unsuccessfully trying to refine. This creative impasse prompted Fitzgerald to reflect on the comparative 'golden age' of ragtime music in his adolescence in which the Basil and Josephine stories are set. Other reasons for Fitzgerald's dependence on the soundtrack of his youth during this period are the fact that he was in Europe from March 1929 to September 1931, where American songs clearly still had an influence (as the European courtship via American phonographs in *Tender is the Night* demonstrates) but hits were disseminated more slowly and sparsely. The emergence of Zelda's mental illness could also have been a catalyst for Fitzgerald to revisit his generally happy youth in his work, whilst the bills that Zelda's illness generated certainly caused Fitzgerald to crave the financial stability that regularly published short stories afforded.

Although jazz served as a constant for Fitzgerald in this tumultuous period, music has notoriously amorphous evolutionary tendencies. Especially in the vernacular cultural spheres of jazz and blues music, divisions into temporal segments, or into distinct

genres, can be confusing or even arbitrary. To over-simplify drastically the music of the American interwar period collectively known
under the loose umbrella of 'jazz', the following account gives an
overview of the generic transitions of the music that influenced
Fitzgerald so profoundly.[15] The demise of the syncopated dance
music known as ragtime by around 1917 led into the age of jazz,
the popularity and dissemination of which was fuelled by the Great
Migration of African Americans from Southern states to Northern
urban centres, bringing half a million African Americans north
between 1916 and 1919, and continuing into the 1920s. Divisions
and subdivisions of jazz are of limited usefulness, given that they
often directly or indirectly rely on racial divisions in trying to establish musical genealogy. The notion of 'hot jazz' as a shorthand for
music performed by black musicians such as Cab Calloway, Bessie
Smith and Jelly Roll Morton, and marketed on a relatively small
scale as 'race records', has given way to a more plural and less segregated understanding of the production and dissemination of this
music. None the less, in 1931, Fitzgerald refers to these as 'bootleg
negro records with their phallic euphemisms that made everything
suggestive' in 'Echoes of the Jazz Age' (*MLC*, 135).

'Sweet jazz', played by and marketed to white Americans, which
'enjoyed widest distribution on recordings and the radio and signi-
fied jazz for almost all white Americans and Europeans', was typi-
fied by much of Tin Pan Alley's 1920s output, and incorporated the
work of bandleaders such as Paul Whiteman, whose concerts are
often also described as belonging to the genre of 'symphonic jazz'.[16]
Despite the porous intermingling of musical styles and influence
at this busy historical moment, it is clear that jazz undoubtedly
originated in African American traditions. David Savran identifies
four loosely distinctive features of jazz music: fast tempo duple or
quadruple time signatures, an emphasis on brass and woodwind
instruments, syncopation, and the use of blue notes.[17] Kathy Ogren
also includes in her definition improvisation; antiphony, or 'call
and response' exchanges; and polyrhythms.[18]

The cusp of the third and fourth decades of the twenti-
eth century was characterised by the rise of 'swing' music. The
Charleston gave way to dances such as the Lindy Hop and the
Balboa. Accolades were transferred from the songwriters and

composers on to the arrangers of this rhythmically propulsive music, designed for big bands that included multiple soloists. Sigmund Spaeth states: Swing was 'nothing more than carefully organised, prearranged "hot jazz", lacking in spontaneity, but impressive as an exhibition of individual and collective skill . . . the average tune was merely a starting point for jazz or swing treatment of varying complexity'.[19]

Predating all of these musical forms was the blues, a secular folk music that developed in the aftermath of the American Civil War, largely in the rural South. It served as a conduit for African Americans to channel and process their experiences, and was influenced by work songs and spirituals, although the precise roots of the music are unknown, as it was an orally transmitted form. In the early 1920s, there was a vogue for blues songs, and a flurry of records was made exploiting the classic blues form of twelve bars, three lines and three chords (tonic, subdominant and dominant), utilising flattened thirds and sevenths which could coincide with their natural counterparts in the accompaniment, creating a unique harmonic character. Artists like Ma Rainey and Bessie Smith were joined by white singers singing pseudo-blues. Arnold Shaw observes that what 'started as a black phenomenon quickly became a white, Tin Pan Alley development, and even invaded the Broadway musical theatre'.[20] The pattern of white Americans profiting from African American culture was a repetitive feature of American history during this period.

In 'Rags Martin-Jones and the Pr-nce of W-les' (1924), the characters enjoy a blues singer's set at a rooftop cabaret, in a curious and filmic interlude. Rags does not recognise the singer, and the entertainment continues with a comedian, the blues singer having been only a brief interlude in Rags's impatient anticipation of the royal arrival:

> A negro girl, thin as a reed, emerged suddenly from a masked entrance into a circle of harsh barbaric light, startled the music to a wild minor and commenced to sing a rhythmic, tragic song. The pipe of her body broke abruptly and she began a slow incessant step, without progress and without hope, like the failure of a savage insufficient dream. She had lost Papa Jack, she cried over and over with a hysterical monotony at once

despairing and unreconciled. One by one the loud horns tried to force her from the steady beat of madness but she listened only to the mutter of the drums which were isolating her in some lost place in time, among many thousand forgotten years. After the failure of the piccolo, she made herself again into a thin brown line, wailed once with a sharp and terrible intensity, then vanished into sudden darkness.

'If you lived in New York you wouldn't need to be told who she is,' said John when the amber light flashed on. (*ASM*, 103)

The fact that Rags has no idea who the singer is serves to undermine the episode's captivating description and emphasises the disjointed-ness of the interlude. The story progresses without further comment on the singer or her act, marking out the episode as self-contained and isolating it from the story. Fitzgerald chooses not to make links between the performance and the protagonists explicit, but if he had done, there would have been parallels to be drawn between the enchantment of the singer, stuck in monotonous madness, and Rags herself, who is characterised by her boredom and ennui, until this very evening. The musicians, trying to break the singer out of her fixed state of mind, are creating entertainment to try to cause an awakening in her, just as John tries to entertain Rags and break the spell of her apathy. The melodic instruments are anthropomor-phised into concerned bystanders, trying one by one to rescue her from the rhythm of the drums, which represent 'the steady beat of madness'. The presence of primitivist images in the descriptions of the 'barbaric light', the 'savage insufficient dream' and the ancient 'lost place in time' collectively undermines the modernity and glamour of the performance – traits that Rags is noted for on both sides of the Atlantic. The fact that the songstress sings herself into oblivion, 'wail[ing]' before 'vanish[ing]', is a worrying premonition of what will happen to the 'old' Rags. She is destined to fulfil the traditional flapper trajectory of decreasing conspicuousness: adventure, domestication and marriage. The story's inclusion in a collection palpably about 'All the Sad Young Men' but which also includes stories about women's sometimes difficult transitions into married life and motherhood is pertinent, most obviously in the 1925 story 'The Adjuster'.

Another, more radical reading of this passage could interpret

Fitzgerald's reference to the 'negro girl, thin as a reed', who performed with 'a slow, incessant step' and sang of losing 'Papa Jack' as an allusion to specific blues singers of the early 1920s such as Bessie Smith and Ethel Waters. Waters in particular, standing at 5 feet 9½ inches and known as 'Sweet Mama Stringbean', is a good candidate for an analogue to the singer here, especially in the early 1920s when she was particularly slim.[21] In the early 1920s it was rumoured that Waters had a relationship with the dancer Ethel Williams.[22] This detail could add an extra layer to our interpretation of Rags and her expression of (heterosexual) love as a purely financial transaction that is conveniently, readily available. 'It looks like a bargain to me,' she says, choosing John at the story's close (*ASM*, 112).

As it stands, the episode serves as a self-contained pastiche of female blues singers in the early 1920s. It is a pastiche rather than a parody because Fitzgerald chooses not to comment on the links between the performance and the story, so we instead encounter 'an imitation of another critical style' – that of female blues singers, 'without critical distance', in Simon Dentith's phrase.[23] The effect of this self-contained performance is rather postmodern, and in addition, the musicality on the page draws our attention to the limitations of a written story in conveying music with sensory verisimilitude. As we have seen, Fitzgerald is rather fond of such forays into metafiction.

Manhattan rooftop blues performances were not common occurrences for most of Fitzgerald's readership, and few among his readers would actually have had access to such fashionable and luxurious entertainment. Revisionist accounts of the 1920s challenge common stereotypes of the decade. Notably, Paul A. Carter raises pertinent questions about how certain periods of history, especially the 1920s, come to be reinterpreted by each subsequent generation, who 'take from – or react against – whatever in that earlier timespan speaks most clearly to its own condition'.[24] This is precisely what Fitzgerald is doing in his portrayal of the ragtime generation in the Basil and Josephine stories. Music's strangely self-cannibalising relationship is a practical example of this reinterpretative tendency, with standards of yesteryear being covered and reimagined by new generations, often with new time signatures or performance styles. As Spaeth reminds us, 'the average tune was merely a starting point'.[25]

Carter insists that whilst a minority of Americans were enjoying the new cultural freedoms of the 1920s, millions more were working too hard to notice, especially in the rural population, amongst whom poverty was widespread. In fact, Howard Zinn contends that 'one tenth of one per cent of the families at the top received as much income as 42 per cent of the families at the bottom' such as 'the tenant farmers, black and white, the immigrant families in the big cities either without work or not making enough to get the basic necessities'.[26] Fitzgerald does not focus on this 42 per cent of families in his fiction, but that is not to say that he was not aware of their struggles and of the inequity of his country. Peter L. Hays notes that 'Fitzgerald did not write about the poor. There are no manual laborers or shopgirls among his main characters, few farmers or truck drivers.'[27] He instead represented the interactions between old and new money, whose financial equivalence could never translate to a state of social equivalence, and the tendencies of the upper-middle classes to attempt to emulate the very wealthy. In the 1920s, it is true that Fitzgerald focused on what the narrator of *This Side of Paradise* (1920) called 'a new generation dedicated more than the last to the fear of poverty and the worship of success', but by the 1930s, especially in light of the national struggles, he was undoubtedly more sensitive to the plight of the poor, and several of his stories were set against the backdrop of the Depression.[28] Writing about the 1920s in 'Echoes of the Jazz Age', Fitzgerald reflects that 'it was borrowed time anyhow – the whole upper tenth of a nation living with the insouciance of grand ducs and the casualness of chorus girls' (*MLC*, 138).

Although Fitzgerald grew to rely on loans and advances to maintain financial security, he also worked hard, one of the few major American authors of his time to support himself solely on the proceeds of his literary output. Most others had a secondary source of income, through marriage or other family resources.[29] Fitzgerald's sheer output – over 170 stories and four completed novels in a twenty-year career – confirms the apocryphal nature of Fitzgerald's supposedly all-consuming hedonism.

Such reassessments of the 'Roaring Twenties' can better help us to understand the seemingly strange relationship between Fitzgerald the *bon vivant* and Fitzgerald the professional author. Fitzgerald does not intend for his protagonists to be read as being straight-forward representatives of the United States, especially during the Depression years, but they served a specific purpose in the market-place. Revisionist accounts of the 'Roaring Twenties' like Carter's can remind us that the vast majority of people reading the *Saturday Evening Post* in the 1920s were ordinary people, enjoying a return to normality after the First World War, rather than flappers and sheiks. Many of these readers were none the less eager to hear all about the escapades of the so-called Flaming Youth. Fitzgerald's stories, two-fifths of which were published in the *Post*, and almost all of which were offered to the *Post*'s editors first between 1925 and 1936, form a narrative of the few for the entertainment of the many.[30] One of the key ways in which Fitzgerald positions himself as an expert on the young flappers and sheiks, gaining the trust of the white-collar worker and suburban housewife, is through his use of popular music. He displays an air of authenticity by knowing exactly which songs young people are listening to, but selecting and representing them judiciously enough so as not to alienate his readership. When Fitzgerald considered himself too old to unironically participate in youth culture, his daughter Scottie provided his lens through which to interrogate and review proceedings. In his later stories such as 'No Flowers' (1934) and the Gwen stories (1936), he shows how easily he is able to tap into this new generation coming of age in the 1930s, and their leisure pursuits.

'"Blow, Ye Winds, Heigho!"': 'The Ice Palace' and Fitzgerald's Early Use of Popular Music

In 'The Ice Palace', written in December 1919, two months after *This Side of Paradise* was accepted for publication, there are two instances of musical interlude. Published in the *Saturday Evening Post*, it is the story of Southern belle Sally Carrol Happer's first (and only) visit to her one-time fiancé Harry's Northern city, which was based on St Paul, Minnesota, Fitzgerald's home town. Choosing to visit in January, when Minnesotan temperatures seldom rise above 23 degrees Fahrenheit (–5 degrees Celsius), Georgian Sally

Carrol is out of her comfort zone in more ways than one, disliking the cultural differences she encounters as much as she despises the weather. She becomes lost in the eponymous labyrinth constructed of ice blocks, the main feature of the St Paul winter carnival. Traumatised by her experience and thoroughly fed up with ice and snow, Sally Carrol retreats back to the South, we infer that the engagement has been broken off, and the story languidly concludes in the Georgian sunshine where it began.

Through careful use of musical references, Fitzgerald juxtaposes North and South, past and present, and stasis and vigour. The first musical interlude occurs when Sally Carrol is on the train up to Minnesota. She is already very cold but takes her newly visible breath in her stride with 'naïve enjoyment'. She is moved by her excitement at being in 'the North – her land now!' to sing '"then blow, ye winds heigho! / A-roving I will go"' 'exultantly' (F&P, 44). This is part of the chorus of a sea shanty called 'Ten Thousand Miles Away', which was popular in the 1910s and featured in compendiums of college songs during this period. The chorus continues:

> I'll stay no more on England's shore,
> To hear sweet music play,
> For I'm on the move to my own true love,
> Ten thousand miles away![31]

The parody version of the song, 'A Capital Ship' (c. 1890), blends elements of the sea shanty with a nonsense poem called 'The Walloping Window-Blind' by Charles Carryl. Sally Carrol's name may purposefully echo Charles Carryl's, and Fitzgerald draws attention to her fondness for her double-barrelled forename, and dislike of being called solely 'Sally'. The lyrics of 'A Capital Ship' modify the chorus to:

> So, blow ye winds, heigh-ho
> A-roving I will go
> I'll stay no more on England's shore
> So let the music play-ay-ay
> I'm off for the morning train
> To cross the raging main

I'm off to my love with a boxing glove
10,000 miles away.[32]

It is impossible to know whether Fitzgerald was thinking of the
sea shanty or the parody when he has Sally Carrol chant the song,
though the setting, on a train, and the imminent hostilities which
are about to befall her and her 'love' would suggest the latter version, based around Charles Carryl's poem for children. Sally Carrol
is associated with childish pursuits throughout the story, from
painting paper dolls to wanting to toboggan in Minnesota, and
then swim in waterholes and eat green peaches in Georgia. The
song reflects her optimism and spirit of adventure in this moment,
but also undermines this confidence with the hint of foreboding,
suggesting that when she reaches Minnesota, known as 'the land of
ten thousand lakes', things may not go entirely according to plan.

Singing a song based on a nineteenth-century sea shanty whilst
travelling on a train in 1920 puts Sally Carrol in a strangely pal-
impsestic position. She is a rather morbid girl, spending time
in the graveyard back in Tarleton, Georgia, amongst the rows of
Confederate dead, who make her 'happy', and hallucinating the
appearance of a long-dead girl in the Ice Palace whose gravestone
she visited back in Georgia. Shanties themselves came into prominence in the United States in the years leading up to the Civil War.
By the end of the nineteenth century, steam power and machinery
rendered motivational work songs unnecessary on ships, but this
coincided with the vaudeville circuit's growing prominence and
the rise of new recording technologies in the early twentieth century that preserved these cultural artefacts, though their contents
and authorship became slippery. Singing a sea shanty while on a
train can be read as a representation of the conflict in Sally Carrol
between older processes and the relatively new industrialism of
the North, as well as subtly echoing the influence of the Civil War
context on her.

By quoting an old song with plainly antiquated lyrics, to pledge
her allegiance to the progressive North, we have a hint that all will
not end well, a suggestion that is corroborated by the melody's
melancholy key of B♭ minor. The choice of the verb 'chanted' solid-
ifies Sally Carrol's invocation of the song as a hymn to hard work;

though spirituality has a large presence in the story in the form of ghosts and graves, the chanting here suggests a group identity, and the etymology of 'shanty' itself, rather than an incantation or prayer. Just as she calls upon the Confederate dead in the graveyard for 'strength', Sally Carrol finds fortification in numbers by singing the song, even though she is singing alone. In a tactic repeated later in the story, by inciting contemporary readers to join in and hear the chorus as they read it (for it was a well-known song in 1920), Fitzgerald provides Sally Carrol with an extra-literary companionship.

Sally Carrol finds antiphony within the narrative also, when in the typical call-and-response style of a shanty, the confused Pullman porter replies to her chorus by politely asking her to repeat herself, and Sally answers with a lie and a command: 'I said, "Brush me off"' (*F&P*, 44). Associated with the Civil War through George Pullman's loan of a car to house Abraham Lincoln's coffin in 1865 (and Pullman's own use of a hired substitute in the Union Army), the Pullman Company employed a large number of African American men as Pullman porters in the 1910s and 1920s, whose duties included brushing off the clothes and coats of the passengers, as well as shining their shoes. Another connotation of the phrase 'brush me off' is 'just ignore me', and this works well as a narrative signal that Sally Carrol's impromptu performance has ended.

Sally Carrol is met at the station by Harry and his family, but finds herself unable to shed the performative identity she assumed in singing her song on the train; when Harry enquires whether she is glad to have made the trip, she replies, 'Where you are is home for me, Harry,' but the narrator tells us that 'as she said this, she had the feeling for the first time in her life that she was acting a part' (*F&P*, 51, 47). Charm comes naturally to her in her capacity as a Southern belle, but in the North, Sally Carrol finds artifice. She has a mixed day, with Harry's racist criticism of the South driving her to tears when he exclaims 'Those damn Southerners! . . . They're sort of – sort of degenerates – not at all like the old Southerners. They've lived so long down there with all the colored people that they've gotten lazy and shiftless' (*F&P*, 52–3). They have a quarrel, which leads to a hasty resolution and a reconfirmation of their impending March wedding date.

That evening they go to a vaudeville performance, which concludes with an orchestral rendition of the song 'Dixie'. This stirs up 'something stronger and more enduring than her tears and smiles' within Sally (*F&P*, 54). Though there is no vocalist, as the final or 'chaser' acts of vaudeville performances were usually 'dumb' to accommodate patrons noisily leaving the theatre, Sally joins the performance, at least in her mind, where she provides the lyrics – 'Away, away, away down South in Dixie' – and stages a ghostly production, all whilst 'gripping the arms of her chair until her face grew crimson'. Her extra-literary companionship is restored through Fitzgerald's quotation of four lines of the extremely recognisable chorus, but not before Sally Carrol retreats into her Confederate dream world, watching 'her own old ghosts marching by' (*F&P*, 54). This prefigures the later appearance of the ghost of Margery Lee, whose gravestone Sally Carrol and Harry had visited near the rows of Confederate dead back in Georgia. Lee appears to Sally Carrol as she realises she is trapped within the 40 cm-thick walls of the Ice Palace, and Sally Carrol imagines herself nestled amongst Margery Lee's plentiful hooped skirts. The anthemic, march-like tempo of 'Dixie' is again revisited when marching soldiers parade outside the Ice Palace before they enter it. Sally Carrol realises her emotional entrapment in the vaudeville theatre just as her physical entrapment is realised in the Ice Palace. Both events profoundly affect her, and Fitzgerald uses 'Dixie' to stir the readers' emotions and sympathy for Sally Carrol, who defends her Southern countrymen as some of 'the finest men in the world' (*F&P*, 53).

A favourite of Abraham Lincoln, who played it to mark General Robert E. Lee's surrender in 1865, 'Dixie' was reportedly originally written by Daniel Emmett around 1859. Beginning as a minstrelsy song, it was later assumed as an anthem of the Confederacy and became emblematic of the old South. The racist stereotype of the homesick slave is utilised in the narrative of the song, and when minstrelsy was gradually eclipsed by the rise of vaudeville, it became a vaudeville standard. In Sally Carrol's viewing of the spectacle in the Minnesotan vaudeville theatre, she transcends the role of observer and becomes part of the performance. She disappears from the conventional narrative, and thus she cannot hear

Harry's whispers to her as she watches her own parade of 'ghosts marching by'.

Alice Hall Petry has identified Sally Carrol's struggle to choose between North and South as a psychic schism in which she is trying to decide between marriage (represented by the North) and Southern spinsterhood.[33] The song choices of these two musical episodes, with their solo/group dynamic, show that even though Sally Carrol ultimately chooses to remain unmarried (at least for now), she is not actually alone. They also serve to underpin the thematic links in the story between the contemporary setting of the action and the Civil War. The songs enhance Fitzgerald's characterisation of Sally Carrol – the shanty portraying her adventurous spirit, while 'Dixie' reinforces the image of her as a sentimental girl whose character is inextricably linked to her provenance – but they also deepen Fitzgerald's presentation of theme. Relying on communal knowledge of songs passed down in the oral tradition, he invites these associations to be brought to a reading of the text, though here he makes sure that reader participation is an enhancing, rather than essential, aspect of the reading experience.

In 'The Ice Palace', we find that Fitzgerald uses songs to fulfil a number of the same aims for which he uses them in the novels: he creates a contrast between the immediate moment of the song and an ambiguous relationship with the past; he evokes an extra-literary response from readers; he trusts his readers to interpret references (although admittedly the songs in 'The Ice Palace' are much less obscure than some of those encountered elsewhere); and he uses lyrics as a substitute for characters' articulation of their own feelings. The songs alluded to are chosen not from the bank of popular song Fitzgerald knew of, but from older, more traditional songs transmitted across the generations, perhaps demonstrating Fitzgerald's awareness of the wider readership that the *Post* offered.

Lawrence Levine sets out two definitions of popular culture: cultural output that is enjoyed by a large audience and cultural creations that have 'questionable artistic merit'.[34] In the wake of the turn-of-the-century drive to segregate high and 'popular' culture by transforming public arenas of culture into socially exclusive areas, instituting rules of behaviour when interacting with art and instituting stringent controls over the participation of audiences, 'art was becoming a one-way process: the artist communicating and the audience receiving'.[35] Cultural eclecticism had once thrived in the popularity of a wide range of nineteenth-century American entertainment, from opera to novels: even Shakespearean drama constituted popular entertainment. During much of the nineteenth century, audiences could enjoy serious performances of Shakespeare's plays in larger cities, but throughout both urban and rural areas, excerpts ranging from passages to several scenes were on offer, sometimes interpolated with dances and songs, or performed as parodies of the original. These performances could be delivered by touring companies or single actors, but the popularity of Shakespearean acts in minstrel shows and on varied and inclusive vaudeville bills demonstrates the capacity of American audiences of all social classes to understand and respond to Shakespearean drama in isolation from its original context, implying a widespread familiarity with the plays.[36] This cultural eclecticism found afterlives in the 1920s, first in the collage aesthetic, then in jazz culture's borrowings from eclectic sources, and in musical and all senses of jazz. Finally, the film industry served as a democratising influence that could bring cultural eclecticism back to its purpose as entertainment for all.

Fitzgerald's own developing interest in questioning what (and who) popular entertainment is for was informed not only by his perceptions of the role of the artist in society, but also by cultural commentators like his friend Gilbert Seldes. Seldes sought to rehabilitate the reputation of popular entertainment, and in 1924 he published a book collecting a series of articles under the title of *The 7 Lively Arts*. The number seven was an allusion to the classical concept of seven arts, rather than to seven particular art forms, although in his book Seldes does focus on film, musical comedy, vaudeville, radio, comic strips, ragtime and jazz music, and dance. Seldes argued that these popular arts had the potential to provide just as much artistic merit as the more traditional, so-called 'high' art forms like classical music, which Seldes calls the 'major' arts. The real opposition to the popular arts, according to Seldes, were the 'bogus' arts, by which he meant pretentious and dull art which required quiet and passive reception, in exclusive arenas. In essence, as Michael Kammen has summarised, Seldes was condemning 'a mindless preference for second-rate high culture over first-rate popular culture'.[37]

Fitzgerald does not seem to interrogate the value of popular culture in his early use of songs in the short story. Looking at other Fitzgerald stories during the 1920s, he often shies away from criticising or interrogating the value of popular culture, even when he includes a reference to a song. In his later work, he meditates on the purpose of songs. In his early work, songs function as an escape and diversion, and readers can choose their degree of emotional investment. In 'Myra Meets His Family' (1920), for example, 'Wave That Wishbone' serves as a vehicle for Myra to show her deftness at assuming another identity at a moment's notice, but the song's complicit guilt in aiding Myra to disguise herself is unexamined. In 'Porcelain and Pink' (1920), Fitzgerald includes a song of his own which references a host of real-life products, but his satire is directed at the advertising industry and consumer culture rather than exploring the medium of popular song itself. It may be that Fitzgerald was conscious that the magazine contexts of these fictions would place them in close proximity to other aspects of popular culture, such as the advertisements that enabled magazines like the *Post* to pay Fitzgerald such high prices. In the later years of his career, Fitzgerald would return multiple times to the issue of the value of popular music, in stories such as 'The Intimate Strangers' (1935) and 'Three Acts of Music' (1936).

'The Ice Palace' is a pertinent example of this reluctance to explore the value of popular culture because, though it was only the fifth story Fitzgerald had published in the lucrative *Saturday Evening Post*, it was the first in which he chooses not to focus on the 'jazz-nourished generation' who are the protagonists of the other five stories Fitzgerald published in the *Post* in a flurry between February and May 1920, appearing in three of May's four issues (*F&P*, 111).[38] Though Sally Carrol is clearly a teenager in the story, which has a contemporary setting, we do not hear any ragtime or jazz– only the sea shanty and the old Southern standard, 'Dixie'. Sally Carrol smokes and drinks, the usual markers of the Jazz Age flapper, but Fitzgerald chooses not to associate her with popular music. Arguably, this hints at an imperviousness to the charms of Tin Pan Alley that speaks to the strength of character Sally Carrol possesses. On the other hand, as

Graham remarks, in *This Side of Paradise*, it is when music disappears from the novel that Amory makes his most irresponsible and regrettable decisions, having no outlet for his transient emotions and thus being forced to see through each whim and fancy, with disastrous results.[39] Following this reading, the lack of popular music in 'The Ice Palace' could symbolise Sally Carrol's fragmented and tormented state of mind. While she is trying to decide what to do with regard to her engagement, she retreats into what she knows – the traditional songs which have endured for generations, rather than the transient Tin Pan Alley lyrics. Unlike Josephine Perry, Sally Carrol does not rely on popular cultural fragments to assemble her sense of self.

Fitzgerald's early stories, especially in the *Saturday Evening Post*, curiously contain fewer song titles and quoted lyrics than we might expect from the 'chronicler of the Jazz Age'. Fitzgerald instead invents his own songs and lyrics, or occasionally quotes brief and carefully selected lyrics from popular songs. He also draws on a more mainstream genre of songs that have come from successful musical comedies: 'Head and Shoulders' (1920) is a notable example of this. Fitzgerald might be conscious of the significant number of people yet to acquire a radio in the early 1920s. The first radio broadcast was in 1920, but it was not until 1922 that pre-assembled radio sets were even marketed, and it was later in the decade that radio really flourished, propelling Tin Pan Alley productions to unprecedented levels of success. Fitzgerald might not want to alienate parts of his audience through inviting them to recall specific songs and lyrics that they may not know. Even in 'Diamond Dick' (1924), the song he alludes to is 'Beale Street Blues', a 1916 W. C. Handy song that would have been well known by 1924, and Fitzgerald 'strips' the story of this reference in order to reuse it in *The Great Gatsby*. In his later stories, music was to take a much larger role, and proved central to Fitzgerald's interrogation of his own role in popular and literary culture.

'Everything We'll Ever Know About Life': Fitzgerald, Berlin and the Function of Popular Music

In 'The Intimate Strangers' (1935), a wife and mother named Sara leaves her family to go and live with another man, Killian, in a cabin in the North Carolina woods.[40] They spend a week there together, constantly making music in a bid to assert their identities: 'They had at least six concert hours a day from sheer exuberance, sheer desire to make a noise, to cry "here we are!"' (*ACC*, 312). Sara experiments with this identity, albeit briefly, and then returns to her old life, where she felt that 'it seemed to her that she had no particular self' (*ACC*, 316). The story, which opens just before the First World War, is peppered with popular music, and the adulterous couple play duets on the piano, sharing special moments where they 'rag' on songs and sing a saccharine love song 'with his baritone following four notes and four words after her little contralto – that was the fad then' (*ACC*, 310). Sara is described as an actress who can mould her personality as the occasion dictates, reserving her true self 'for the few' (*ACC*, 316). They are bound together by their interest in music, which, though it brings them pleasure, is also described in slightly portentous terms:

> No one would ever let Killian and Sara stop, no one ever had enough, and as they sang on, their faces flushed with excitement and pleasure like children's faces, the conviction grew in Sara that they were communicating, that they were saying things to each other in every note, every bar of harmony. They were talking to each other as surely as if with words – closer than any two people in the room. (*ACC*, 329)

Fitzgerald implies that the over-exposure and over-reliance on music have replaced language for Sara, recalling Josephine Perry's disastrous substitution of emotional song lyrics for authentic emotion, 'as if they expressed the writer's state of mind more fully than verbal struggles of her own' (*BJG*, 198). She has reneged on the spoken words of her marriage vows and responsibilities, caring only about Killian and therefore music, and vice versa. Their audience will not let them stop and Sara seems happy to be thus enslaved. Fitzgerald does not introduce humour into the situation but merely presents it to us for our judgement. The story's conclusion, in which they communicate with music instead of words, is one of Fitzgerald's most challenging endings and was understandably rejected by the *Post*, given its adulterous theme.

By placing so much importance on popular song in their

relationship, Sara and Killian have built an ominous foundation on impassive ground, each of them, perhaps, 'substitutable', as the title suggests. Sara complains about how 'she felt life crowding into her, into her childish resourceful body' (*ACC*, 308). The pair are described as childish throughout the story, in a subtle judgement of their extra-marital actions. Popular music has caused Sara to become childlike, shirk her responsibilities and cease to question her place in the world, which, it is hinted, is immoral and potentially insecure. Interestingly, we do not hear from Killian until near the end of the story, and do not get a sense of whether he similarly feels that they are transcending language in their musical communications.

Prigozy was unable to identify where the song 'To Let' was taken from in her otherwise comprehensive study, and although Berret suggests two songs that may have influenced Fitzgerald, it is also possible that Fitzgerald included a song of his own design in order to make a subtle statement about the dangers of reading too much into music.[41] It is the first song of the story, which is set in 1914, and the lyrics suggest that Sara's heart is 'to let':

> 'The key is in the door,' she sang,
> 'The fire is laid to light
> But the sign upon my heart, it says "To let"'. (*ACC*, 308)

This sets up a sense of romantic foreboding and also, in its use of the domestic image, hints at the familial chaos to follow. Sara's abandonment of her husband and children undermines this domestic image and calls into question the security of the domesticity the song describes.[42] It is unusual for Fitzgerald to mix genuine songs with his own inventions but here he seems to depart from his usual allusive tactics. By undermining his own use of songs and lyrics to create a shared understanding with the reader, and instead providing deliberately ironic lyrics which are probably his own, Fitzgerald can be seen to be potentially critiquing the popular music, and criticising Sara for her reliance on it to express her emotions. This could be read as a subtle instance of self-parody, Fitzgerald betraying the trust of the reader to dramatise his character's untrustworthiness and fickleness. At the end of the story, having returned to her family, been widowed, and subsequently reunited with Killian by their love of music, Sara's new life is far from secure: Killian confesses that when they had run away together initially, he had not been in love with her but was still mourning his dead wife.

By this point, in 1935, Fitzgerald recognised his inability to produce the stories of young love that established his brand. He explored this crisis in print, both in the 'Crack-Up' essays and in stories that explored artists' roles in society. One such story is 'Three Acts of Music' (1936), which is a curious piece. Written to cover an advance from Arnold Gingrich at *Esquire*, it consists of three stark scenes, or 'acts', which are separated by undetermined lengths of time, charting the bungled relationship between two unnamed protagonists, a nurse from Yonkers and a doctor from 'a conservative old Vermont family' (*TLD*, 5). The story fixates on the inability to make oneself understood but this obscuring of meaning is often wilful: the doctor withholds information several times. He corrects the nurse's pronunciation and grammar, and the missed connections, revisions and false starts in their interruptive and fragmentary speech serve as a metaphor for their fruitless relationship. By the third scene, they accept that 'it's too late' for them (*TLD*, 7).

The opening 'act' of the story has them humming along to Vincent Youmans's ebullient 'Tea for Two', in the flush of young love. The simplistic lyrics and two-note melody fit their situation, and the song's two-step rhythm is mirrored by their snappy repartee in their terse exchanges. Since they are both poor, just beginning their careers, the man suggests flippantly, 'lets spend the rest of our lives going around and listening to tunes' (*TLD*, 3). The next 'act' opens with the explanation, 'This was now years later but there was still music. There was "All Alone" and "Remember" and "Always" and "Blue Skies" and "How About Me"' (*TLD*, 4). All of them Irving Berlin songs, this list comprises four songs explicitly about lost love, and 'Blue Skies', which contrasts the speaker's former 'blue days' with his current joy.[43] The man turns on the radio and 'Remember' is playing. Fitzgerald quotes the opening of the chorus,

> *Re-mem-ber*
> *the night*
> *the night*
> *you said –*

but readers would presumably recall the other lyrics, which include 'deep regret', 'longing to forget' and 'but you forgot to remember' (*TLD*, 4).[44] This soundtrack lends the scene a degree of melancholy and implies the doctor's culpability. The couple then dance to 'Blue Skies', though it is clear that they have not been together in the intervening years and the class boundary has proved too prohibitive, despite the woman's promotions at work. It is a 1927 song and moves repeatedly from E minor to G major, the minor key qualifying the upbeat lyrics with a tentative optimism. It is a song that fights against itself, the lyrics melding happy emotion with a strangely semi-melancholy music, perhaps ironically riffing on the word 'blue'.

The woman asks a series of questions about whether Irving Berlin is happy with his new wife, 'the Mackay girl' (*TLD*, 5). Ellin Mackay, a Catholic heiress, was in love with the Jewish Berlin, whose first biographer described him as 'a dirty, little, barefoot newsboy' as a child, before he amassed his fortune, and the match was violently but futilely opposed by her father.[45] In a situation that is paralleled in the story, though with the genders reversed, Mackay was sent to Europe, where her family hoped she would find other suitors. In 'Three Acts', it is the man who has been in Europe, but both he and Mackay return to America alone.[46]

In the third scene, we meet the couple again, when 'both of [them] are fat and – sort of middle-aged' (*TLD*, 8). The musical accompaniment comes courtesy of Jerome Kern: 'Smoke Gets in Your Eyes' and 'Lovely to Look at' play. The former serves to underline the estrangement of the couple, who have '*heart[s] on fire*' now that it is 'just too late' (*TLD*, 7). The lyrics are interspersed with the dialogue, in italics, to express feelings that the characters cannot quite express in words. Since the pair have not managed to realise an actual relationship fully, they are allowing the songs that play in the background to serve as substitutes for feelings they have missed out on. The music changes to 'Lovely to Look At' (which Fitzgerald misquotes slightly, perhaps deliberately, in order to emphasise their fundamental mismatch):

Lovely
  to look at

Romantic
  to know.

The man asserts that the woman is both of these things but she angrily retorts, 'You should have told me that fifteen years ago' (*TLD*, 7). The man has finally found a way of communicating these feelings to the woman, by quoting popular song, but it is too late for both of them. At the story's close, the woman reflects on the music that they have heard over the course of their meetings:

> All those people – that Youmans, that Berlin, that Kern. They must have been through hell to be able to write like that. And we sort of listened to them, didn't we? [. . .] It was all we had – everything we'll ever know about life. (*TLD*, 8)

The songwriter has a specific function here – not just to entertain, but to provide a means of emotional support, almost therapy, for people going through the experiences being written about. It is a bold claim to make about any artist, and significantly Fitzgerald's short piece is published in *Esquire* rather than the *Saturday Evening Post*, where such an experimental, strange work would have been inconsistent with the general tone of the magazine. Here, as West has identified, Fitzgerald appears to be writing about himself when he writes about the popular songwriter: he argues that real experiences, clothed in song (or fiction), can provoke genuine emotional responses and forge an intimacy between artist and consumer. West finds that:

> The story is almost an *apologia pro vita sua* for Fitzgerald himself. He reveals here his function as a popular artist and tries to explain something about his own tumultuous life. He also expresses the closeness he feels towards the thousands of unknown lovers whose emotions he must have moved over the years through his fiction. Fitzgerald is saying that many popular artists like Youmans, Kern, and Berlin must feel this same closeness.[47]

This is especially true of Irving Berlin in 'Three Acts of Music'. The unnamed woman feels connected to Berlin because of the class boundary he traversed in marrying his second wife – she feels this kinship despite their differing genders and circumstances. It is the social barrier that she was unable to break and has led to a personal life of emotional emptiness, with only her professional life for enrichment. Because Berlin's experience is first hand, and he has lived the heartbreak and the romance that he writes about, the woman finds his songs more genuine: 'it was all that we had – everything we'll ever know about life'. It is telling that Fitzgerald chooses Berlin for this task, since there are many similarities between their lives that can also be related to their art.

Aside from them both marrying women who were their financial and social superiors, there are a number of interesting parallels between the lives of Berlin and Fitzgerald. Both experienced vast success at a young age – by twenty-four. Both were relatively small in stature, and both enlisted in the First World War without actually reaching the Western Front or seeing active service. Both men endured the belittling of their achievements by being popularly considered to be 'naturals' and ignoring the hard work that went into their compositions (although Fitzgerald encouraged this in his early years). Also, each of them was a prodigious but also prolific talent, Fitzgerald producing a staggering 178 stories and five novels (one incomplete) in a career that spanned only twenty years.[48] Berlin's first biographer, Alexander Woollcott (of Algonquin Round Table and *New Yorker* fame) notes as early as 1925 that Berlin was 'the man who has written more than any one man's share of the songs this land has liked'.[49] The same could be said of Fitzgerald's short stories, though no biography of him appeared until 1951. Finally, both men struggled with the delicate balance between creative inspiration and financial necessity. As Woollcott comments on Berlin:

It may be a shock to the ingenuous to learn that scarcely a song in all his long, eventful catalogue was written because his heart was singing and the song could not be kept from bursting out of him. Nearly all of them were written deliberately and a little sulkily by one whose business associates stood around him in a reproachful circle and assured him that, if he did not give birth to something at once, the dear, old publishing house would go on the rocks. The artist in him may be tickled mightily by some neat, unexpected phrase in the chorus he has just written, but the publisher in him will ruthlessly strike it out in favor of some quite routine threadbare word with no disconcerting unfamiliarity about it to stick in the crop of the proletariat.[50]

Fitzgerald certainly felt the pressure to produce stories to fund his initially lavish, then increasingly tumultuous lifestyle, and clearly viewed the short story writing and novel writing experiences as independent. The stories were not simply hackwork, but undoubtedly there were certain constraints within which he had to work, just as Berlin had to consider the marketability of his own creative decisions.

'Three Acts of Music' functions as evidence of Fitzgerald wrestling with longstanding issues of marketability alongside his vocation as an artist, in an experimental mode that Milton Stern argues was innate in his writing all along:

> the Pat Hobby stories [. . .] along with others of his 1930s prose pieces [. . .] signal the marketplace dominance of Hemingwayesque modernism that had always been *a part* of Fitzgerald's own style. [. . .] [They] are a stripping away of evocative lyricism, largely in a diminution of descriptive passages.[51]

There was also a financial aspect to this new terse experimentalism in Fitzgerald's work: he would be paid the same fee regardless of the length of the piece in *Esquire*, so Fitzgerald opted to write a short piece. 'Three Acts of Music' differs from most of Fitzgerald's work in that the stark structure takes the form of three scenes, presented in succession without a link between them. It is possible that he intended it as a kind of postscript to his 'Crack-Up' pieces, which were published in *Esquire* in February to April 1936, with 'Three Acts' appearing in May. These essays had meditated on the role of the artist and concluded that Fitzgerald was a 'cracked plate'. He was, by this point, more famous as a *Saturday Evening Post* short storyist than he was as a novelist, and this undermined his own confidence in his literary capabilities. The critical reception of the 'Crack-Up' pieces was mainly frosty, however, and Fitzgerald returned to Hollywood for a third and final time to try his hand at screenwriting.

In his short fiction, Fitzgerald was working within the confines of a specific genre – the commercial short story – and he managed a surprising amount of experimentalism for such a genre. His narratorial interjections fulfil Daniel Albright's definition of modernism as a 'testing of the limits of aesthetic construction'.[52] He conspires with the reader, in 'Porcelain and Pink', cheekily explaining, in a stage direction, 'Yes, you've guessed it. Mistaken identity is the old, rusty pivot upon which the plot turns' (*TJA*, 116). He makes reference to the illustrations which he knew the *Post* would add to his story, in the collected version of the story that was published without illustrations, in 'The Offshore Pirate' (1920) when Ardita leans up and kisses Toby 'softly, in the illustration' (*F&P*, 35). Especially in his later stories, he often managed to avoid overtly happy endings, leaving hints that all may not in fact be well, and sometimes is more insistent on doleful conclusions, as in 'Three Acts of Music'.

Fitzgerald was well aware of the expectations readers brought to a Fitzgerald story, especially as a *Post* author. Many of his initial reviewers had praised his originality, 'vividness and virility' but predicted that his success would be short-lived.[53] In reviews of his last two short story collections, after the publication of *The Great Gatsby*, there is a recurring theme of reviewers praising a newfound restraint and maturity in his work. His audience expected stories that were 'ironical, and sad, and jolly good fun by turns'; they expected 'a wit and discernment in characterization'; and in his post-*Gatsby* work, 'a satiric slant toward the grown-up children of the jazz age' and 'a melancholy which is new in Fitzgerald's work'.[54] He had cultivated an image of himself that was so closely entwined with his fictional creations that it was inevitable that, as his own life became unhappy, his stories would follow suit. In a letter to Zelda of May 1940, he admitted that 'I lost the knack of writing the particular kind of stories they wanted.'[55] He began, subtly at first, to defy reader expectations of his work, and on closer inspection his sassy, bright heroines can appear morally questionable and vacant, the pulsating rhythms of jazz giving way to hollow repetitions of lyrics and half-remembered melodies.

Fitzgerald repeated and reworked themes over multiple stories. Whilst his novels, especially *The Great Gatsby* and *Tender is the Night*, gestated, he did indeed 'workshop' theme and character in the stories he published during these times. As a professional author reliant on selling his work as his sole source of income, he was conscious of his buyers' preferences and conditions. Yet as West's edition of *Taps at Reveille* has shown, 'during the late 1920s and early 1930s, Fitzgerald was writing mature stories on adult themes for the *Post* but [. . .] these stories were being edited at that magazine to remove forbidden elements'.[56] Fitzgerald's stories still sold in this period but he was pushing the boundaries of saleability to this audience. West's collation of Fitzgerald's final typescript versions of his stories against the stories as published in the *Post* show that even though Fitzgerald knew that references to 'sex, race, and alcohol' would be cut and profanities also cut or toned down, he submitted stories including them anyway.[57] West lists 'alcoholism, suicide, open adultery, incest, racial prejudice, mental illness, homosexuality, and violent crime', commenting that 'One does not find frank treatments of these subjects in very many of Fitzgerald's commercial stories.'[58]

Fitzgerald does, however, manage to refer to several of these banned topics through his musical allusions. For example, the song 'Boulevard of Broken Dreams', featured in 'No Flowers', refers to male and female prostitutes on the streets of Paris. The 'Beale Street Blues', which appears in 'Diamond Dick', warns of the secrets witnessed by the street, the revelation of which would result in infidelities being revealed, marriages ruined and even murders being committed. When, as in 'The Intimate Strangers', Fitzgerald creates his own lyrics to serve his purpose, this demonstrates his confidence in the unspoken contract he had with his audience. He relied on the reader to make appropriate connections between lyric and aural experience but here there is no aural content and so the reader has only the story, and indeed the wider context of the 'typical Fitzgerald story', to supply the links. In 'The Intimate Strangers', when Sara struggles to express herself without songs, Josephine Perry's emotional bankruptcy is called to mind, as a partial consequence of Josephine's quotation of song lyrics in lieu of genuine emotion. This self-referential genre is key to allowing Fitzgerald to create parodic currents in which he references his previous stories. His thematic repetitions, character workshopping and 'for the trade' concessions reposition these repetitions as conscious (as well as unconscious) self-parody.

Although Robert Warshow is writing about the genre of gangster films, if we consider his argument in terms of, for example, the flapper of Fitzgerald's early fiction, like Ardita, their conventions have indeed 'imposed themselves upon the general consciousness'. We do 'go [...] to any individual example of the type with very definite expectations', but even though certain of these narratives appear to be unoriginal, Fitzgerald's clever but subtle manipulations of formulaic expectation, and musical allusions to prohibited themes, show that his 'own field of reference' is wide as well as rich.[59] Repetition, variation and 'ragging', the formulae he worked within, are a vital part of Fitzgerald's literary aesthetics, and such self-parody finds an especially effective home in his stories that engage with the formulaic structures of Tin Pan Alley even as they undermine them.

In Fitzgerald's magazine writing, dance and music were in dialogue in an interrogation of the value of popular culture and its ability to enrich an understanding of modern American identity. Fitzgerald's exploration of the authentic dancer as a metaphor for the literary craftsman is also present in his veneration of the songwriter who can teach 'everything we'll ever know about life'. But in giving his readers shared ownership of his allusions, as Fitzgerald does in his evocative use of popular music, he risks this audience allowing their genre-bound expectations to outweigh or misinterpret the actual words on the page. It would be easy to read Sally Carrol from 'The Ice Palace' and Sara from 'The Intimate Strangers' as two-dimensional Fitzgerald heroines, but each in her own way has transcended the genre of flapper 'confection' through her use of popular music. Just as syncopation and changing time signatures can confuse audience expectations before lulling them back into a sense of familiarity and security, so Fitzgerald aptly manages the expectations that attend his stories, whilst at once self-consciously defying them, to produce some of his best and most challenging work.

CHAPTER 4

'The One about Sitting on His Top Hat and Climbing up His Shirt Front': Fitzgerald and Musical Theatre

Fascinated by musical theatre from a young age, Fitzgerald perceived an intersection between entertainment and morality that characterised his presentation of popular culture.[1] In 1939, Fitzgerald wrote to his daughter:

> If you start any kind of a career following the footsteps of Cole Porter and Rodgers and Hart, it might be an excellent try. Sometimes I wish I had gone along with that gang, but I guess I am too much a moralist at heart, and really want to preach at people in some acceptable form, rather than to entertain them.[2]

As a member of the Triangle Club at Princeton, he wrote the libretti for three musical comedies, and as a student at the Newman School in New Jersey from the ages of 15 to 17, he made the forty-minute journey into New York City often to see the latest musical comedies on Broadway. Fitzgerald grew up amidst something of a golden period of musical theatre composers and lyricists, and he also witnessed the film industry's appetite for remaking Broadway shows and then distributing them to millions of people all over the country, creating the new genre of film musicals in the late 1920s.

Fitzgerald uses allusions to plots and themes from musical theatre in his short stories, especially favouring those in which social-class boundaries are traversed in search of romance. Fitzgerald incorporates specific songs in his novels to allude to themes and plots of popular musicals of the day, which resonate within his texts.[3] In terms of his short stories, Fitzgerald refers to popular songs from musical comedies in the theatre, but also to film musicals. This reflects his deep-seated interest in immersive media in which reader collaboration is key to ascertaining meanings in the texts, but many of these musical theatre references are lost on the modern reader.

Fitzgerald's allusions to musical theatre draw upon the profusion of collage-like interdisciplinary juxtapositions that have become known as the 'collage aesthetic'. Prior to Jerome Kern and Oscar Hammerstein II's landmark production of *Show Boat* (1927), musical theatre very much relied on the aesthetic of vaudeville revues, without integration between song and action. Discrete episodes of entertainment hailing from differing genres, building up to a headliner, constituted a vibrant and original American aesthetic, like jazz, and Fitzgerald was interested in the transposition of this vaudeville style into his writing. His first novel, *This Side of Paradise* (1920), is a kaleidoscopic mixture of prose, poetry, letters and playscripts, and it has also been suggested that *The Great Gatsby* (1925) 'loosely follow[s] a vaudeville show's format . . . in order to elucidate economically a number of *Gatsby* themes'.[4]

As well as quoting from Broadway songs, Fitzgerald on occasion chooses to tailor his musical allusions perfectly by inventing his own lyrics, drawing on the skills he honed during his undergraduate Triangle Club years. In the one-act play, 'Porcelain and Pink', collected in *Tales of the Jazz Age*, we meet two sisters, one of whom, Julia, is in the bath, while her sister Lois is waiting to get into the bathroom. Lois's beau, calling up to her through a high window, mistakes the bathing Julie for his beloved. Julie sings while she is in the bathtub, imagining 'wild applause' after her rendition of 'The Imperial Roman Jazz':

When Caesar did the Chicago
[. . .] He gave them an awful razz
They shook in their shoes
With the Consular Blues
The Imperial Roman Jazz. (*TJA*, 116)[5]

As Anthony Berret has noted, this combination of the classical world with modern slang is comparable to T. S. Eliot's sense of cultural hybridity in *The Waste Land* (1922).[6] Fitzgerald was fond of drawing comparisons between ancient civilisations and his contemporary society, and an early draft of *The Great Gatsby* was entitled *Trimalchio*, named after a character in Petronius' *Satyricon* dating from AD 1.

As well as drawing farcical comparisons between ancient and modern society by 'jazzing Caesar', Fitzgerald also used the copious reach of advertising as a target for his satire. Just before Julie hears Lois's boyfriend at the window, she gives a rendition of this strange little song, also penned by Fitzgerald:

> When the Arrow-collar man
>> Meets the D'jer-Kiss girl
> On the smokeless Santa-Fé
>> Her Pebeco smile
>> Her Lucile style
> De dum da-de-dum one day – (*TJA*, 120)

The references here are taken from the world of advertising and show how Julie is immersed not just in the bath but in the world of consumerist pleasures. 'The Arrow-collar man', of Arrow shirts fame, was from a series of illustrated advertisements from 1920 onwards that were successful enough to warrant fan mail. He also features briefly in *This Side of Paradise*, when Myra's attraction to Amory is described as 'arrow-collar taste' and 'the quintessence of romance'.[7] The song imagines this man (actually based on a series of different men) meeting the D'jer-Kiss girl, an illustrated Kerkoff perfume advert with bobbed hair, drawn by Malaga Grenet and described by James West as 'epicene and nymphlike'.[8] The place for this union is given as 'the smokeless Santa-Fé': that is, the cross-country Atchison, Topeka and Santa Fé railway line, powered with bituminous (and thus supposedly smoke-free) coal. Her smile is courtesy of Pebeco toothpaste, who secured an expensive full-page advertisement on the back cover of the *Saturday Evening Post* in 1920, and her modern style comes care of Lucile, the couture house of Lady Duff-Gordon, the designer and socialite whose modern designs lowered necklines and split skirts. The lyrics are then obscured by humming, and so we never do find out what happens when these two characters meet. Such obfuscation fits in with the theme of concealment of both identity and the female body, and as Sharon Hamilton has noted, 'this story announced an author unafraid to take chances in the subject matter he chose for his art. Naked girls in bathtubs were *not* the stuff of standard magazine fiction in those days.'[9] Fitzgerald referred to 'Porcelain and Pink' as a 'vaudeville sketch' in a letter to his agent Harold Ober in 1923. It is worth noting that this risqué vaudeville sketch appeared in *The Smart Set* rather than in the family-centric *Post*.[10]

The references need glossing for most contemporary readers, but for Fitzgerald's 1920 audience these companies' advertisements would have provided regular paratextual interruptions to the reading experience itself, especially in the ad-heavy 'slick' magazines. Responding to these advertisements, Julie sees herself as the desirable 'Djer-Kiss girl' and begins a flirtation with her sister's boyfriend under false pretences, before fleeing the scene when her sister arrives. The boyfriend is undoubtedly confused and the obscured lyrics at the song's close could signify the uncertain resolution of this case of mistaken identity. Though he is being flippant in tone, and the song's situation creates physical humour through Fitzgerald's satire on consumption practices (this consumerist girl is naked rather than clothed in a Lucile gown), Fitzgerald seriously posits that these advertisements have been assimilated into modern life and are fair game for allusive purposes. He economises on description through the short but evocative phrase 'the Arrow-collar man' and relies on his readers to supply the context for the reference.

Musical Theatre and the Collage Aesthetic

The influence of vaudeville's patchwork aesthetic was strong throughout the 1920s, and in musical theatre itself, songs were frequently self-contained narratives with little interaction with the overarching plot. Fitzgerald imports these features from musical theatre into his 'playlet' and infuses them with popular cultural references. As a writer of song lyrics, Fitzgerald frequently calls upon contemporary popular culture in this way, naming brands as well as summoning up images of the advertisements themselves.

The Arrow-collar man was immortalised by his allusive appearance in *The Great Gatsby* but also in Irving Berlin's song, 'Puttin' on the Ritz', in which Berlin asks:

> Have you seen the well-to-do,
> Up and down Park Avenue?
> On that famous thoroughfare
> With their noses in the air
> High hats and Arrow Collars,
> White Spats and lots of dollars,
> Spending every dime
> For a wonderful time.[11]

The Arrow collar here serves as shorthand for a well-dressed rich man, interested in 'a wonderful time' at any cost.[12] However, these lyrics are modified ones that Berlin added to the song for the 1946 Fred Astaire film musical, *Blue Skies*. The original lyrics for the 1929 song (as featured in the 1930 film musical, *Puttin' On the Ritz*) describe 'the well-to-do / up on Lenox Avenue' and ask 'why don't you go where Harlem sits / Puttin' on the Ritz'.[13] Berlin's portrayal of fashionable black urbanites on Lenox Avenue contrasts with the image of Harlemites propagated by the Harlem nightclubs which were frequented by white New Yorkers, in which 'black men and women were portrayed as primitive dancing fools, whose sensuality civilised whites could not hope to match'.[14] Philip Furia identifies in the song extreme innovation stemming from its embodiment of mixing: mixed rhythms, mixed accents (musical and verbal) and the so-called 'misfits' of the song, black Harlemites dressed in 'spangled gowns', which recall Berlin's depiction of Josephine Baker in *As Thousands Cheer*, lamenting becoming 'too damned refined . . . With Harlem on my mind'.[15]

Though 'Puttin' on the Ritz' itself fails to feature in Fitzgerald's œuvre, his admiration for Berlin is cemented through the many mentions of Berlin's other songs. None the less, 'Puttin' on the Ritz' offers an insight into both the music industry and what Kathy Ogren aptly summarises as the commercial 'appropriation of black musical idioms'.[16] The song has an infectiously destabilising rhythm, described by music critic Alec Wilder as:

a rhythmic device that is probably the most complex and provocative I have come upon, by any writer. It is, naturally, in a form of $\frac{4}{4}$, but cut time. If one wishes to break this into time signatures which indicate more simply the stressed notes, it could be done this way: $\frac{3}{4}, \frac{3}{4}, \frac{4}{4}, \frac{6}{4}$.[17]

The song confounds aural expectations not only by utilising syncopation, hardly a new tactic by 1929, but also by further disguising the beat through a seemingly unstable and shifting time signature. By relying on the audience's complicit, even instinctive, understanding of $\frac{4}{4}$ time, Berlin deconstructs it and confuses it, then pauses, before reanchoring the listener with the title phrase (in quavers forming a simple descending scale). It is thoroughly modern, almost experimental, and Furia's description, that 'the musical accents break down sentence, phrase, and word into tiny Cubistic fragments fitted "mosaically" to musical shards' speaks to this destabilising element.[18] The comparison to cubism is apt: the beginnings of the cubist movement coincided with the ragtime dance craze of the pre-war years. From around 1907, Pablo Picasso and Georges Braque pioneered a new way of representing their experiences of the world, just as the Castles and James Reese Europe were revolutionising how people spent their leisure hours.

Picasso, Braque and other cubists juxtaposed fragments of multiple different perspectives of the same subject: in viewing many perspectives at the same time we are left with a tonally diverse patchwork that exposes the benefits as well as the limitations of such an aesthetic statement. Berlin's treatment of the established formula of a Tin Pan Alley popular song speaks to many of these same aims.

Berlin's malleable treatment of an established formula is also reminiscent of Fitzgerald's clever and subtle manipulation of the *Post*'s expectations of the short story genre. In his characterisation, Fitzgerald presents us with many different perspectives on the archetype of the flapper, which leads us to recognise the limitations of each perspective. Other ways in which Fitzgerald manipulates the *Post*'s usual formula for short stories includes his use of unhappy (or only superficially happy) endings, as in 'Babylon Revisited'; latent ironies in his use of coincidence and plot resolution; and his incorporation of profoundly ambivalent portrayals of popular culture. Destabilisation of genre is reliant on audience complicity in agreeing upon the characteristics of that genre, as Robert Warshow reminds us.

This sense of audience complicity is also a key feature of musical entertainment in this era. In 'Puttin' on the Ritz', the call-and-response antiphonal style so fundamental in hot jazz, as well as energetic syncopated rhythms, is cleverly manipulated into a neatly repetitive AABA structure by Berlin and marketed successfully to a mass audience.[19] Part of the song's success is due to the way in which Berlin's lyrics capture a specific moment in the history of American life. Harlem, by 1929, was extremely overcrowded and was beset by attendant sanitation and health problems. Nicholas Evans explains that by 1930, 'approximately 72% of Manhattan's African American population lived in Harlem'.[20] Berlin's lyrics describe well-dressed African Americans spending 'their last dime' on entertainment, but Harlem was also famous for the nightclubs and cabarets to which Manhattan's white populations flocked for 'authentic' experiences of jazz, despite many of the nightclubs, like the Cotton Club, operating whites-only entrance policies.

The question of why 'Negrophilic' whites were so interested in experiencing (and appropriating) African American culture is a complex one. Much cultural discourse of the period posited that African American culture provided a link to primitive states of being. For example, in 1923, Gilbert Seldes assessed jazz music and segregated it into white jazz and 'Negro jazz', the latter of which he considered to be a natural expressive asset of the 'Negro', differing from more 'intellectual' white jazz:

> In words and music the negro side expresses something which underlies a great deal of America – our independence, our carelessness, and our frankness, and gaiety. In each of these the negro is more intense that we are, and we surpass him when we combine a more varied and more intelligent life with his instinctive qualities.[21]

Some white Americans were keen to indulge these 'intense' and 'instinctive' qualities sparingly, rationalising that they needed to address their 'primitive' impulses in order to keep them in check: in effect, 'civilising' them.[22] Irving Berlin and Fred Astaire are two examples of this 'civilising' force at work, taking two traditionally African American leisure activities – jazz and tapdancing – and 'sanitising' them for mass consumption, as the Castles had done with ragtime dance just before the First World War. Though undeniably talented, self-taught Berlin lacked the keyboard skills of the great ragtime pianists such as Scott Joplin and he greatly benefitted from the innovation of the 'transposing piano' which allowed him to access different keys by moving a lever, rather than confining himself to his proficiency with solely the black keys, and thus the solitary key of F♯ major.

In his plundering of African American rhythms and harmony as established by composers such as Joplin and James Reese Europe, Berlin thought he was acting respectfully. As Robert Dawidoff explains:

> Berlin, Kern, and the Gershwins did not intend racism, as they understood it. A genuine part of their project was to eliminate what they felt was American race prejudice, to respect what they recognized as African-American racial genius, to express a fellow feeling as victims of oppression.[23]

All four were first- or second-generation European immigrants, and their tendencies towards appropriation emerged from the tradition of minstrelsy that had so profoundly influenced vaudeville. Both these media were heavily populated by European immigrants who made use of blackface, both literally and figuratively. Jews were a recent immigrant group who faced marginalisation, and blackface functioned as a means of disguising Jewishness and gaining acceptance in American culture. Many Jewish entertainers, most notably Al Jolson and Eddie Cantor, used blackface on stage and in films. This use of blackface was tied up in a complex set of emotions: in Jewish minstrelsy, a sense of near-nostalgia for slavery and exile coexists with an elusive dream of a homecoming of sorts. Michael Alexander emphasises how 'Jewish depictions of blackness were explicitly and unambiguously understood by Jews as a form of identification. Jews believed they saw their own history re-enacted before them in the form of African-American culture, and longed to participate in that culture.'[24]

African Americans were largely effaced from this apparent representation of their culture – it was a white performance of African American identity as seen through the perspective and projected desires of white performers. In his classic study of minstrelsy, Eric Lott summarises this cultural praxis: 'What was on display in minstrelsy was less black culture than a structured set of white responses to it which had grown out of northern and frontier social rituals and were passed through an inevitable filter of racist presupposition.'[25] When Berlin writes about 'the well to do . . . high browns . . . all misfits' in 'Puttin on the Ritz', he actually tells us more about himself than he does about well-dressed Harlemites of the late 1920s.

Seldes imagines Irving Berlin as 'A neat, unobtrusive, little man with bright eyes and an unerring capacity for understanding, appropriating, and creating strange rhythms in the foreground, attended by negro slaves'.[26] The image of the attendant slaves is an uncomfortable one. Berlin himself rose from immigrant poverty to great wealth, and amassed his fortune, as Seldes has identified, from 'appropriating' musical and rhythmic idiom, but to portray the Belarusian Jewish immigrant, born as Israel Beilin, as a slave-master is rather incongruous. Interpreting the image in another way, it is possible to see Berlin as the controller of a culture industry in his musical empire. Berlin's production and dissemination behemoths included, by 1921, a New York City theatre exclusively showing Berlin-penned musicals, and remarkably, Berlin's extraordinary popularity endured, throughout his 101 years.

Evans argues that Fitzgerald's work shows evidence of his protagonists '"borrowing" the behavioural inflections of the socially disempowered [in order for] Fitzgerald's protagonists [to] gain access to the masculinity that revitalizes their manly authority'.[27] By situating the cultural appropriation debate in the context of masculine insecurities and anxieties, which recalls Basil's anxieties on the dance floor, Evans calls upon the work of T. J. Jackson Lears, who argues that the pursuit of an 'authentic' identity became the task of many Americans who felt that they were in a cultural crisis provoked, for the most part, by the accelerating speed of the modern world and its technologies.[28] Rather than turning towards more conventional 'antimodernist' avenues such as the artisanal, for Fitzgerald, this authentic identity can be constructed in kaleido-scopic, or collage, fashion: through assembling various selves col-lated from popular culture influences, as the song from 'Porcelain and Pink' demonstrates.

In April 1920, Fitzgerald wrote to Perkins with his selection of seven stories for the collection, *Flappers and Philosophers*, along with six poems that he also wanted to include.[29] As West notes, this 'mixing of literary forms was logical, since *This Side of Paradise*, though technically a novel, was in fact an experimental book made up of fiction, poetry, and long passages of drama dialogue'.[30] Such an eclectic mixture tapped into the frenzied and contradictory zeit-geist of the early 1920s, and also overlapped with the ascendancy of the collage aesthetic in fine art, which was a medium that exerted considerable influence on literature of the Harlem Renaissance. Rachel Farebrother finds that, in collage, 'techniques of juxtaposi-tion and stylistic incongruity' and 'the democratic mixing of dispa-rate components, is inevitably subversive'.[31] Farebrother goes on to relate the collage aesthetic to African American vernacular culture such as jazz and blues, finding 'the practice of incorporating musi-cal quotations into early American jazz' to be a musical impulse that is reflective of the collage aesthetic.[32] Though Fitzgerald was not labouring under the oppression that African American prac-titioners of the collage aesthetic operated within in the interwar years, his interest in eclectic form, whether in a novel peppered with playlets and poetry, fiction imbued with snippets of song, or a short story collection that oscillated between prose and poetry demonstrates an intellectual investment in 'the democratic mixing of disparate components'.

Fitzgerald's style was deeply infused by modernism, romanti-cism, realism and, for a period in the early 1920s, naturalism. As Kirk Curnutt observes, 'that Fitzgerald's works are often categorized within opposing literary traditions testifies to the diversity of his talent'.[33] His forays into heavily symbolic didacticism in stories such as 'The Cut-Glass Bowl' and 'The Four Fists' (both 1920) usu-ally ended up in lower-paying magazines with smaller circulations and less commercial outlooks, such as *The Smart Set* or *Scribner's*, but these stories demonstrated the extent of Fitzgerald's proficiency with differing genres even though they failed to command large fees. 'The Diamond as Big as the Ritz' (1922), now recognised as one of Fitzgerald's most successful stories, commanded a mere $300 from *The Smart Set* (as compared to $1,500 for 'The Popular Girl', which appeared in the *Post* in 1922 in two parts, written in November 1921, only a month after 'Diamond') and demonstrated the ongoing influence of the Romantics on Fitzgerald: Coleridge's poem 'Kubla Khan' informing descriptions of the family home, and the diamond itself standing as a symbol of modern avarice, complete with its self-destructive loneliness. The story's cynical climax sees the family destroy their home rather than revealing the secrets of their wealth.

This 'mixing of disparate components' reflects a wider cultural context, linked to the concepts of cubism in fine art and relativity in science, that recognises the limits of single perspectives and seeks to build up a representation of something through many perspectives of the same object. These multiple perspectives can cross genres, shift tones and mix high art and popular entertainment. Picasso combined everyday found objects like newspapers and bottle labels with fine art techniques to create collages and sculptures. For Fitzgerald, the importation of thematic and formal ideas taken from the worlds of popular cultural entertainments is a major means by which he achieves the eclecticism that gives his work its lively character. When Fitzgerald breaks the fourth wall and addresses the reader directly, he is drawing upon the vaudeville revue aesthetic, which influenced many of the major artists of his time, such as Josephine Baker, and the idea of mixing different influences leads to a new combination of existing perspectives, creating something new through the repetition of their disparate parts. His quotations of song lyrics and allusions to musical theatre shows and stars all populate his world and reflect his interest in social realism, but these references also serve to add modernist texture to his writing.

Fitzgerald's multiple flappers with their variations and repetitions fulfil this goal of the reconstruction of fragments into a collage patchwork of meaning. By revisiting the same character archetype, Fitzgerald creates a self-reflexive field of reference. As with a collage, you can view the whole (the flapper) or break down your interpretation into responses to individual pieces (or characters). Repetition with a difference is a defining characteristic of parody, and these repetitive currents exist in dialogue with one another and give the reader an active role in interpretation.

This strain of interpretation must permit all fragments to interact as well as to stand alone, as Farebrother explains:

> Faced with collage, viewers are forced to piece together meaning actively: they must tease out relationships between parts – each fragment is perceived in relation to other fragments, to the whole (and possibly to other collages) and to its origin. These meanings remain suspended in dynamic play. It is the viewer's task to identify cultural pieces and to hold them in view, never suppressing the heterogeneity of elements.[34]

This perception of the fragment in self-referential relation to other fragments echoes Warshow's conception of the type. This interrelation is fundamentally dialogic, with various components speaking to one another across chronological and artistic divisions. As Lawrence Levine reminds us, culture does not exist in a vacuum, and is constantly in flux, with intertextualities abounding: 'Culture is a process not a fixed condition; it is the product of unremitting interaction between the past and the present.'[35]

As well as temporal fluctuations, Levine also explores the idea of cultural superiority, writing about the development of hierarchy in culture, and demonstrating that in the nineteenth century, rather than segregating art into high and low, vaudeville promoters in the United States ensured that their programmes were mixed in order to try to appeal to as many spectators, and thus sell as many tickets, as possible.[36] In the early twentieth century, in the 'symphonic jazz' of Whiteman's 1924 Aeolian Hall concert, we can witness a similar mingling of traditionally respectable, high culture in the form of classical music with apparently 'low', popular music, known as jazz. Ann Douglas identifies the songwriter Berlin in strikingly similar terms, overlapping popular and elite cultural spheres: 'Like Jolson and Whiteman', she writes, 'Berlin was a parodist, a splicer of high and low art.'[37] In his short fiction, this is homologous to the role that Fitzgerald often played. He draws upon the popular arts, writing in the formats that are acceptable to popular magazines and building on the character archetypes they solicit, but it is possible to see Fitzgerald's serious, 'high' treatment of the short fiction, if we analyse his stylistic and thematic achievements, especially as they pertain to the performance and consumption of popular culture.

Popular culture functions as an opportunity for Fitzgerald to explore the new behavioural freedoms heralded by the profusion of dance floors and picture houses, and the impact these leisure activities had upon gender and class boundaries, but also, as Berret argues, to depict the violence and discord brewing in the culture and finding their release through music, dances, theatre and film. The parodic appearance of 'the voluptuous chords of the wedding march done in blasphemous syncopation' in 'The Camel's Back' (1920) is frantic, and initially comic, but in the context of a story in which threatened violence and outright coercion simmer away, the jazzy march takes on new significance and a tone of manic, frightening loss of control: control of one's liberty, identity and even marital status (TJA, 54). Fitzgerald is parodying the mixture of popular and the seemingly sacred 'high culture' by jazzing a tune that is associated with the sanctity of marriage rites.

Musical theatre was the ideal conduit for the expression of cultural concerns about the conflict between highbrow and lowbrow entertainment: David Savran finds 'countless' productions from the 1920s that take this antagonism as their theme.[38] George and Ira Gershwin were prominent figures in 1920s Broadway and challenged the hierarchy of high art versus popular entertainment by copiously mixing styles. Colloquial and formal discourse coexisted in song lyrics; syncopated jazz was fused with classical music and George Gershwin had success with both concert pieces and Broadway songs, each genre influencing the other as Gershwin imbued the classical with motifs and techniques from blues and jazz music. The critical and commercial success of the Gershwins' work supported Gilbert Seldes's exhortation that the 'Lively Arts', like jazz and musical theatre, should be digested and criticised with the same care and attention afforded to those art forms traditionally regarded as high culture, such as opera and fine art.

This fusion of disparate styles and components was a key characteristic of much modernist art during the late teens and 1920s, and is on show in both Gershwin's Broadway melodies as well as his concert pieces:

The modular construction of the Concerto in F, and of all Gershwin's concert pieces, links it to a central modernist preoccupation with the fragment and to the fixation on constructing large canvases, poems, or musical works through the use of collage, the appropriation and recombination of shards of images, texts, or music (cubism is perhaps the clearest example of this technique).[39]

Such 'shards of images, texts, or music' permeate Fitzgerald's short fiction, coexisting with more traditional narrative techniques, to great effect.

Fitzgerald was heavily associated with his depictions of his flapper heroines, one reviewer of *Tales of the Jazz Age* (1922) remarking that it is 'the "flapper yarn" for which the author is famous'[40]. An early review of Fitzgerald's first collection, *Flappers and Philosophers* (1920), proclaimed that 'Flappers are the same the world over – temperament varies, but never the innate markings – and so are the flappers of Mr Fitzgerald's acquaintance.'[41] This same reviewer remarked upon Fitzgerald's deftness at manoeuvring within established character archetypes:

> Hand in hand with Fitzgerald's faculty of piercing discernment is the ability to draw characters as unusual from the accustomed fiction type in their delineation as in their conception, a knack for writing sparkling, realistic dialogue that is dialogue, and a blessed style and writing ability that creates literature.[42]

Although complimentary to Fitzgerald's writing style and ability, the criticism that 'Flappers are the same the world over', including Fitzgerald's flappers in this assessment, must have been an exasperating judgement for Fitzgerald to bear. In 1937, he wrote a curious story in which he channelled his frustrations with being associated with flappers and 'glamor girl[s]' (*LK*, 226).[43] Although it was not published during his lifetime, 'A Full Life' is a strange addition to the genre of stories in which we witness Fitzgerald reflecting on his own role as an author, such as 'Three Acts of Music' and 'Two Wrongs'. In three parts, opening in 1923 and dramatically concluding in 1937, the story features a man named Dr Wilkinson, who has three encounters with Gwendolyn Davies, a woman whose mysterious life Wilkinson has been following in reported fragments since their paths crossed when he treated her in hospital in 1923. Their encounters culminate in Wilkinson's threat to reveal Davies's identity as a runaway, which prompts Davies literally to blow herself up: '"The joke's on you – I'm full of dynamite"' (*LK*, 226). The story, as Horst Kruse has persuasively argued, serves as an allegorical exploration of Fitzgerald's relationship with his flapper heroine, who was no longer in demand by the mid-1930s but was no less important to Fitzgerald, despite the fact that his literary fortunes seemed to have waned alongside the popularity of his 'glamor girl' heroine.[44] In 'Gretchen's Forty Winks' (1924), Fitzgerald had his protagonist drug a young heroine who was struggling to adapt to a quiet life as a married mother, causing her to sleep for a full twenty-four hours. But in 'A Full Life', Fitzgerald goes to the extreme measures of exploding his heroine, not just sending her to sleep.

Parodying his golden girl flapper to such a flippant degree, Fitzgerald reveals himself to be at a transitional point in both his life and career. On the cusp of his final trip to Hollywood, he has been through his 1936 *Crack-Up* and is looking towards the future, cognisant of the fact that he is unable (and unwilling) to produce the enormously successful flapper confections with which he launched himself on to the literary scene in 1920. He writes to Kenneth Littauer, the editor of *Collier's* magazine, in the summer of 1939: 'I know what's expected of me, but in that direction the well is pretty dry and I think I am much wiser in not trying to strain for it but rather to open up a new well, a new vein.'[45] But despite opening this new vein of inspiration, the flapper would linger in Fitzgerald's imagination. In 'A Full Life', Fitzgerald describes the elusive draw of his charismatic flapper: 'She was the girl for whom a part of him was always searching at cafés and parties and theatres' (*LK*, 223). Her significance for Fitzgerald dictated that she was given an appropriate farewell that befit her revolutionary status and rebellious nature. The fact that Fitzgerald chooses to have Davies break with propriety by donning an inflatable suit and jumping out of a window on the fifty-third floor shows just how frustrated he had become with his association with the golden girl characters he used to portray with ease, as well as his irritation at no longer being able to create saleable fiction in this strain. Gwen Davies's definitive break with expectations of conventional behaviour is a metaphor for Fitzgerald's own new direction.

Dr Wilkinson expresses sentiments similar to those expressed by the unnamed nurse towards songwriters in 'Three Acts of Music':

> He felt that he knew her, in some such manner as one might know a composer or a writer one had never seen – he knew her though she had written only on air and there was a mysterious compulsion that made him follow her career with admiration and curiosity. (*LK*, 224)

The phrase 'written only on air' is reminiscent of the gravestone of Fitzgerald's favourite poet, John Keats, which is inscribed with the words, 'Here lies one whose name was writ in water.' The tombstone comparison is apt, given that Davies's body dangerously makes its mark upon the air at the story's opening, and repeats this daring feat, this time as a precursor to her death, at the story's conclusion. Her 'perfect parabola' through the air recalls Fitzgerald's first and most important flapper muse Zelda's daring parabolas diving off Riviera cliffs into the sea, and Davies's spur-of-the-moment dive off a cruise ship into the Atlantic recalls Rags Martin-Jones pushing an unsuspecting John Chestnut off a dock and into the Hudson river (*ASM*, 97).

Contrary to the moralistic rehabilitation endings of flapper films, Fitzgerald chooses to explode his flapper heroine, at a circus off the beaten track, not even with the status of headliner billing. This ending was preferable to reformation. As well as killing herself, Davies's explosion kills Dr Wilkinson, symbolising a kind of creative rebirth and emancipation from previous generic constraints and Fitzgerald's readiness for the fresh start his sojourn in Hollywood promised. The story's sardonic closing line, 'And so another glamor girl passes into history' (*LK*, 226), betrays Fitzgerald's frustrated mindset at this point in his career. His relationship with the flapper archetype declared to be over in such dramatic style, Fitzgerald turns his attention to Hollywood, which had its own set of stock figures to explore.

Some degree of Fitzgerald's talent for manœuvring within these 'accustomed fiction type[s]' in order to create 'literature' may be indebted to his early fondness for musical comedies. Musical

theatre of the 1920s had a set of conventions and stock characters, and Fitzgerald draws upon these, especially some of the stock
plots concerned with traversing class boundaries. Writing about
these musical comedies of social mobility, Savran outlines how
'The characters as a rule are stock comic figures that include the
young lovers (the ingénue and juvenile lead), foolish parental
figures, an eccentric sidekick or two, as well as other comic foils
(many of them clearly derived from vaudeville).'[46] Examples of
these stock characters in Fitzgerald's fiction can be found in stories
such as 'Myra Meets His Family' (1920), 'Dice, Brassknuckles and
Guitar' (1923) and 'The Unspeakable Egg' (1924). Berret finds the
'romance between a high class person and a popular entertainer'
to be a common theme of shows of the 1920s, and this theme
certainly pervades many of Fitzgerald's stories of the period.[47]

One show of the 1920s that was acknowledged as 'pivotal' and
praised for its rejuvenating effect on musical comedy was 1921's
smash hit, *Shuffle Along*.[48] It was the first all-black revue to reach
Broadway in the 1920s, with a plot that was based on vaudeville
sketches and a cast that included future stars Josephine Baker,
Adelaide Hall and Florence Mills. On its debut, composer Darius
Milhaud praised the show's 'exquisite musicality', while the pia-
nist and critic Samuel Chotzinoff found that the show's 'verve,
simplicity and ardor . . . rejuvenated the spineless and degenerate
American musical-comedy'.[49] This rejuvenation actually took place
by looking backwards, into the cultural archives of minstrelsy, as
well as vaudeville, both of which provided inspiration for the col-
lagistic form of *Shuffle Along*.

Noble Sissle and Eubie Blake created *Shuffle Along* quickly, blend-
ing together different vaudeville acts and managing to expand the
plot of a sketch of theirs called *The Mayor of Dixie* into a musical
length show. Some of the songs were even written after Sissle and
Blake acquired some cheap second-hand costumes: 'Bandana Days'
was composed over the phone, to facilitate the company's use of
a batch of cotton-pickers' costumes they had bought in a job lot,
and then this plantation number was shoehorned into the plot.[50]
Sissle and Blake themselves referred to their creation as a 'musical
mélange' and the integration between story and song was loose at
best, as was the case for most musical comedies of this time.[51]

The advent of the sophisticated integration of song, dialogue and movement to convey theme is commonly dated to the premiere of Hammerstein and Kern's *Show Boat* in December 1927, and in 1921 *Shuffle Along* wore its patchwork, fragmented structure with pride, an element that was evidently part of its appeal. A review in *Variety* praised it as 'lively entertainment' with 'an excellent score', and with musical numbers 'worthy of a real production, which *Shuffle Along* lacks entirely'. The reviewer dismissively refers to 'whatever book there is and the comedy business' as being contributed by vaudeville.[52]

As well as the kaleidoscopic material and form of the show, as Savran has argued, aspects of the musical are open to 'a kind of double reading'.[53] A number like 'Bandana Days' can be interpreted in the 'coon song' vein, with stereotypes of plantation nostalgia where 'Dearest mem'ries will live always. / In those dear old bandana days, / Cane-and-cotton-ne'er-forgotten bandana days.'[54] Savran suggests that much of the musical can be interpreted 'as an ironic reinvention of a racist formula that freely appropriates and satirizes the conventions of both minstrelsy and musical comedy'.[55] Just as in Baker's performances, parodic currents prove to be a destabilising force, where stereotypes are undermined and performers articulate their virtuosity by simultaneously reproducing and redefining genres.

Josephine Baker's early reviewers tended to emphasise the presumed improvisatory nature of her performances, and Baker, ever the promotion-savvy performer, fanned this fire by claiming to be 'driven by dark forces I didn't recognise'.[56] In a similar vein, the orchestra of *Shuffle Along* performed without sheet music for the entirety of the show, giving the impression to some that they were improvising, rather than having memorised the entire score. Eubie Blake explained that this was because 'People didn't believe that black people could read music – they wanted to think that our ability was just natural talent.'[57] Playing to the audiences' prejudiced expectations like this fed into the show's appeal, and the racial diversity of the audience was testament to these dual interpretations on offer.

Ann Douglas locates in this double interpretation an innovation she terms 'affectionate parody': '*Shuffle Along*'s happy mongrel idiom rediscovered and reinvented the omnivorously affectionate parody mode, half flattering mimicry, half creative insult, of which Jones, Whiteman, Jolson and Berlin were the masters.'[58] She finds the 'Shuffle Along' cast to be paying 'mock homage' to the minstrel show:

> Its heady ragtime numbers, 'Dixie' songs, fisticuffs, and comic dialogues full of fractured and exaggerated Negro dialect, its anti-reform impulses and comic electioneering drama serving weakly as plot, were all staples of the old minstrel stage; minstrel fans had thought nothing funnier than the Negro's thoughts and antics when faced with those activities half-forbidden to him, voting and running for office. The comedians and librettists Aubrey Lyles and Flournoy Miller performed in blackface.[59]

Yet the ever-present subtext of parody undermined the employment of so much minstrelsy humour and provided dual readings of the show to complement the integration of white and African American audiences.

'All We Can Do Is Watch It in the Movies': Fitzgerald and the Film Musical

Shuffle Along acknowledged its influences proudly but such open admission of source material was a rarity, especially when those sources originated in African American culture. Linda Mizejewski conceives of this as a whitening process: 'As moving pictures took over the American musical, black musical elements would be whitened beyond recognition', or the African American inheritance would be acknowledged by the use of blackface, 'which effectively displaced black performers'.[60] In RKO's Swing Time (1936), a Fred Astaire and Ginger Rogers vehicle set in New York City, Astaire performs a number in blackface called 'Bojangles of Harlem'. Ostensibly a tribute to famous African American tapdancer Bill 'Bojangles' Robinson (who was alive and actively performing throughout the 1930s), 'Bojangles of Harlem' features Astaire dancing with three enormous shadows of himself. The sequence was filmed with special effects that took days of filming, and weeks of post-production work were needed to generate a performance that lasted for just a few minutes. The use of blackface is rather incongruous and marks the 'Bojangles of Harlem' sequence out as a self-contained interlude contrasting with other numbers that work in a more integrated way to enhance the themes and advance the plot. Despite this, the film was a great success and the 'Bojangles of Harlem' sequence was nominated for the Academy Award for Best Dance Direction.

Famously, in the 1930s, there was an abundance of film musicals produced, despite the financial pressures of the Depression affecting audience figures. In 'No Flowers' (1934), eighteen-year-old Marjorie Clark reprimands her mother while preparing to go to her first university prom: 'Mother, try and realize you've had your fun, all that luxury and everything, but all we can do is watch it in the movies, and as often as not have to go Dutch treat to the movies' (*ACC*, 238). Set in 1933, 'No Flowers' conceives of its Depression-era setting as a 'tin age' to counteract with the 'Golden Age' of the post-war years and the 'Gilded Age' of the pre-war years.

But in 1933, despite being steeped in the 'tin age', Warner Brothers produced two of the most iconic movie musicals of all time: *42nd Street* and *Gold Diggers of 1933*. The lavish and complex dance sequences of both were choreographed by Busby Berkeley, who specialised in innovative kaleidoscopic shots of large numbers of dancers, especially enjoying the use of high overhead shots, breaking the traditional constraints of the stage. The public appetite for glamorous musicals had waned by 1932, as Hollywood, identifying a money-making trend, had flooded the market with a huge number of hastily made musicals, and the public grew weary of the formulaic films. Busby Berkeley's 1933 Hollywood debut reinvigorated the form, and paved the way for many more iconic musical films to be made throughout the 1930s and into the 1940s.

Another Fred Astaire and Ginger Rogers vehicle, *Top Hat*, was released in 1935, and featured sumptuous sets and luxurious costumes. It was a roaring success, and dance critic Arlene Croce argues that it is 'a Thirties' romance of the Twenties, the sins of the decade wiped clean by a flow of lyrical optimism.' She explains that:

> The whole film starts from a non-literal premise. In the class-conscious
> Thirties, it was possible to imagine characters who spent their lives in

evening dress – to imagine them as faintly preposterous holdovers from the Twenties, slipping from their satin beds at twilight, dancing the night away and then stumbling, top-hatted and ermine-tangled, out of speakeasies at dawn. It was a dead image, a faded cartoon of the pre-Crash, pre-Roosevelt Prohibition era, but it was the only image of luxury that most people believed in, and *Top Hat* revived it as a corrected vision of elegance.[61]

This sense of urbanity and luxuriousness pervades many of Fitzgerald's short stories from the 1920s, and in his post-Crash fiction he imports this 'corrected vision of elegance' into his work via his use of nostalgia, set against the backdrop of the Depression, as in 'No Flowers'.

The Wall Street Crash of October 1929 serves as the midpoint of Fitzgerald's two-decade career. Fitzgerald would struggle to throw off the associations he had accumulated with images of 1920s luxury, despite writing many stories about Americans facing harder times. As Bruccoli has noted, there was a moralistic angle to Fitzgerald's wane in popularity after the Crash: 'Fitzgerald came to symbolise the excesses of the boom decade. The Twenties had spoiled and rewarded him. The Thirties would disparage him.'[62] As symbols of the Roaring Twenties, Scott and Zelda were both born at the century's outset (in 1896 and 1900, respectively), a fact which lends itself to the Fitzgeralds' representative status. As Prigozy identifies, 'the parallels between his life and American history continued with the national recovery and the author's artistic renewal, but Fitzgerald's physical resources were depleted and he died with his new novel [*The Last Tycoon*] incomplete and his fame far in the future'.[63] In terms of this 'national . . . and artistic renewal', it is tempting to interpret Fitzgerald's more moralistic depictions of modern vices leading up to the Crash as warnings (especially if we focus on his much-quoted 1931 essay, 'Echoes of the Jazz Age') but the reality was more complex than this reading suggests. Fitzgerald has a unique combination of qualifications for writing about the pre- and post-Crash worlds: he is writing from the perspective of someone who has lived in the United States and in Europe, viewing problems at home with the unique perspective of an expat; by 1929 he had both been very wealthy and struggled to pay his bills; his constant geographical transit, even within the United States, gave him an insight into multiple areas of the country, East and West; and his role on the proscenium of public life, as a celebrity author who saw his books fall out of print in his lifetime, gave him a privileged insight into this transitional period.

Only six months after writing 'The Bridal Party', which conveys a sense of optimism in the wake of the Crash, Fitzgerald wrote another story that gives a different reading of life in the Depression. This was 'The Hotel Child' (1931), in which he addresses:

> the erosion of old values, the gulf that had arisen between the generations during the boom, the new morality which appeared to lack definition or recognizable goals and he felt was reflected in the activities of corrupt and rootless Americans, sycophants of a decadent European aristocracy.[64]

A satire, 'The Hotel Child' complicates a simple reading of Fitzgerald's work pre- and post-October 1929, in its meditation on the differences between Americans and Europeans. Set in Lausanne, 'the continually sagging American stock exchange' is cited as the reason 'so many hotels [were] begging to be filled' (*TAR*, 290), and although the Schwartz family are still prosperous in the wake of the Crash, they find themselves surrounded by and preyed upon by bogus and impecunious aristocrats, and rejected by their fellow Americans. Fifi's naïveté and innocence initially assure a sympathetic interpretation of her character, but as the story unfolds, she is increasingly associated with what Thorstein Veblen coined 'conspicuous consumption', especially of the sartorial variety.[65] At the story's conclusion, 'as [Fifi] went out looking for completion under the impression that she was going to the *couturier*', her status as distinct from the 'corrupt and rootless Americans' is somewhat undermined (*TAR*, 309). Other stories Fitzgerald wrote in this period, also depicting expatriates, such as 'One Trip Abroad' (1930) and 'Indecision' (1931), feature expats blithely continuing about their business, either ignorant of or unmoved by the plight of their compatriots.

Key to the creation of the special atmosphere in which 'the sins of the decade' vanish in the wake of 'lyrical optimism' is the use of musical and film allusions. The Depression is conspicuously absent from many musicals of the 1930s, which provided a distraction from the difficult times facing most Americans. Fitzgerald has a particular fondness for the music of Irving Berlin, one of the most successful purveyors of Depression-era entertainment. 'Too Cute for Words' was published in 1936 and focuses on the different perceptions of a parent and child during the Depression, a theme Fitzgerald had poignantly explored in 'No Flowers'. Fitzgerald uses the songs of Berlin to explore ideas about his own successes and failures as an artist, his potential and lack of fulfilment, and ultimately to interrogate the value of popular culture, whether in popular music or popular short stories. 'Too Cute for Words' was written in December 1935 whilst Fitzgerald was staying in Hendersonville, North Carolina. It appeared in the *Saturday Evening Post* on 18 April 1936, intended to be the first in a series of stories featuring the protagonist Gwen Bowers, loosely based on the exploits of his teenaged daughter, Scottie, who was fourteen at the time. 'Too Cute' is a five-part story that chronicles Gwen's visit to Princeton for the annual Princeton versus Harvard American football game – a trip that results in her gatecrashing the prom only to run into her father, who is serving as a chaperone. It is a story palpably about father–daughter relationships and teenagers' obsessions with popular culture, but at its heart is a fundamental concern with the limitations of language.

The story opens with an uncertainty: 'Bryan didn't know exactly why Mrs. Hannaman was there' (*BJG*, 289). The very title speaks to the inexpressible: 'Too Cute *for Words*'. 'Cute' is Gwen's latest slang, overused to the point that her father Bryan utters it ironically at the story's close, to Gwen's horror. Uncertainties of expression and shortfalls of language characterise Bryan and Gwen's relationship, the story meditating on the politics of listening and silence, and offering music as a potential alternative method of communication. The 1935 Irving Berlin song 'Cheek to Cheek' becomes a leitmotif in the story, appearing five times. Gwen is encouraged to 'play music of her own choice' on her phonograph, though she is not allowed to listen to the radio, in an effort to encourage her to be a discerning consumer of popular culture. However, Gwen has secretly seen the 1935 film *Top Hat* several times, and her obsession with the film's score permeates the narrative. Gwen's record of

'Cheek to Cheek' has been broken, though its remains 'preserved to remind her to get another' – she retains the totemic object and plays the abbreviated remnants of the record, much to her father's bemusement (*BJG*, 292).

Music serves as a guide in the story, as Gwen and her friends follow the audio trail to reach the Princeton prom, where they '[huddle] silently' while 'a sonorous orchestra proclaimed a feeling that someone was fooling, announced that someone was its lucky star, and demanded if it wasn't a lovely day to be caught in the rain' (*BJG*, 299–300). These references each foreshadow events to follow: the 1934 song 'Fun to be Fooled' ruminates on the ability to trick oneself into believing that the fleeting is eternal. Marion Lamb, a debutante from the girls' school, is caught in this practice when the girls witness the following exchange on having found Marion alone with a boy outside the prom:

> 'I went to school with these girls and I know they won't tell. Anyhow, they know it's not serious – that I get engaged every few weeks or so.'
>
> 'Marion,' cried the young man, 'I can't stand hearing you talk like that!'
>
> 'Oh, Harry, I didn't mean to hurt you!' she gasped, equally upset. 'You know there's never been anyone but you.'
>
> He groaned. (*BJG*, 301)

Marion's words lose their value for Harry. 'Too Cute for Words' can be read as a satire on the conventions of romantic song, as well as formulaic love stories found in the *Post*. The 1935 song 'You Are My Lucky Star' describes the singer's fanatical reaction to watching his love interest from a distance and comparing her to a beguiling celebrity. Gwen and her two friends engage in this kind of celebrity worship as they find themselves an unobserved vantage point at the prom, described as 'an orchid-colored dream in which floated prototypes of their future selves, surrounded, engulfed, buoyed up by unnumbered boys' (*BJG*, 300). Being 'buoyed up by unnumbered boys' calls to mind the elaborate choreography of Busby Berkeley, and the anonymous proliferation of dance partners also recalls the vogue for Tayloristic dance troupes and chorus lines.

'Isn't This a Lovely Day (To Be Caught in the Rain)', the third *Top Hat* number mentioned in the story, is a playful *pas de deux* in its film context. A jodhpur-clad Ginger Rogers and characteristically dapper Fred Astaire, trapped by a rainstorm under a park gazebo, perform a mirrored tap routine, without making any physical contact until the last 30 seconds of the 4½ and a half minute sequence. The song prefigures the lack of contact with boys in 'Too Cute' (who have remained in New York unexpectedly), as well as the entrapment in a small physical space, and the story emulates the light-hearted screwball tone of the film. RKO's most profitable film of the decade, *Top Hat* infiltrated Scottie Fitzgerald's life profoundly, as she remembers in Eleanor Lanahan's biography, *Scottie*: 'Our whole little group went to see *Top Hat* seven times, saying the lines with the actors which infuriated the people sitting near us. Astaire and Rogers seemed the epitome of grace and beauty, all that we wanted to be.'[66] When Bryan 'facetiously' suggests dancing to the song, Gwen looks at him 'with infinite compassion' and enquires, 'Who do you imagine you are, Daddy? Fred Astaire?' (*BJG*, 294). Fitzgerald went on to exonerate Bryan in summer 1937, arranging for Scottie to meet Fred Astaire when she visited her father in Hollywood. In the story, 'Cheek to Cheek' represents the romantic possibilities of future selves, the pull of imitative identity and the lure of celebrity culture.

As a leitmotif, the recurrence of the song is not as problematic as some of Fitzgerald's other formulaic story devices, such as the multiple coincidence or mistaken identity plots. Its repeated appearances serve to illustrate the saturated market of music and film of this period – the song is heard everywhere. For Gwen, though, the song is imbued with a romance and nostalgia found frequently in Fitzgerald's œuvre, and at the story's close, when Bryan remarks on the Harvard band 'jazzing old marching songs' when Gwen would prefer them to play what he calls 'Cheek by Jowl', Gwen disappears from the moment, like Sally Carrol, instead listening 'to that sweeter and somehow older tune' (*BJG*, 307). For Gwen, it summarises the limitless romantic potential of her future – a future she glimpsed at the prom, when she danced 'in a breathless trance' to the same music. Contemporary music is tied up with this kind of forward-looking nostalgia in several of Fitzgerald's stories from this period, including 'No Flowers', which is also set at Princeton.[67]

These stories are hopeful but also contain an inescapable melancholy. The romantic potential of these young protagonists' futures coexists with the bittersweet romantic experiences of the past. When unable to produce the romantic stories of young love that the *Post* wanted, instead Fitzgerald parodied his earlier work and interrogated the role of the artist (whether they were writer, dancer, singer, musician or filmmaker) in society. Interested in all popular cultural forms, Fitzgerald's short stories tapped into a wider modernist desire to represent experience in a collage aesthetic, most at home in the musical theatre Fitzgerald had so highly prized from his adolescence onwards.

Music is the cultural measure by which Fitzgerald reassures himself that there is still quality to be found in the popular, whether it is a popular song or a popular short story, and that readerships are fundamentally plural in their interpretations. It was this conviction that led him back to Hollywood to interrogate the value of the newest commercial venture in storytelling.

CHAPTER 5

'A More Glittering, a Grosser Power': Fitzgerald and Film

F. Scott Fitzgerald was born just eighteen months after the Lumière Brothers created their pioneering 1895 film *Sortie de l'Usine Lumière de Lyon*, which laid the foundations for modern cinema.[1] He was fascinated by the movies throughout his youth, and despite his irrepressible passion for musical theatre, film was a pervasive influence on Fitzgerald. Alan Margolies recounts how a young Fitzgerald met with director D. W. Griffith at his Mamaroneck, New York, studios and unsuccessfully submitted script suggestions to Griffith as well as to David O. Selznick, although Fitzgerald did go on to write intertitles for a 1923 Paramount picture and the scenario for a Clara Bow vehicle, *Grit*, released in 1924.[2] Far from turning to Hollywood as a last resort, Fitzgerald had been interested in the movie industry from the very outset of his career, and he spent brief periods in Hollywood working on screenwriting projects in early 1927 and late 1931. These forays into the industry were described by him as 'failures' in 1937, when he was on the train to Hollywood for his third and final screenwriting stint, which was to affect him, and his work, profoundly.[3] Contrary to the stereotype of the alcoholic Hollywood hack, Fitzgerald's final days in Hollywood were spent in productive work on his final, unfinished, novel, which was to have been an exploration of the inner workings of the film industry – both decent and sordid.

In April 1925, Fitzgerald wrote a letter to his Princeton contemporary, John Peale Bishop, in which he asserted that 'I'm too much of an egoist and not enough of a diplomat ever to succeed in the movies.'[4] As early as 1925, Fitzgerald was already conscious of the emerging studio system's lack of democracy – he was aware that his temperament as an artist would not be happily reconciled with the Taylorian mass-production line in which contributions were valued only in so far as they formed part of a process, with little (if any) individual ownership of the created product for the vast majority of contributors. This must have been disheartening advice for Bishop, who was undertaking a stint at Paramount Pictures in New York at the time. But despite knowing this in April 1925, Fitzgerald still took screenwriting jobs in Hollywood on multiple occasions. Unsuited to collaborative authorship, Fitzgerald inevitably struggled with the demands placed upon him as an author in Hollywood. As his satirical hack Pat Hobby remarks in 'Mightier Than the Sword' (1941), 'They don't want authors. They want writers' (*TLD*, 200), and Fitzgerald's reconciliation of his novelistic authorship with his writing of short stories was tempestuous. In February 1939, Fitzgerald explained to Perkins, 'Conditions in the industry somehow propose the paradox: "We brought you here for your individuality but while you're here we insist that you do everything to conceal it."'[5] In spite of these struggles, Fitzgerald's fascination with Hollywood and the film industry was unwavering.

In the summer of 1939, Fitzgerald wrote to a fiction editor at *Collier's* magazine, reflecting on the trajectory of his self-referential love stories:

> it isn't particularly likely that I'll write a great many more stories about young love. I was tagged with that by my first writings up to 1925. Since then I have written stories about young love. They have been done with increasing difficulty and increasing insincerity. I would either be a miracle man or a hack if I could go on turning out an identical product for three decades.[6]

Fitzgerald's consciousness of one of his major themes being revisited with decreasing levels of success shows his objective professionalism as well as his acknowledgement that the stories lost their originality due to 'increasing insincerity'. His self-assessment of his 'type's relationship with previous incarnations of the type', in Robert Warshow's phrase, is startlingly honest. Simultaneously part of his love-story 'field of reference' and separate from it, Fitzgerald marks out his later, more 'insincere' love stories as inferior.

Even in the later period of Fitzgerald's career, when he had given up on flapper stories, self-parody through variations on a theme was still an important facet of his work. For example, Nell Margery in 'I Got Shoes' (1933) is happy only when she is working, and her independence is depicted as almost archetypal: she 'seemed to bear with her, as she moved, a whole dream of women's future' (*ACC*, 200). Like Rags, she describes herself in terms of commerce: 'I'm just a sort of shopkeeper,' echoes Rags's conception of love's 'bazaar' (*ACC*, 208; *ASM*, 99).

As critics such as Michele Hannoosh explain, parody requires a mastery of a subject before revealing something new about it by showing it from a different, or exaggerated, angle.[7] In Fitzgerald's use of dance, music and musical theatre, he both appropriates the cultural forms to demonstrate their innate power and desirability, and takes the forms in a different direction – to show how they can be misused, how there are dangers inherent in over-reliance upon them, and how there is potential that sits within them, unfulfilled. Fitzgerald's use of film and the filmic in his short fiction is consistent with this approach to popular culture.

Fitzgerald sometimes calls upon the enticing glamour of music, dance and film, and is highly critical of them at other times, mocking those who build their identities on such seemingly superficial foundations. Fitzgerald's ambivalence towards popular culture is visible in his satirical portraits of gimmicky jazz bands in 'May Day' (with a flautist playing whilst standing on his head) but also more subtly, in Amanthis's involuntary foot-tapping when she hears jazz provoking both excitement and annoyance (*TJA*, 91, 281). Fitzgerald uses music to enhance a narrative's mood, as in 'Winter Dreams', where Dexter listens to soft piano music floating across the romantic darkness (*ASM*, 50). But Fitzgerald also warns against those who invest too heavily in music, chastising characters like Josephine Perry who replace their emotions with quoted song lyrics (*BJG*, 198). Similarly, Josephine Baker's performances are alluringly glamorous but can also be read as examples of inauthenticity: the seasoned performer is delivering a choreographed, not spontaneous, performance. Fitzgerald's apparent 'double vision' in writing about these cultural forms – that is to say, his ambivalence – can be read as a simultaneous presentation and rereading of these cultural forms' contribution to popular culture and, indeed, national identity.

Simon Dentith uses the term 'parody' as 'the generic term for a range of related cultural practices, all of which are imitative of other cultural forms, with varying degrees of mockery or humour'.[8] Fitzgerald imitates other cultural forms on two levels – by seeking to portray the dances, songs and filmic tendencies of his day accurately, but also by imitating their distilled essences to reveal something new and sometimes disturbing – the dry roots and Parisian arabesques of Josephine Baker tell us about the vertical but oppressive psychology of New York City. The formulaic assembly line of Tin Pan Alley demonstrates the ubiquity of mass-marketed leisure products, the consumption of which operated as the means 'of gaining or retaining a good name', as the average American moved away from producing (things, fun, entertainment) towards an unstoppable culture of consuming.[9] The previous chapters have shown how Fitzgerald satirises popular culture by creating his own advertising jingles and song lyrics (in 'Porcelain and Pink' and 'The Intimate Strangers'), as well as his own dances ('the Florida Drag-Out', 'Memphis Sideswoop' and 'slow Chicago' in 'Dice, Brassknuckles and Guitar'). In film, his parody of popular culture is visible in his satire of studio hacks, producers, actors and screenplays in the Pat Hobby series of stories, as well as in 'Jacob's Ladder' (1927) and 'Magnetism' (1928). His satirical portraits imply the need for reform, in order for film to reach its potential as a great American art form.

'A Mechanical and Communal Art': Fitzgerald's Responses to Hollywood

Fitzgerald was quick to recognise the earning potential inherent in the medium of film for an author.[10] When *The Great Gatsby* (1925) failed to sell as many copies as he expected on its release in April, Fitzgerald wrote to Maxwell Perkins explaining:

> In all events I have a book of good short stories for the fall. Now I shall write some cheap ones until I've accumulated enough for my next novel.

When that is finished and published I'll wait and see. If it will support me
with no more intervals of trash I'll go on as a novelist. If not I'm going to
quit, come home, go to Hollywood and learn the movie business.[11]

As Walter Raubicheck has noted, in this period, the film industry
and the popular story market were similar in their lucrative production of popular culture.[12] At this point, in 1925, Fitzgerald is
contemplating (perhaps humorously) learning a new trade that he
thinks will be both financially and artistically rewarding: filmmaking. One prevalent Hollywood narrative suggests that writers were
lured west by the promise of easy money, only to find their talents
under-appreciated and eventually eroded. Tom Cerasulo formu-
lates this as 'the vampire myth' in his study.[13] He questions the
validity of this Hollywood myth and reformulates the relationship
between scriptwriting work and these writers as a dialectic exchange
that was actually beneficial to them rather than a one-way, crushing
relationship. As he points out, writers do not go to Hollywood
to be writers; they become screenwriters, which means something
quite different to any conception of authorship. The studio system
did not permit the Romantic notion of singular, inspired authorship that Fitzgerald especially identified with. Screenwriters were
fundamentally collaborative (in practice, if not in temperament)
and were fairly low in the filmmaking hierarchy, despite the cachet
studios capitalised upon of having a certain famous author working
for them. Cerasulo argues that, contrary to popular belief, the fact
'that they were workers in the culture industry was never artistically
devastating, and it was never a vocation killer'. 'In fact', Cerasulo
continues, there was a 'shift in the vocation of authorship, from a
late modernist pose of the disaffected genius who stands outside of
society to a later role as an engaged laborer in industrial America.'[14]

Whilst it is true that Fitzgerald underwent something of a political awakening during his last years in Hollywood, he also cherished
the position of the outsider. In writing *The Last Tycoon* (1941),
with a privileged insight into the workings of the studios despite
his lack of screenwriting success, Fitzgerald emulates his 'poor boy'
heroes of his early fiction, being simultaneously granted entry to
this glamorous new world, all the while perceiving its flaws and
vanities with objective clarity. In January 1927, during his first

Hollywood sojourn, Fitzgerald's stance towards Hollywood is quite light-hearted: he writes to his cousin, Mrs Richard Taylor, that 'this is a tragic city of beautiful girls – the girls who mop the floor are beautiful, the waitresses, the shop ladies. You never want to see any more beauty. (Always excepting yours).'[15] His crystallised fictional responses to Hollywood begin to appear in stories like 'Jacob's Ladder' and in 'Magnetism', written in June and December 1927, respectively, and in the latter he uses notably darker language, describing the landscape as hellish and the studio workers as 'souls in purgatory' (*ASM*, 410).

Perhaps it was Fitzgerald's lack of success as a screenwriter that began to colour his perception of Hollywood; more likely it was the simple fact of spending longer in the industry. He feuded with a collaborator in 1931, returning home $6,000 richer but more disillusioned. In January 1938, he felt deeply betrayed by Joe Mankiewicz's rewriting of his and Ted Paramore's script for *Three Comrades*. But there was discipline as well as disappointment: prior to the *Three Comrades* debacle, Budd Schulberg remembers Fitzgerald having 'plunged into a study of film-making that even included a card file of the plot lines of all the pictures he had seen', and Margolies writes of how, directly after finishing on *Three Comrades*, Fitzgerald began an intensive viewing of Joan Crawford's films, dividing them into acts and noting montages in particular when preparing to write a script for her in February 1938.[16] In his three years and nine months of work in Hollywood, Fitzgerald shockingly managed only one screen credit: a sought-after measure of worth second only to salary.

In his introduction to the published screenplay of 'Babylon Revisited', Budd Schulberg diagnoses Fitzgerald's screenwriting failures as being ultimately hubristic:

> Instead of rejecting screenwriting as a necessary evil, Fitzgerald went the other way and embraced it as a new art form, even while recognizing that it was an art frequently embarrassed by the 'merchants' more comfortable with mediocrity in their efforts to satisfy the widest possible audience.[17]

Fitzgerald put a lot of pressure on himself to succeed in this 'new art form': he thought that screenwriting could finally provide the mutually beneficial coexistence between art and commerce that he chastised himself for failing to effect in his commercial short story writing. Fitzgerald aimed for both literary acclaim and 'satisfy[ing] the widest possible audience', but previously he had managed to accomplish this only in his two separate personas of novelist and short storyist. In Hollywood screenwriting he tried to combine the two, despite the fact that since he left Princeton, he had had limited success with playwriting: his political satire, *The Vegetable; or, From President to Postman* (1923) closed after disastrous Atlantic City tryouts, and Linda Paterson Miller describes it as 'lack[ing] unity as either political satire or burlesque'.[18] It is an entertaining and ambitious piece but the surviving script is unfortunately uneven.

Christopher Wixson finds that the play possesses 'a Marx Brothers lunacy and anarchy' and finds it 'emblematic of the paradox of the Jazz Age itself, replete with corruption, experimentation, vigor, and the loss of the center'.[19] Such experimental features are only now beginning to be appreciated for their ambitious complexity, rather than being dismissed for their apparent flippancy, and in Fitzgerald's detailed, idiosyncratically elaborate stage directions, we can anticipate the criticisms of his approach to screenwriting. Fitzgerald seems to have channelled the dramaturgical aspirations nurtured by writing plays as a teenager in St Paul and his Princeton Triangle Club libretto days into his Hollywood work. Despite referring to 'the never dying lure of another play' in 1924, Fitzgerald never completed another play after *The Vegetable*'s lacklustre critical reception.[20] This means of working through his failures as a screenwriter, when the 'merchants' were rejecting and revising his work, was a route he had taken before: to rationalise an artistic crisis, he began writing about the writing process. Reaching its crescendo in *The Last Tycoon*, this method of processing his Hollywood shortcomings began after his 1927 trip, with stories such as 'Jacob's Ladder', 'Magnetism' and 'Crazy Sunday' (1932).

Fitzgerald's third and final period in Hollywood began optimistically: he aimed to write a screenplay that would be so wonderful on its own that no collaborators would be needed and no revisions requested. In July 1937, he wrote to Scottie that 'I must be very tactful [. . .] until, in fact or in effect, I'm alone on the picture.'[21] He hoped that he would even be able to direct what he had written, to become what we would now recognise as an 'auteur'. In 1950, his ex-supervisor and screenwriting adversary, Joe Mankiewicz, succeeded in both writing and directing a film, *All About Eve*, but by then Fitzgerald had been dead for six years.

Fitzgerald's interest in taking on an auteur role, 'alone on the picture', is reflected in his preoccupation with exploring the role of the artist in society. As we have seen, he uses the dancer figure as a metaphor for the literary craftsman seeking to marry critical and commercial acclaim, and prizes the songwriter's role in helping people to make sense of their lives. For Fitzgerald, the filmmakers of Hollywood had the potential to combine artistic merit and commercial success to a greater degree than the author, dancer or songwriter. The special medium of film, combined with the funding assuring a wide distribution, was an irresistible combination. One major setback was the fact that the filmmakers who employed Fitzgerald did not rate his screenwriting skills very highly.

His early attempts at scripts were too heavily reliant on words to convey meaning – Fitzgerald even compared screenwriting to a word game, calling it 'a sort of tense crossword puzzle game'.[22] In his work on *Three Comrades* in 1937, Fitzgerald argued in favour of including a graph representing German National Wealth, seemingly reluctant to comprehend that moving images could convey this poverty effectively. At the other end of the spectrum, he was occasionally too flippant in his proposed screenplays, once suggesting a scene showing St Peter manning a telephone switchboard. But Fitzgerald's work on *The Women* and *Infidelity* in 1938 was more inventive, proposing the use of imaginative tracking shots, and revealing feelings through small eye movements and gestures, demonstrating more of an aptitude for screenwriting than his sole screen credit might suggest.[23]

Despite his shortcomings as a screenwriter becoming evident on each of his three visits to Hollywood, Fitzgerald was none the less drawn repeatedly to analysing Hollywood's artistic potential. He was especially fond of identifying with Hollywood as the locus of celebrity and the lucrative marketing of talent. In 'My Lost City' (1932), he conceptualises his early professional life as living 'in my own movie of New York', and describes how he fails as an actor, as 'it was demonstrated that I was unable to play the role' (*MLC*,

109). Thinking of his early days in terms of a film alludes to the arc of overnight success that some movie stars enjoyed. Fitzgerald also enjoyed dramatically sudden notoriety, recounted in 'Early Success' (1937), when 'all in a space of three days, my book was published, I married my girl, and they were pounding out copies as they pound out extras in the movies' (*MLC*, 188). He conceptualises his books as extras in the film of his life. Furthermore, his self-diagnosis in 'My Lost City' (1935) of being 'not only [. . .] spokesman for the time but [. . .] typical product of that same moment' aligns himself with the movie stars of the era (*MLC*, 110). In 1936's 'Crack-Up' essays, he speculates that 'It seemed a romantic business to be a successful literary man – you were not ever going to be as famous as a movie star but what note you had was probably longer-lived' (*MLC*, 139). This acerbic tone reveals, through his satirical jibes at the film industry, an innate desire to dominate it.

His most famous assessment of the film industry comes from the 1936 *Esquire* essay, 'Pasting It Together', second in the series of three articles known as the 'Crack-Up' essays, which were written the year before Fitzgerald's final, and longest, foray into the Hollywood 'dream factory'. He writes:

> I saw that the novel, which at my maturity was the strongest and supplest medium for conveying thought and emotion from one human being to another, was becoming subordinated to a mechanical and communal art that, whether in the hands of Hollywood merchants or Russian idealists, was capable of reflecting only the tritest thought, the most obvious emotion. It was an art in which words were subordinate to images, where personality was worn down to the inevitable low gear of collaboration. As long past as 1930, I had a hunch that the talkies would make even the best selling novelist as archaic as silent pictures. People still read, if only Professor Canby's book of the month – curious children nosed at the slime of Mr. Tiffany Thayer in the drug-store libraries – but there was a rankling indignity, that to me had become almost an obsession, in seeing the power of the written word subordinated to another power, a more glittering, a grosser power . . . . (*MLC*, 148)

Filled with binary phrases and making copious use of oppositions posed between 'and' and 'or' compounds, Fitzgerald's assessment of the unstoppable rise of film is both scathing and self-congratulatory. He credits the almost Darwinian 'subordinat[ion]' of the novel to the medium of film with contributing to his 'Crack-Up' but simultaneously credits himself with having foreseen this predicament 'as long past as 1930'.

Fitzgerald implies that the general purpose of the novel is to 'convey' thought and emotion from one person to another, whereas Fitzgerald's own manifesto, heavily influenced by Joseph Conrad's more impressionistic notions of the role of the novel, emphasised a model of 'conveying thought and emotion' that was more interactive than Hollywood's 'mechanical and communal art'. Expressed in the Preface to *The Nigger of the 'Narcissus'*, Conrad distinguishes between thinkers and artists:

> The thinker plunges into ideas. [. . .]. They speak authoritatively to our common sense, to our intelligence, to our desire of peace, or to our desire of unrest; not seldom to our prejudices, sometimes to our fears, often to our egoism – but always to our credulity.

The artist appeals 'to our less obvious capacities [. . .]. His appeal is less loud, more profound, less distinct, more stirring — and sooner forgotten. Yet its effect endures for ever.' Conrad goes on to explain that the task of the writer is to appeal 'primarily to the senses', and

> by the power of the written word to make you hear, to make you feel – it is, before all, to make you *see*! That – and no more: and it is everything! If I succeed, you shall find there according to your deserts: encouragement, consolation, fear, charm – all you demand; and, perhaps, also that glimpse of truth for which you have forgotten to ask.[24]

Conrad's instructions for the writing of fiction formed the keystone of Fitzgerald's literary philosophies. In a letter to H. L. Mencken of 1934, Fitzgerald called Conrad's Preface 'the greatest "credo" of my life, ever since I decided that I would rather be an artist than a careerist'.[25] In the same year, he paraphrased Conrad in a letter to Hemingway: 'the purpose of a work of fiction is to appeal to the lingering after-effects in the reader's mind as differing from, say, the purpose of oratory or philosophy which respectively leave people in a fighting or thoughtful mood'.[26] Allowing his readers to hear, feel and see these performative leisure activities in his short fiction is an effective way to accomplish this. Whilst critics such as Kirk Curnutt link Fitzgerald's allegiance with Conrad's aesthetic principles to Fitzgerald's capacity to move his readers with the lyrical beauty of his prose, causing it to linger in the mind after reading, it is clear that Fitzgerald also sought to accomplish Conrad's manifesto through the vivid incorporation of dance, song, theatre and film references into Fitzgerald's fiction.

For Curnutt, the clearest evidence of Fitzgerald's esteem for Conrad's prescription is found in his effusive, elaborate lyricism, which is at its peak in what Curnutt describes as 'rhapsodic' passages: 'Rhythmically propulsive, these passages are often built out of chains of conjoined sentences, sometimes cadenced for parallelism, or else they link appositives and subordinate clauses to structure a crescendo in emotion.'[27] Curnutt cites the ending of 'My Lost City', which uses the rhetorical technique of apostrophe, favoured by the Romantic poets Fitzgerald so admired, to serve as a climax for a concluding section that virtuosically alternates between humour and 'rhapsody': 'Come back, come back, O glittering and white!' (*MLC*, 115). In the passage about the 'mechanical and communal art' of film quoted above, from 'Pasting it Together', we find evidence of such 'rhythmic propulsion', parallel cadence and 'structured crescendo in emotion'.

The concept of rhapsody as a rhetorical technique embodying highly enthusiastic emotion is closely linked to the classical music genre of rhapsody, in which fragmented and contrasting episodes are united by a loose structure. Gershwin's 'Rhapsody in Blue' is an iconic example of the genre, which was also a reflection of the collage aesthetic in 1920s culture more widely. Carl Van Vechten suggested to Gershwin in February 1924 (two days after the debut performance of 'Rhapsody in Blue') that Gershwin should consider mixing the disciplines of film and music: '[I]nvent a new *form*. I think something might be done in the way of combining jazz and the moving-picture technique. Think of themes as close-ups, flash-backs, etc!'[28] This potential mixing of different media is what excited Fitzgerald about Hollywood: a multi-sensory means of making the audience 'hear, feel and see'.

But when Fitzgerald describes the purpose of film with the negative superlatives 'tritest' and 'most obvious', he denigrates the studios' target audience. Fitzgerald spent a great deal of time lamenting how difficult it was to marry popularity with critical esteem, but here he chastises the film industry for courting large sales without giving enough thought to the quality of the product, its 'worth' and its success in representing 'truth'.

Fitzgerald's almost parenthetical observation of 'personality worn down to the inevitable low gear of collaboration' fails to make it clear whether the 'personalities' are writers or other movie professionals, such as producers or actors, but there is a convenient lack of recognition of his own dependence on a kind of pop cultural intertextuality to help him follow Conrad's prescribed path of appealing 'primarily to the senses'.

In criticising the lack of subtlety in the movies' appeal to the senses, and the 'indignity' inflicted upon the novel in the process, Fitzgerald ends up sounding rather old-fashioned and Victorian – the opposite of his profligate 'chronicler of the Jazz Age' mantle. It is possible that this antiquated pose is deliberate, serving the purpose of distancing himself from his perceived reputation as a Riviera playboy during a time of national economic crisis. However, it is important to note that this entire diatribe is prefaced by Fitzgerald's admission that this was the 'obsession' of his dark nights during his 'Crack-Up', his time of mental despair and instability. 'It was strange to have no self,' he writes (*MLC*, 149).

It is not the first time Fitzgerald has shown insecurity when confronted with 'glittering [. . .] power': he prefaces his admonishment of the film industry with his confession that 'I have never been able to stop wondering where my friends' money came from, nor to stop thinking that at one time a sort of *droit de seigneur* might have been exercised to give one of them my girl' (*MLC*, 147). Despite eloquently professing that he is 'rankled' at the 'indignity' of 'seeing the word subordinated to a more glittering, grosser power' (*MLC*, 148), Fitzgerald in this moment is reminiscent of his 'Winter Dreams' (1922) protagonist Dexter Green, the poor boy 'who could not afford the luxury of proms, and [who] had stood outside the gymnasium and listened' (*ASM*, 50). Professional success in screenwriting would prove to be just as elusive and frustrating for him.

Fitzgerald's filmic metaphors in his essays thus reveal an author who is both excited and intimidated by the industry. The 'glittering, grosser power' that Fitzgerald writes of actually served positive social purposes, despite its conspicuous use and display of wealth (*MLC*, 148). Paula Marantz Cohen explains how early film, from the late 1910s and early 1920s, served an important role in terms of disseminating American culture to its newest settlers:

> The consumerism generated by film was of special value to Americans in the first three decades of the twentieth century. A large immigrant population had deluged the cities and, lacking the skills necessary to express themselves in words, were seeking alternative routes to becoming American as quickly and efficiently as possible. Women were also poised on the brink of changing roles, and the consumerism they learned from films gave them a leverage in the marketplace that would help them to gain the vote. The stars operated as representatives and guides for these groups.[29]

The importance of women in the marketplace of the interwar period should not be underestimated. As consumers of leisure and material goods, women helped to contribute to the emerging culture of almost theatrical display embodied by department stores. The shopgirl narratives of early silent films such as *The Shop Girl* (1916), as well as later films such as *It* (1927), show how the culture of display was bisected by issues of consumerism and desire. Carmen M. Mangion explains: 'The shopgirl becomes a part of, as well as a consumer of, this gendered culture of pleasure through the display and presentation of seductive consumer goods.'[30] Fitzgerald explores these issues through his meditations on the instability of identity and the increasing theatricality of quotidian life, both of which are themes that feature heavily in his fiction about Hollywood.

In the early 1920s, Fitzgerald had performed a similar function as 'representative and guide', not for immigrants but for his readership, who wanted to experience the leisure pursuits of his young and wealthy protagonists vicariously. His celebrity was assured by the enormous success of *This Side of Paradise*, published in March 1920, the same month that Mary Pickford and Douglas Fairbanks were married, and as we have seen, Fitzgerald conceptualised this novel's success in filmic terms: 'they were pounding out copies as they pound out extras in the movies' (*MLC*, 188). In a 1922 interview, Fitzgerald recognised that 'the movies are here to stay', and described 'the feet of Charlie Chaplin' as 'lyrical', perhaps expressing his early stylistic affinity with the silver screen, as well as with the parodic mode in which Chaplin excelled.[31] As Cohen observes, alongside escapism, early film served the important function of facilitating naturalisation and cultural acclimatisation. Film provided Fitzgerald with exciting opportunities to explore various facets of identity, such as the impact of theatrical identity on self-knowledge that he was simultaneously exploring in his use of references to dance and music. In these early Hollywood films, as Cohen emphasises, a particularly American inflection of identity is invoked because of the cultural assimilation that they offered, in tandem with their mandate of entertainment.

The riskiness of imbuing film with the authority to disseminate guidance on American cultural identity is explored in Fitzgerald's Pat Hobby stories. The Pat Hobby stories dramatise the tribulations of the unsuccessful screenwriter over the course of seventeen short pieces sold to *Esquire* between September 1939 and June 1940. Pat had once been a successful screenwriter, but in the story sequence, he 'scavenges a living as a hanger-on at the studio'.[32] He has been read by Milton Stern as 'a metaphor for the national fatuities of a culture that determines and dissolves human identity; and the stories are a chronicle of the connection between the culture and the tenuousness of identity'.[33] Pat Hobby functions as a critique of an industry, and by metaphoric association, Stern suggests, he also operates as an indictment of the national culture, circa 1939–40.

The most striking feature of the Pat Hobby stories is their style, which markedly differs from the well-known lyrical style of Fitzgerald's earlier work. Although, by the late 1930s, Fitzgerald was increasingly unwilling to self-censor his themes and profanities in order to satisfy the 'slicks', Stern has shown that Fitzgerald, ever the professional, adapted his style to suit his publication contexts, as he had done with regard to the *Saturday Evening Post* more than a decade earlier: 'Fitzgerald limited himself to one aspect of his stylistic capacities, not because the subject was Hollywood but because the context was *Esquire*.'[34] The aspect of his stylistic capacities to which Stern refers was Fitzgerald's tightly controlled prose, much closer to cablese than anything else in his œuvre, and described by James West as 'compressed'.[35] Such a 'compressed' style works well to satirise metafictively the voice of Pat Hobby, consummate Hollywood hack who contributes the minimum possible effort to each project, composed by Fitzgerald whilst he was simultaneously working on *The Last Tycoon*, his unfinished magnum opus.[36]

Because of their length, at around 1,800 words each, critics sometimes refer to the Pat Hobby stories as vignettes, sketches or simply 'pieces', but Fitzgerald was clear that he considered them to be short stories. He wrote to Arnold Gingrich, *Esquire*'s editor, to say 'I wish to God you could pay more money. These have all been stories, not sketches or articles and only unfit for the big time because of their length.'[37] Fitzgerald referred to the 'Crack-Up' essays as 'sketches', creating a cloud of generic doubt that leaves one reluctant to use 'sketch' to describe a piece of short fiction such as the Pat Hobby stories.[38] Since being published in *Esquire*, the Pat Hobby stories have appeared in standalone collections, the first of which was the 1967 Penguin collection, which includes an introduction written by Gingrich. This inevitably implies that the stories are a collection to be read in sequence. There are some problems with this approach, however: despite the fact that they were written with the intention of being read in sequence, this sequence would have been punctuated by monthly breaks and would have welcomed new readers to each new story with restatements of major plot points and setting, along with deft character sketches. Fitzgerald spent time and effort advising the *Esquire* staff on his intended publication order, revising it when he thought necessary, but publishing the Pat Hobby stories in book form means that a reader will encounter the same introductory material, the same type of plot twist that serves Hobby his comeuppance and the same cynical descriptions of the movie world in such close proximity as to cause the stories to seem clichéd and overly repetitive.[39]

Fitzgerald did write the Basil and Josephine stories as a sequence, which appeared at intervals in the *Saturday Evening Post* over 1928 to 1931, but the major difference here is that Basil and Josephine develop as characters, in a way that pays homage to the *Bildungsroman* genre.[40] The *Post*'s subscription rates were much more stable than the newcomer *Esquire*'s, and Fitzgerald knew that there were precedents in the *Post* for series that revisited a character. Tim Prchal differentiates the Pat Hobby stories from other such sequences because 'Hobby does not evolve psychologically, morally, or in virtually any other way.'[41] When the stories are read individually, as intended, this lack of evolution does not pose a serious problem. But this stasis is an overwhelming flaw when the stories are read sequentially. The repetition of character exposition and plot mechanics, complete with formulaic twists, shows that Fitzgerald, a veteran of magazine fiction, was writing to his audience.

There was a practical, as well as aesthetic, reason for the brevity of the Pat Hobby stories: *Esquire* paid between $200 and $250 regardless of the length of piece submitted, so Fitzgerald knew that it made no professional sense to turn in his usual 6,000- to 8,000-word stories that had earned him $4,000 at the *Post*. Fitzgerald also benefitted from the fact that Arnold Gingrich, the editor of *Esquire*, was a fan of Fitzgerald's work and would accept virtually anything Fitzgerald submitted for publication. 'Between 1934–1941, Fitzgerald appeared [in *Esquire*] 45 times, more than any other writer in the history of the magazine,' as West reminds us.[42]

In the Pat Hobby stories, Fitzgerald shows his skill in being able to write in a more pared-down, crystallised mode, which John Kuehl describes as 'functional rather than figurative'.[43] The theme and setting of the Pat Hobby stories, however, offer us further examples through which to interpret Fitzgerald's ambiguities as parodic. In the Pat Hobby stories, written about the performance industry, we witness the full spectrum of material Fitzgerald has parodied elsewhere, in his earlier short fiction: the performative personality of the teenaged flapper reaches its apex in tersely but vividly sketched actresses who, divas off the set, stand in almost metonymically for all actors. Disguise features both in the farcical plots, like 'Pat Hobby and Orson Welles' (1940), and in the costumes and sets that saturate Hobby's world. The industry is built upon exploiting the chasm between popular and high culture, and though Fitzgerald addresses this more fully in *The Last Tycoon*, here we find evidence of Fitzgerald exploring his longstanding conflict between art and commerce, albeit through the presentation of a cautionary, self-parodying possibility of a future identity. The significance of these concise pieces is wide-ranging.

Far from the stories being autobiographical, some critics have found the overarching mode of the Pat Hobby series to be satirical. Stern finds them to be 'episodes in satiric revelation', whose overriding theme is 'an exploration of belonging, of the precariousness of personality in a world in which one's very identity is dependent upon modes of behaviour and appearance most shallowly conceived'.[44] Christopher Ames finds that the stories function as a metafictive commentary on the state of screenwriting and motion pictures themselves:

> The intentionally clichéd and predictable plots of the stories satirize the hackneyed nature of Hollywood storytelling at its worst [. . .]. We must not forget that *The Pat Hobby Stories* are stories about a writer, fictions about a fiction maker, and thus are inevitably self-referential and meta-fictional. So when we identify the narrative characteristics of these stories – their brevity, their clichéd plots, their predictable structures – we should get the ironic point: they satirize similar conventions in motion pictures and they satirize, by example, the degraded state of Pat Hobby's narrative imagination.[45]

This reading favours Fitzgerald's artistic choices over the more practical considerations pertaining to the stories' serial publication context, in which repetition serves to avoid the alienation of new readers, and as a means of replicating a successful format. As an aesthetic choice, such metafictive technique is a characteristic of postmodernism, but the 'predictability' of the formulaic narratives sits in tension with this interpretation.

Fitzgerald's earlier short fiction was also accused of having 'clichéd plots'. For example, John Higgins refers to Fitzgerald's 'popular romance formula' in Fitzgerald's early stories, and Kenneth Eble finds that in Fitzgerald's early magazine work, 'His reliance upon plot often forced the conclusion of a story or led it to a final twist that might have embarrassed O. Henry.'[46] Fitzgerald himself identified O. Henry's influence on stories such as 'Two for a Cent' (1922), in which a simultaneous reversal of fortunes hinges on the loss and discovery of a penny.[47] Ames argues that Fitzgerald intentionally makes his stories' plots clichéd in order to satirise the 'worst' kind of 'Hollywood storytelling' in the movies. Yet, in the context of Fitzgerald's earlier sustained accusations of being 'formulaic', Fitzgerald can also be seen to parody himself, drawing parallels between his job working as a *Post* writer and Hobby's job in Hollywood. Both aim to produce stories that would appeal to the masses, working within clearly agreed editorial guidelines of decency, and both are (or at least have been) handsomely paid for their work. Ultimately, since Fitzgerald failed to find success in screenwriting, it was a bold and self-assured move to begin a series about a hack writer in Hollywood who is down on his luck after having had prior success.

The concept of metafiction makes related appearances elsewhere in popular culture of the post-First World War period, such as in songs like 'Alexander's Ragtime Band', in which the singer sings about hearing the song 'The Swanee River'.[48] It recurs in Josephine Baker's self-referential parodic performances of performance, and in the ragtime 'barnyard' dances like the Turkey Trot, in which their accompanying songs narrate instructions of how to dance their dances. Additionally, Fitzgerald's work often recourses to the metafictive mode, in which we are reminded of the stories' literariness. He gleefully pushes narratorial voice to the limits, encouraging the reader to embrace the tale as an artificial rendering of reality, and thus invites questions about the purposes of fiction. This narrative voice sometimes encourages readers to acknowledge the intertextuality inherent in his works. Though not controlled by Fitzgerald, he none the less invites us to consider how our reading experience is necessarily mediated through the lens of our knowledge of popular culture forms. In 'Dice, Brassknuckles and Guitar', he interjects, 'Now if this were a moving picture' (*TJA*, 278), not only encouraging us to read his work in the context of the available contemporary material in that medium, but also giving us a hint to look out for other filmic devices he has included in his fiction. In encouraging us to read stories filmically, and importing aspects of filmic technique into his stories, Fitzgerald thus invites us to read, watch and hear his stories as an immersive experience.

By the time Fitzgerald comes to write the Pat Hobby stories, he is still interrogating the potential of film to marry artistic and commercial ambitions: in focusing exclusively on a few key characters, with an appropriately objective aesthetic distance, with clear and succinct plot development (though arguably without much development at all in some individual stories), and without his characteristic rhetorical flourishes and lyrical evocation, the Pat Hobby stories invoke – in both form and content – the medium of film. Higgins, drawing on the work of Ellen F. Moers, even likens the terse stories to silent screen comedies.[49] As a whole, the Pat Hobby series could be read as individual scenes constituting a whole film, albeit a fairly badly edited and poorly paced film, due to the terse, sparse style and repeated story elements from story to story. This terse style has been remarked upon by many critics, including Stern, who finds that several of the stories 'seem deceptively plotless'. He argues that 'the "plotless" style of these stories is a foreshadowing of what came to be the norm in popular magazines of literary sophistication such as *The New Yorker*'.[50] Once more, Fitzgerald's work appears to be straddling the commercial, performative arts and literary art.

One of the most sophisticated features of the Pat Hobby stories, aside from their brevity, is their voice. Stern continues, 'There are moments' in 'Pat Hobby's Christmas Wish' (1940) 'when the satiric quotidian style of a character's dialogue becomes that of the invisible narrator'.[51] Known as 'free indirect discourse' or *libre indirect*, this is a narrative technique often employed by Fitzgerald, as well as many other modern writers, such as Joyce, who used free indirect discourse in *Dubliners* as a symbolic motif as well as a narrative technique, representing the struggle of characters to assert their choices and individuality, as Mark Corcoran has identified.[52] The ambiguities brought about by the use of free indirect discourse remind the reader of the impossibility of omniscience, emphasising the narratives as a series of representational and interpretative decisions. Though free indirect discourse features heavily in the Pat Hobby stories, Fitzgerald had been proficient in its usage for many years. As Curnutt explains,

Fitzgerald no doubt felt comfortable writing in FID [Free Indirect Discourse] for a very simple reason: its main attribute is that it creates ambiguities of motive and morality that perfectly enabled the author to plumb his ambivalence toward the ethical balance between self-control and indulgence. [. . .]. [It] requires readers to assess the moral valence of the protagonist's thoughts without benefit of an authorial baseline. [. . .] As such, FID is a device not only for engaging audiences in the narrative but for layering it with the formalist complexity that was a hallmark of modernism.[53]

In imbuing the Pat Hobby stories with 'ambiguities of motive and morality', Fitzgerald again enters into an unspoken contract with his readership just as he does with his musical allusions: he devolves responsibility for assessing 'the moral valence' to his audience and creatively exploits the ensuing ambiguity to his advantage.

In 'Jacob's Ladder' (1927), Fitzgerald demonstrates his agility with free indirect discourse in describing Jacob Booth's infatuation with Jenny Prince: 'His own well-ordered person seemed for the first time in his life gross and well-worn to him as he knelt suddenly at the heart of freshness' (*ASM*, 335). This contrasts greatly with our introduction to Jacob, sitting in the sweaty courtroom for want of anything better to do, and marks the turning point in Jacob's inner life, as he feels himself being drawn to the vibrant shopgirl. The parallelism of the compound adjectives 'well-ordered' and 'well-worn' encapsulate and foreshadow Jacob's present and future emotional states. But are we to read Jacob's concern with his appearance in the face of 'freshness' as an indication of his superficiality? Or are we to interpret his captivation by Jenny as genuine? By the end of the story, he has only her image, 'in the vast throbbing darkness' of the movie theatre. Are we therefore to interpret this as a just ending (*ASM*, 358)? Fitzgerald is playing with the idea of seeking serious meaning from the filmic image, even invoking religious imagery to parody the worship of celluloid goddesses: Jenny has 'the face of a saint, an intense little madonna', and at the story's close, Margolies notes a potential allusion to the Song of Solomon in the narrator's description of Jacob's interpretation of the sign announcing Jenny Prince's name: '"Come and rest upon my loveliness," it said. "Fulfill your secret dreams in wedding me for an hour"' (*ASM*, 357).[54] Such hints of blasphemy, along with the story's unhappy ending, make it all the more surprising that it was published in the *Saturday Evening Post*. Margolies also notes a tendency for critics to place 'too much emphasis on the story's autobiographical characteristics', given Fitzgerald's alleged romance with the actress Lois Moran, and it seems that Fitzgerald's Hollywood fiction is particularly vulnerable to autobiographical readings, perhaps because in these writings he interrogates performative personality and the cult of celebrity in a way that overwhelmingly focuses on the individual.

One of Fitzgerald's best-known Hollywood stories, 'Crazy Sunday', famously draws upon Fitzgerald's own experiences at one of Norma and Irving Thalberg's parties in Hollywood. It is ostensibly the story of screenwriter Joel Coles, but the split focus between Coles and the director Miles Calman (a precursor of Monroe Stahr, and partly based on Irving Thalberg) confuses this narrative emphasis. Based in part on Fitzgerald's own experiences in Hollywood and on his 1931 writing assignment at MGM, it has been described by Kuehl as 'Fitzgerald's last major story', and by Ruth Prigozy as a 'masterpiece', save for 'Fitzgerald's division of focus: Joel Coles is the central consciousness, Miles Calman the center of interest'.[55] This results in a 'limited omniscient point of view' that mediates the action of the story through the perspective of Joel Coles, who freely admits at the story's outset that he had spent his peripatetic childhood 'trying to separate the real from the unreal' (*TAR*, 5).[56] Though it raises the spectre of narratorial reliability, and the limits of fiction to represent lived experience accurately, this mediated focus also gives us an insight into life as a junior screenwriter, in which the directors' (and producers') presence can be keenly felt even in lieu of their physical presence.

Prigozy finds the plot of 'Crazy Sunday' to be 'simple', while Kuehl describes it as 'more structured than plotted', which recalls Fitzgerald's verdict of his 1934–6 stories often being 'built rather than written'.[57] Indeed, the story essentially consists of two parties followed by an outing to the theatre, peppered with discussion of infidelity and the climactic news of Calman's death. Raubicheck offers a valuable reading of the structure in which he suggests that 'the love triangle appears to be a parody of the romantic plot typical of both the short story and of Hollywood film in the early 1930s'.[58] This parody delicately coexists with Fitzgerald's sparing use of romantic rhetoric (deemed 'happily' absent by Prigozy), but arguably present in the climactic description of Calman's untimely demise: 'Meshed in an industry, he had paid with his ruined nerves for having no resilience, no healthy cynicism, no refuge, only a pitiful and precarious escape' (*TAR*, 21). Whilst not in the same league as his rhetorical 'rhapsody' in stories like 'The Swimmers' (1929), here the emphasis on human vulnerability and illness sits in tension with the commercial demands forced upon Calman by his state of being 'meshed in an industry'. Connoting a predatory spider's web or a fishing net, as well as the industrial image of cogs and engaged gearwheels being meshed together to power a machine, Calman's 'escape' from the industry that had, perhaps ominously, 'not *yet* broken' Coles (the emphasis is mine), represents Fitzgerald's own predictions of the sublimation of the novel by 'a mechanical and communal art' reliant on 'the inevitable low gear of collaboration' (*TAR*, 5; *MLC*, 148). It is for this reason that Fitzgerald is careful to emphasise Calman's 'artistic conscience', investing potentially mundane decisions with a moral dimension.

Following Raubicheck's reading of the story as parodic, as we have seen, parody entails repetition with a difference. In alluding to 'the romantic plot typical of both the short story and Hollywood film in the early 1930s', Fitzgerald challenges our generically conditioned expectations by writing a 'startling' ending 'that render[s] any clear-cut assessment of the outcome impossible'.[59] In Joel's refusal of Stella's grief-stricken advances, he reflects on how Calman 'made her a sort of masterpiece' (*TAR*, 22), in a subtle nod to the nascent star system that had also produced Jenny Prince in 'Jacob's Ladder'. Raubicheck's assertion that Coles's future will include '"making love," in both senses of the term to the art object created by Miles Calman' invokes both the Pygmalion myth and the ending of 'Jacob's Ladder', in which Jacob Booth is 'wedded' to Jenny Prince 'for an hour' whilst he watches her film play 'in the vast throbbing darkness' (*ASM*, 357–8).[60] Coles's ambiguous oath, uttered 'with a certain bitterness' at the story's conclusion, dramatically references an implied sequel in which he will return to Stella's life: 'Oh, yes, I'll be back – I'll be back!' (*TAR*, 23). The ambiguity of his statement draws upon the position of Coles in his relationship with Calman: in their appositional partnership, if Calman is the 'artistic conscience', Coles, the survivor, represents the inauthentic artist. In his earlier fiction, inauthentic artists are vulnerable to Fitzgerald's judgement but Coles's position is complicated by Stella's existence, perhaps alluding to Philip Sidney's Renaissance sonnet sequence *Astrophil and Stella*, as beloved 'art object', in Raubicheck's phrase. Thus we are left to judge whether the production of Calman's artistic labours, Stella, is worthy of his sacrifice. This reading justifies her centrality in the narrative, which has been criticised for its shift of focus away from Miles.[61] Ultimately, the parodic undertones in the destabilising ending serve to draw attention to the difficulties of resolving Fitzgerald's artistic crisis of art versus commerce. By paring down plot and limiting his recourse to rhetorical rhapsody, Fitzgerald conveys his predicament, negotiating the path between his artistic and commercial needs, whilst beginning to interrogate the potential of the medium of film to provide some resolution to these deep-seated concerns.

In the Pat Hobby stories, Fitzgerald is prompting a specific reader response and then indulging in self-parody. Having recently adopted such an exposed and confessional authorial standpoint in his 'Crack-Up' essays, Fitzgerald must have known that some would read Pat Hobby as a self-portrait. By penning these stories in a terse, controlled style, absent of his previously favoured lyrical descriptions, he is flexing his literary muscle, whilst risking an overly literal interpretation of his parodic depiction of Pat Hobby. Though there was an undeniable financial function served by the Hobby pieces, Matthew Bruccoli also finds in them a cathartic function: 'The character's grotesque adventures in Hollywood provided a kind of therapy for the author and purged the bitterness that might otherwise have found its way into the novel.'[62] This may be true to an extent but another reading situates Fitzgerald as a professional author writing saleable stories to the appropriate magazine. His bitterness about being an ostensibly unsuccessful screenwriter plays very little part in the Pat Hobby stories. Indeed, Pat Hobby himself was once a successful screenwriter, even meeting the President, as recounted in 'A Patriotic Short' (1940). Fitzgerald's screenwriting failures were, paradoxically, his fiction-writing strengths. He cared about mood and the almost intangible aspects of a scene as well as its dialogue: this is a trait of the fiction writer, not the screenwriter. As Ronald Berman writes of Fitzgerald's fiction, he sometimes even expresses colours as 'possibilit[ies] rather than characteristic[s]':

One of Fitzgerald's most important stylistic techniques is the replacement of description by perception. Given that [*The Great Gatsby*] is often romantic and lyrical, we expect it also to be intensely evocative. But it is often denuded of description, focused not affectively but on line, mass, space, and motion. It deals with color, as in the brief description of Daisy's hair, as a possibility rather than as a characteristic.[63]

'Possibilities' do not translate well into screenplays, but Fitzgerald's modernist assumption of a spectrum of interpretative possibilities is a destabilising and even disruptive force when read in light of his parodic presentation of dance, music and film in his stories. Using 'Magnetism' (1928) as a case study, an examination of the filmic techniques Fitzgerald imports into his fiction illustrates these interpretative possibilities.

'Now if This Were a Moving Picture': Filmic Technique in Fitzgerald's Stories

En route to Hollywood for the final time, Fitzgerald expressed the belief that he could forge a new path as a writer who oversaw a film from a raw idea through to production as a kind of proto-auteur, but this belief was held only briefly. He wrote to Scottie in July 1937, reflecting on his two earlier visits to Hollywood:

> I want to profit by these two experiences – I must be very tactful but keep my hand on the wheel from the start – find out the key man among the bosses + the most malleable among the collaborators – then fight the rest tooth + nail until, in fact or in effect, I'm alone on the picture. That's the only way I can do my best work.[64]

He had, in fact, been profiting from the film industry since as early as 1920. Much of his early work was – by coincidence or design – suitable for adaptation to the filmic medium, and several of his early stories were indeed made into films. Three 1920 stories were adapted: 'Head and Shoulders' became Metro's *The Chorus Girl's Romance*; 'Myra Meets His Family' (1920) became Fox's *The Husband Hunter*; 'The Offshore Pirate' was produced by Metro in 1921, retaining Fitzgerald's title; and 'The Camel's Back' (1922) became a 1924 Warner Brothers production called *Conductor 1492*. Critics such as Margolies have argued that Fitzgerald wrote some of these stories with a view to selling them to Hollywood, and whilst that may be true, he was under a more immediate pressure to make the stories saleable to the 'slicks' like the *Saturday Evening Post*.[65] Furthermore, incorporating filmic attributes does not necessarily denote a desire for the fictions to be filmed. In some cases, such as in 'Dice, Brassknuckles and Guitar', film could be being deployed to show off his familiarity with the innovative conventions of film and develop his idiosyncratic narrative presence, without actually angling for the film to be made. Fitzgerald audaciously explains:

> Now if this were a moving picture (as, of course, I hope it will be some day) I would take as many thousand feet of her as I was allowed – then I would move the camera up close and show the yellow down on the back of her neck where her hair stopped and the warm color of her cheeks and arms. (*TJA*, 278)

Jesse Meyers labels the importation of filmic technique as 'subliminal screenwrit[ing]' in his analysis of Joyce's story 'Araby', and cites a strikingly similar passage in Joyce's 1914 story: 'The light from the lamp opposite our door caught the white curve of her neck, lit up her hair that rested there and, falling, lit up the hand upon the railing.'[66] John McCourt finds that Joyce took 'inspiration from cinema's capacity to absorb other art forms', and this integrative impulse is also on display in Fitzgerald's work.[67] Of course, Fitzgerald self-consciously draws our attention to the filmic potential inherent in the scene, although such brazen asides are relatively rare in his stories, and generally he is more subtle with his use of the filmic, even in the stories that were adapted into films. He incorporates a range of filmic technique in his fiction for their aesthetic effects, from camera angles to montage.

The example above, from 'Dice, Brassknuckles and Guitar', shows Fitzgerald's familiarity with the concept of the close-up, which he also deploys in 'Magnetism'. The story of actor George Hannaford, who cannot help but attract and charm women, encompasses a foiled blackmail plot and the averted adultery of his wife. Set in

Hollywood, it is a story that makes use of several cinematic techniques. In establishing the character of Kay Tomkins Hannaford, the narrator describes how 'her face was round, young, pretty and strong; a strength accentuated by the responsive play of brows and lashes around her clear, glossy, hazel eyes' (*ASM*, 413).[68] This is a shot familiar to us from silent films: for example, the iconic close-ups of Garbo's face in the 1926 film *Flesh and the Devil*, which was directed by Clarence Brown and produced by Irving Thalberg, whom Fitzgerald greatly admired. The face and the eyes, in particular, are highlighted as the main means of expressivity for actors in a theatrical medium that, for the first time, provided the entire audience with the same intimate view of the simultaneously accessible and remote stars.

Another example of a close-up occurs later in the story when would-be blackmailer Margaret Donovan describes George's head in terms that read almost as stage directions: 'your hat has squashed your beautiful hair down on one side and you've got dark circles, or dirt, under your eyes' (*ASM*, 424). There are several more filmic techniques used in the story, from the slapstick physical comedy of Dolores the housekeeper, who 'tripped on the broom and fell off the stoop' (*ASM*, 407), to the use of a soundtrack to accompany the confrontation with Margaret: 'George felt as if a band which had been playing for a long time in the distance had suddenly moved up and taken a station beneath his window' (*ASM*, 425). In contrast, we are also provided with two silent sequences in the story, which was written in December 1927, three months after the premiere of *The Jazz Singer*; this was 'the first feature-length picture incorporating spoken dialogue' and also included songs, such as Fitzgerald's favourite, 'Blue Skies'.[69] The second silent scene is described brusquely – 'They dined in silence' (*ASM*, 414) – whilst the first is more explored in a more filmic manner:

> She stood a long time with her back to him at one point, and when she turned at length, their eyes swept past each other's, brushing like bird wings. Simultaneously he saw they had gone far, in their way; it was well that he had drawn back. He was glad that someone came for her when the work was almost over.

Dressed, he returned to the office wing, stopping in for a moment to see Schroeder. No one answered his knock, and, turning the knob, he went in. Helen Avery was there alone.

Hannaford shut the door and they stared at each other. Her face was young, frightened. In a moment in which neither of them spoke, it was decided that they would have some of this out now. Almost thankfully he felt the warm sap of emotion flow out of his heart and course through his body. (*ASM*, 412–13)

This scene describes George's emerging realisation of the unintended effects of his effortless charm. By removing dialogue, Fitzgerald calls upon the reader to recognise the non-verbal forces at work, as well as to convey an intensity of attraction and withdrawal that would perhaps be belittled in its transposition into words. George's life is frequently described in terms of 'scenes' and 'actors', and this scene belongs to a silent melodrama. The fixed point of view (or camera angle) affords a stasis to their encounter that would, in George's recent past, have been dictated by the large, immobile cameras of early cinema. The emphasis on the expressivity of eyes is also typical of silent film, especially melodrama, and is an aspect of body language that Helen and George, as actors, would spend much of their professional day focusing on. Helen and Kay in particular are associated with emotionally demonstrative eyes throughout the story, almost to the point of metonymically signifying George Hannaford's watched status as a movie star (*ASM*, 411, 415). Cohen describes how 'facial expressiveness was most closely identified with women in silent films [. . .] where it complements the bodily expressiveness of men'. She goes on to suggest that the close-up offers the audience 'intimacy without involvement', which dovetails well with a plot in which all of the protagonists happily continue acting after their working day at the studio has ended.[70]

D. W. Griffith was especially famous for his use of the close-up in his films, and became known for creating an acting style that bridged the near-histrionic gesturing of the earliest silent films (most of the actors having come directly from the stage) and the more naturalistic style that became common during the mid-1920s.[71] The last aspect of the early style to disappear was the exaggerated facial expressions focused on during close-ups. This cemented a narrative semiotics in which audiences interpreted motivations and reactions through the mere movements of a seemingly unobserved face. Audiences thus projected their interpretations on to the literal projection of the film, as with the face of starlet Jenny Prince in 'Jacob's Ladder': 'Her face, the face of a saint, an intense little madonna, was lifted fragilely out of the mortal dust of the afternoon' (*ASM*, 335). Just as with the Griffith heroines, the audience (including Jacob Booth, the story's protagonist) project their beliefs and desires on to the giant porcelain faces on screen. Lewis Erenberg identifies a similar process in the interaction between chorus girls and patrons at Broadway revues: 'their ever-present smiles invited customers to project their desires onto their faces'.[72]

As well as close-ups, another filmic technique Fitzgerald uses is the dream sequence, which is related to the disguise-laden twist-ending story he favoured in his earliest works, such as 'The Offshore Pirate'. In fact, 'The Offshore Pirate', in its original version, contained a coda (cut by the *Post*) in which Ardita awakens to discover the events of the story had been a dream.[73] To return to 'Magnetism', the dream sequence begins unannounced, leaving the reader to deduce gradually that the described events are not real: 'Mechanically he went upstairs, undressed and got into bed. Just before dawn Kay came to him in the garden' (*ASM*, 419). We are told that there was a river, with boats moving by, but given Fitzgerald's opening descriptions of Hollywood's lavish incongruity of architecture and population, a garden moat of some sort does not necessarily strike the reader as impossible. Two-thirds of the dream sequence are given over to setting: the starlight, the damp grass, and the tableau of Kay '[holding] up her face as one shows a book open at a page' (*ASM*, 419). It is one of several passages that Fitzgerald reused in *Tender is the Night*, which led to his description of 'Magnetism', along with 'Jacob's Ladder' in his Ledger, which recorded his story sales and earnings, as 'Stripped and – Permanently Buried'.[74] Fitzgerald is borrowing from himself at the same time as borrowing techniques from a different (and happily intertextual) medium.

In the dream, Kay is submissive, adoring and fragile – a far cry from the real Kay, in whom he saw only that evening 'something veiled and remote in [her] eyes that he had never seen there before' (*ASM*, 416). The dream sequence plays on the layers of selves we find in the story – private, public, acted, imagined, demonstrated and impersonated. The studio system of the 1920s was notorious for its slippery attitude to biography, as we see in 'Jacob's Ladder', where Jenny Delehanty is expertly groomed into becoming Jenny Prince. As Brooks Robards has noted, though popular in films of the 1920s, such as the Buster Keaton vehicle *Sherlock, Jr.* (1924) (which also purposefully blurs the boundaries between dream and reality in a film-industry setting), dream sequences were even more popular in the 1910s: 'The fact that half as many of the films made in the twenties use dreams as a plot device as those in the teens suggests that the early popularity of dream sequences as a narrative device was gradually exhausted.'[75] The declining popularity of the dream sequence by the 1920s (before its renaissance in the big-budget musicals of the 1930s) situates George Hannaford in transition between the Griffith films and the imminent 'talkies'. His liminal situation between an older and a younger actress supports this reading.

To continue exploring the extensive use of filmic techniques in 'Magnetism', at the story's climax, George mentally adds a soundtrack to the pivotal scene in which he realises and accepts some culpability for the events that have unfolded: 'George felt as if a band which had been playing for a long time in the distance had suddenly moved up and taken a station beneath his window' (*ASM*, 425). The following enigmatic sentence hints that Fitzgerald is referring both to the film industry and to George's dawning consciousness of how his charm affects women: 'He had always been conscious that things like this were going on around him.' Yet he struggles to separate his own application of the film industry to his daily life from real life itself. He cannot easily ascertain where film ends and his life begins: 'the faint music of these emotions in his ear seemed to bear no relation to actual life. They were phantoms that he had conjured up out of nothing; he never imagined their actual incarnations' (*ASM*, 425). Fitzgerald subtly demonstrates that George Hannaford's 'magnetism' is illusory.

More than acting as a quintessential 'rags to riches' leading man, plucked from obscurity as a one-time movie lot electrician and forced to fill in as an actor, George Hannaford can be read as a metaphor for the motion picture industry itself (*ASM*, 411). He 'was young and extraordinarily handsome', but aside from his aesthetic appeal, he also has charm and good character (*ASM*, 407). If we read George as one aspect of the film industry – representative of the potential that emerged through the values of 'rags to riches' aptitude, good character and desire to work hard enough to feel one's success was 'solid beneath his feet' in a notoriously fickle industry, Helen Avery can be read as representing a contrasting aspect of the business. She is a star who attracts, generates and demands attention, but also displays selfish and difficult behaviour on set and shows little respect for George's marriage, telephoning him multiple times at home. We do not find out about her background, but we know that both George and Kay fell into filmmaking accidentally and turned out to be very talented. They embody the Romantic notion of the artist whose talents are innate and natural, and find themselves fulfilled through an expression that brings joy to others – except that they clearly are not fulfilled, as the cracks in their marriage begin to reveal.

Helen, younger than both George and Kay, can be read as representative of the Hollywood that had 'offended' George at first: 'the almost hysterical egotism and excitability hidden under an extremely thin veil of elaborate good fellowship' (*ASM*, 411). We are told that 'he was critical of Helen Avery' and despite his almost involuntary gravitation towards her, he manages to check himself, sacrificing the romantic epiphany he anticipates: 'He had felt that they both tolerated something, that each knew half of some secret about people and life, and that if they rushed towards each other there would be a romantic communion of almost unbelievable intensity' (*ASM*, 411). It turns out that he is not in love with Helen Avery, and this expression may be no more than a role he tries on for size, or a virtuosic exploration of the power he knows is latent in the loaded glances and stylised gesture he has capably learned in the silent film industry.

George is clearly worshipped by the public and well respected by his peers. When visiting the set, 'An actor in evening clothes, his shirt front, collar and cuffs tinted a brilliant pink, made as though to get chairs for them but they shook their heads and stood watching' (*ASM*, 410). This respect is amplified by Fitzgerald to an almost comic degree that does, in fact, accurately represent the state of awe such celebrities commanded: 'figures [. . .] turned up white faces to George Hannaford, like souls in purgatory watching the passage of a half-god through' (*ASM*, 410). In this curious mixture of Catholic doctrine ('purgatory') and classical mythology ('half-god'), we are reminded of the allure of the potential union of mortals and divine beings for which Jacob waits, in the liminal space of the movie theatre, at the close of 'Jacob's Ladder'.[76] George settles the situation with his charm just as he tries to heal the rift in his 'perfect' marriage with his characteristic 'magnetism', but ultimately this is accomplished only when Kay confronts the thought of losing not George but $50,000. By the story's close, Kay loses some of our sympathy, but so too does George. When Kay tries to end things with George and starts to cry, we are told that 'Face to face with what was apparently a real emotion, he had no words of any kind' (*ASM*, 421). This implies not only that Kay rarely presents him with authentic emotion, but also that he rarely calls upon his genuine empathetic responses, coasting through life on an automatic charm offensive. Fitzgerald punishes both. Though we are told that '[George] had come near to making something bright and precious into something cheap and unkind', by the story's end we are no longer convinced of the solidity of the Hannaford marital situation, nor the integrity of any of the protagonists (*ASM*, 61).

George is 'a star of the new "natural" type then just coming into vogue' and in the story's binary opposition of old 'Griffith-era' stars and their modern counterparts, George thinks himself philosophically aligned with 'the old crowd' of 'the early Griffith pictures' who 'had a dignity and straightforwardness about them from the fact that they had worked in pictures before pictures were bathed in a golden haze of success. They were still rather humble before their amazing triumph' (*ASM*, 413–15). He was, in fact, in a Griffith western as a boy and so straddles the old crowd and the vanguard, embodying the conflicts inherent in technological progress in the industry, if in a fractured way, with multiple George Hannafords pervading the story. His appeal is not lost on Dolores the housekeeper, who fantasises about having a relationship with him, and we hear that old ladies 'believed in him' (*ASM*, 416). Dolores, her association with gesture bookending the story, represents the early days of silent film, specifically comedy, with her slapstick stumble over her broom and ambiguous closing gesture, 'express[ing] either ecstasy or strangulation' (*ASM*, 429). This gesture takes place on the stoop of the Hannaford home, proscenium between private and public versions of the Hannafords.

Finally, George is established as more than an actor; more than acting royalty, even. When he is en route to Margaret's house and is confronted by Kay's would-be lover, he assumes the role of writer, or even producer. He reads the scene, surveys his theatrical options and rejects them all:

> In a flash the scene that would presently take place ran itself off in George's mind. He saw himself moving through the scene, saw his part, an infinite choice of parts, but in every one of them Kay would be against him and with Arthur Busch. And suddenly he rejected them all. (*ASM*, 421)

Parts of his daily life end up on the cutting-room floor even as he experiences them, as he lives a selective reality. It is an enticing kind of power but, as the story's title reminds us, magnetism both attracts and repels. By the end of the story, when he discovers Margaret's suicide attempt, not even George can bear to look himself in the eye: 'he closed his eyes with a sudden exclamation of distaste, and abandoned the intention of brushing his hair' (*ASM*, 429). His face, the canvas for the projection of people's hopes and desires, as the Griffith heroines' faces had been in the 1910s, is concealed by the closing of his eyes and symbolic avoidance of his reflected image. He ultimately rejects his role and status, unable, we infer, to respect himself in his embodiment of such an artificial industry.

All is not what it seems in Hannaford's world: the pink-shirted actor from 'Magnetism' was attired thus so that the early film cameras could pick up the shirt sharply and it would register on the black-and-white screen as a pure white. This artificiality pervades silent cinema and is, in fact, symptomatic of the industry itself, whose innate contradiction stipulates that we accept artifice as reality for the duration of the film – that we wilfully substitute the reel for the real. There are two aspects of this artificiality that warrant further discussion here: firstly, the way Fitzgerald uses film, in Alan Bilton's phrase, 'as a metaphor for artificiality and falseness'; and secondly, the link between this falseness and parody.[77] 'Magnetism' is a good example of Fitzgerald using the characters as metaphors for the industry's inherent artificiality. Characters describe themselves as living 'scenes' and being 'actors'. The theatricality of self is a theme that is more fully explored in *Tender is the Night* (1934) but performative identities also permeate the stories, varying from the polishing of Jenny Delehanty into Jenny Prince in 'Jacob's Ladder', to the spontaneous skit Joel Coles stages on his 'Crazy Sunday'. As with so much in Fitzgerald's work, this was an autobiographical trait: in *The Far Side of Paradise*, Arthur Mizener quotes a *New York Tribune* review by Heywood Broun, in which Fitzgerald is castigated for his demonstrative performance of identity:

> The self-consciousness of Fitzgerald is a barrier which we are never able to pierce. He sees himself constantly not as a human being, but as a man in a novel or in a play. Every move is a picture and there is a camera man behind each tree.[78]

This was published in 1920 and Fitzgerald is certain to have read it, since he pasted it into his scrapbooks. Curnutt quotes the same review as evidence of a larger cultural shift towards 'the art of personality' promulgated and marketed by early film stars like Pickford and Fairbanks. Curnutt notes that some of the public were rightly sceptical about the relationship between, for example, the celebrity endorsement of cosmetics and the 'externaliz[ation] of innate but untapped traits'. Fitzgerald (himself having acted as a celebrity judge in a 1926 beauty contest) explored the idea of performative identity, as Curnutt notes, though the disguise motif in his work, but also in his own approach to authorship.[79]

As a *Post* writer, Fitzgerald played his role, with his own 'marks' to hit. He was sufficiently talented to vary the formulae enough almost to obscure them but found certain other stipulations of a *Post* author's role difficult to adhere to creatively. This can be witnessed in the 2014 Cambridge Edition of *Taps at Reveille*, which restores content in the stories that was deemed unfit by the *Post* editors at the time. Despite this editorial censorship, Fitzgerald was much more adept at working within the confines of his role in story writing than he was in screenwriting. Early arrogance aside, when he went to Hollywood for the third time, in 1937, he seriously prepared (or perhaps, rehearsed) for his role, which included making index cards recording plots and noting montage sequences.[80] The fact that he failed to succeed in scriptwriting despite applying himself so industriously is usually attributed to his apparent inability to cede authority to the image in motion pictures; for him, despite stating in 1936 that 'film was an art in which words are subordinate to images' (*MLC*, 148), his 1937–40 stay was spent interrogating that notion, both in his stories and in *The Last Tycoon*.[81]

The tensions between the written and the gestural, as embodied by Fitzgerald's depictions of the artificiality of the pink shirts and exaggerated facial expressions familiar to silent film, are indebted to pantomime, burlesque and, above all, parody. Bilton identifies a critical tendency to see Fitzgerald's use of filmic metaphor and descriptions as 'a kind of literary inoculation, an ingestion of the cultural poison of the age only so as more effectively to repudiate it'.[82] This is a fascinating choice of metaphor, recalling the lexis of disease encountered in criticism of dance and jazz music. This literary inoculation can be expressed in parodic forms – taking on a little of the culturally significant established norms in order to push forward into new territory and to fashion new meanings.

Fitzgerald's 'self-consciousness' may be just that in 1920, but before long, he learns that in order truly to 'make it new', he needs to show he is adept at the old. The problem with parody, as Josephine Baker found, was that by demonstrating confidence with the rules of the status quo, one runs the risk of being seen to endorse them. In his exploration of film, calling into question 'the dominant and hegemonic systems of signification', in Henderson's phrase, Fitzgerald invites us to interrogate these cultural practices and generate more nuanced responses to them.[83] What appears initially to be ambivalence can be read more usefully as Fitzgerald's attempt to convey through language the multiple strata of intertextual interpretative possibilities inherent in each dance, song and filmic allusion. Far from mere period details, his references to popular culture serve to remind us of the very complex ways in which people perform, enact and consume popular culture in order to derive pleasure. Through his work, we can see Fitzgerald trying to explore the inexpressible disconnect between what dance, music and, most fluently, film, can achieve in comparison to, and in partnership with, literature.

Fitzgerald's parodic treatment of popular culture is pronounced in his use of film for several reasons. He conceptually identifies Hollywood as a site of great artistic potential, though also finds himself intimidated by the threat to novel-writing posed by the movies. He is drawn to the new medium but the threat inherent in it renders it ripe for satire. He recognises that though filmmaking has great potential, it is reliant on great filmmakers with the vision to strive for artistic merit and not just commercial success. This mission was one he identified with personally, and his belief in the power of the screenwriter, producer and other filmmakers relates to his similar investment of authority (and even a degree of responsibility) in other artists such as songwriters, dancers and authors. He also personally identifies with the speedy trajectory from unknown to success that many of the early Hollywood stars enjoyed, having had a similar journey into the public eye himself.

Moreover, the tension between the written and the gestural, combined with the potential to distribute films to millions of people, was unique to the medium, and this connection between creator and audience was one Fitzgerald thrived on. Audience engagement had long been a major goal of Fitzgerald's work, and his use of popular culture often functions as a means of drawing his audience into a collaborative position, and into a shared interpretative space.

In film, Fitzgerald saw the manifestation of his society's preoccupation with theatricality and artificiality: his years of exploring performative identity through interactions with popular culture and use of disguise motifs culminated in his reactions to Hollywood. The film industry also enacted the battles in the growing chasm between popular and high culture which so fascinated and concerned Fitzgerald. Reconciling the drive for artistic acclaim with commercial recompense was Fitzgerald's professional goal, and he believed that film had the potential to do better than expressing 'the most obvious emotion' and could fulfil his aim, if only he could break free from the 'low gear of collaboration'.

Cohen writes of D. W. Griffith: 'The close-up was the means through which Griffith reconciled a literary concern for the subtleties of feeling and thought with a medium that favoured action and spectacle.'[84] A lifelong admirer of Griffith, Fitzgerald's version of Lilian Gish's eloquent porcelain face is his invocation of loaded allusions to popular cultural forms. Through textual context and intertextual inference, the reader projects and imbues these references with meaning, all the while having been guided by Fitzgerald to see a 'Memphis Sideswoop' as much more than just a dance, 'Blue Skies' as more than a disposable Tin Pan Alley production, and the burgeoning film industry as the most exciting and terrifying cultural site of all: the place where Conrad's manifesto – 'to make you hear, to make you feel [. . .], to make you *see!*' – could be achieved, and 'the replacement of description by perception' could be most fully realised.[85]

Conclusion: 'All My Stories are Conceived Like Novels'

Popular culture richly impacted upon the literary aesthetics of Fitzgerald's short fiction. Whether in his groups of linked stories or in his discrete stories, there are several unifying features of a Fitzgeraldian story that help to create a self-referential space through which Fitzgerald can enact his self-parodic techniques. These unifying patterns include the conceits of disguise and mistaken identity, an unmistakably Fitzgeraldian tone of lyrical nostalgia, and the recourse to dance, music and film to explore what it means to be a modern American. Fitzgerald's short stories give us an insight into his response to modernity, as well as the intertextual dialogue that took place in the 1920s and 1930s between Fitzgerald's short stories and several other modernists' attempts to confront modernity as manifested in popular culture.

Putting Fitzgerald's stories in the context of their foundations in early twentieth-century culture enables us to value them beyond their role in facilitating Fitzgerald's composition of novels. Fitzgerald's habitual ambiguity can be reread in the realm of parody: his interrogations of dominant cultural practices simultaneously risk endorsement or acquiescence through their faithful reproduction of their parodied targets. Fitzgerald's representations of popular cultural forms meet the criteria of what Linda Hutcheon coined in the late 1980s 'complicitous critique', and it is through these parodic portraits that Fitzgerald offers a more nuanced response to these cultural practices than is initially apparent.[1] Fitzgerald deploys two modes of parody: he uses parodic plotting and characterisation (to make the formulae used for stories in the 'slicks' his own); and he also makes use of self-parody, both intentionally and subconsciously, often in an attempt to try to retain his audience, who had enjoyed his romantic stories of the early 1920s.

Ambiguity and parody are key features of African American cultural practices in the period between 1920 and 1940. It was during this same period that the Harlem Renaissance, in particular, was helping black writers, artists and performers find new subject matter that could speak to their early twentieth-century lives at the level of both form and content. Parody, satire and imitation were vital forces in the shaping of modernism, both white and black. Jazz music and dance celebrated imitative and improvisatory practices in radical new ways, and the aesthetics of repetition, ragging and variation are key elements of Fitzgerald's aesthetics, as shown by his subtle self-parody in portraying flapper figures. Hybridisation and cultural exchange inform Fitzgerald's literary experimentation, and with recourse to case studies of songs, dances, musicals and films, Fitzgerald's interactions with primitivist modernism can be traced.

Undoubtedly, Fitzgerald's lifelong appreciation of popular music and dance infused his stories. Michael Nowlin has suggested that 'Fitzgerald playfully identif[ies] with a figurative "black" America to represent his enmeshment – by both desire and economic necessity – in the entertainment business and America's mass culture of celebrity.'[2] As I have shown, this identification is particularly visible in Fitzgerald's allusions to dance, music and film of the interwar period. It is in Fitzgerald's depictions of dance and music that his racially inflected, parodic portrayals are most clearly delineated: in Josephine Baker's 'chocolate arabesques', in Myra's Al Jolson-inspired 'syncopated appeal' and in Charlotte's Topsy-infused Charleston (*TAR*, 161; *F&P*, 244; *ASM*, 303).

Both Baker and Fitzgerald are working within established formulae and managing the expectations of their audience. By adopting a satirical tone, they are able to find a commercially viable creative position from which they can satisfy the majority of their audiences, who do not notice the parody in their performance, whilst also connecting with those audience members who do perceive the parodic undertones, all the while delivering financial returns that can sustain their roles as artists. Fitzgerald explores dancers as metaphors for the literary craftsman: the authentically inspired artist attaining critical acclaim, whilst the uninspired performer receives only pay cheques.

Music influences Fitzgerald's literary aesthetics on both a thematic and a formal level: repetition, ragging, variation and quotation are integral to jazz music, and Fitzgerald adopts these techniques in his subtle self-parody, destabilising our expectations of what a typical Fitzgerald story entails. Fitzgerald reinterprets the formulaic strophic structures of Tin Pan Alley in his treatment of his flapper heroines, providing inviting, song-like hooks of characterisation that appeal to his readership, whilst subtly undermining the prescriptions he laboured within to create memorable, marketable fictions that on closer analysis transcend their formulae.

In Fitzgerald's representations of the film industry, he shows how cultural media can function as models of identity for consumers, a theme common to music, dance and musical theatre but perhaps reaching its apex in Fitzgerald's depictions of Hollywood. Fitzgerald's parodic representations of the film industry, especially in the vehicle of Pat Hobby, expose Hollywood conventions whilst satirising archetypal figures such as the hack screenwriter, ingénue starlet and matinée idol. Fitzgerald imports filmic techniques into his fiction, interrogating the capabilities of the new medium through stories that incorporate the use of filmic techniques such as montage, dream sequences and close-ups. The film industry also offers Fitzgerald the opportunity to explore more fully the impact of the cult of celebrity and performative personality, as well as to evaluate Hollywood as the potential site for the union of the commercial success and creative fulfilment that he had so relentlessly sought.

During the composition process of *The Great Gatsby*, in 1924, Fitzgerald distinguishes the 'purely creative work' of writing his novel from the 'trashy imaginings' of his short stories, a quotation with which I began the introduction.[3] Yet the representations of popular culture in his short stories suggest that his commercial fiction is often imbued with an experimentalism that, though subtle, betrays a more nuanced engagement with popular culture than the term 'trash' suggests. Popular cultural references in Fitzgerald's short fiction thus do not simply serve as temporal markers nor solely to set the tone and mood of a scene, but actually often function as subversive agents that destabilise our expectations of a commercial Fitzgerald story whilst sitting in tension with Fitzgerald's lyrical prose style. The tropes of disguise and performance are of paramount importance to Fitzgerald's literary modernism, which is often racially coded. Fitzgerald's use of these cultural media, centred around the concepts of performance and leisure, show his subtle manipulation of our expectations of his short fiction.

Fitzgerald's struggle to reconcile his artistic and commercial needs leads him to demonstrate that popular and high culture could profitably coexist in his short fiction, through his efforts to situate popular cultural references in the context of serious literary craftsmanship. He contributes substantially to the leisure debate that was topical in the 1930s, and his treatment of dancers, musicians and those working in the film industry serves as a metaphor for his conception of the popular short story genre. The well-worn notion of Fitzgerald's 'double vision' and 'ambiguity' can be reread in terms of the palimpsest and conflict between contrasting ideas as symptomatic of the parodic mode.

In these ways, Fitzgerald was not merely faithfully portraying his era, but rather evaluating and critically engaging with it. Like Joel Coles and George Hannaford, who serve as actors and directors in their daily lives on and off the set, Fitzgerald assembles his surroundings into an artistic response to his lived experience, even as he lived it. Fitzgerald's short stories should be appreciated not only in their function as supplementary to novel-writing, but also as interdependent entities, valuable for their own aesthetic merits and for the insights they give us into Fitzgerald's writing processes and aesthetic techniques, as well as their representations of Fitzgerald's undoubtedly 'radiant world'.[4]

Fitzgerald's work can also be fruitfully considered alongside more obviously innovative cultural practitioners. Gertrude Stein, for example, sought to make language achieve that which visual art could accomplish, and D. W. Griffith 'wanted to turn the literary into the visual – to find objective correlatives for what literature could do'.[5] Throughout his career, Fitzgerald explored the disconnect between what language can undertake and what dance, music and film can achieve. Fitzgerald's fondness for Joseph Conrad's exhortation to use fiction to make readers hear, feel and see, as well as his respect for his friend Gilbert Seldes's defence of the 'lively' arts, helped him to formulate his ideas about the inexpressible divide between what dance, music, musical theatre and film can achieve in comparison to, and in partnership with, literature.[6] Moving beyond the limitations of language, through his invocation of dance steps, song lyrics and filmic techniques, Fitzgerald makes his readers hear, feel and see in a modern, multi-modal way that draws upon the collage aesthetic which had characterised his first novel, *This Side of Paradise*. Fitzgerald's interest in eclectic form and extra-literary expression leads him to imbue his fiction with snippets of song, snatches of dances and allusions to popular musical theatre plot arcs, and to include filmic techniques in his short fiction.

In alluding to these popular cultural forms on both formal and thematic levels Fitzgerald seeks to represent the interrelated layerings and fragmentation of experience that were being explored by other modernists on both sides of the Atlantic, such as James Joyce, Gertrude Stein, Sherwood Anderson, Dorothy Parker and T. S. Eliot. In his short fiction, Fitzgerald explores modernist concerns such as plastic spatiality, the abandonment of temporality, loneliness in an increasingly competitive society and the concept of the epiphany. These comparisons hold up: for example, in 1923, Clive Bell famously described Eliot as 'a product of the Jazz movement', and Eliot's use of the collage aesthetic in *The Waste Land* (1922) grapples with questions of representation and the construction of meaning.[7] These questions are also at the heart of Fitzgerald's work. The parodic undercurrents running through Fitzgerald's short fiction emphasise the myth of cohesion in modern society. Fitzgerald's golden girl flappers can indeed be read as escapist 'confections', but by utilising self-parody, along with metafictive techniques, composite characterisation and the collage aesthetic, Fitzgerald interrogates the ambiguities that form the foundations of both modern culture and his own literary endeavours.[8]

Fitzgerald's use of dance, music, musical theatre and film references in his short fiction is a reminder of the complex ways in which people perform, enact and consume popular culture. Fitzgerald seeks to convey through language the multiple strata of interpretative possibilities embedded within each allusion to popular culture. He demonstrates the desirability and power innate in these popular cultural forms but also shows how there are dangers in emotional over-investment in them. Whilst Fitzgerald profoundly feared the moral repercussions of dance, music, musicals and film of the 'Jazz Age', he is still irresistibly drawn towards them. In 1939, Fitzgerald wrote to his daughter, 'I guess I am too much a moralist at heart, and really want to preach at people in some acceptable form, rather than to entertain them.'[9] In punishing several of his fictional consumers of popular culture for their inauthentic performances and reception of popular dance, music and film, Fitzgerald surely succeeds in moralising and entertaining simultaneously. In so doing, he finds some resolution for his deep-seated anxiety about the fracture between his work's artistic and commercial success.

APPENDIX: FITZGERALD'S SHORT STORY COLLECTIONS

Fitzgerald's four short story collections contained the following stories:

Flappers and Philosophers (1920)
'The Offshore Pirate'
'The Ice Palace'
'Head and Shoulders'
'The Cut-Glass Bowl'
'Bernice Bobs Her Hair'
'Benediction'
'Dalyrimple Goes Wrong'
'The Four Fists'

Tales of the Jazz Age (1922)
'The Jelly-Bean'
'The Camel's Back'
'May Day'
'Porcelain and Pink'
'The Diamond as Big as the Ritz'
'The Curious Case of Benjamin Button'
'Tarquin of Cheapside'
'O Russet Witch!'
'The Lees of Happiness'
'Mr. Icky'
'Jemina, the Mountain Girl'

All the Sad Young Men (1926)
'The Rich Boy'
'Winter Dreams'
'The Baby Party'
'Absolution'
'Rags Martin-Jones and the Pr-nce of W-les'
'The Adjuster'
'Hot and Cold Blood'
'"The Sensible Thing"'
'Gretchen's Forty Winks'

Taps at Reveille (1935)
'Crazy Sunday'
'Two Wrongs'
'The Night of Chancellorsville'
'The Last of the Belles'
'Majesty'
'Family in the Wind'
'A Short Trip Home'
'One Interne'
'The Fiend'
'Babylon Revisited'

NOTES

Introduction

1. Fitzgerald, *Life in Letters*, 67 [c. 10 April 1924]. The quotation in the chapter title is also taken from Fitzgerald, *Life in Letters*, 67 [c. 10 April 1924].
2. Cowley, 'Third Act and Epilogue', 66. This essay originally appeared in *The New Yorker*, 30 June 1945.
3. Bryer, 'The Critical Reputation of F. Scott Fitzgerald', 211; Letter from Fitzgerald to Anne Ober, in Fitzgerald, *Life in Letters*, 352 [4 March 1938].
4. Henson, *Beyond the Sound Barrier*, 1. For excellent overviews of the dramatic social and cultural changes during the 1920s, as well as histories of the continuities between the 1910s, 1920s and 1930s, see Currell, *American Culture in the 1920s*, Douglas, *Terrible Honesty*, and Dumenil, *Modern Temper*.
5. See, for example, Fass, *The Damned and the Beautiful*.
6. The Fitzgeralds lived in France and Switzerland between March 1929 and September 1931; following her breakdown in April 1930, Zelda was treated in a clinic near Paris, before discharging herself eighteen days later. She was readmitted to a clinic near Montreux, Switzerland, and promptly transferred to Rives de Prangins, near Nyon, where she remained for fifteen months.
7. This preface was composed in December 1934.
8. Currell, *The March of Spare Time*, 3.
9. West III, 'Explanatory Notes', *Flappers and Philosophers*, ed. by West III, 351–80 (373).
10. See Erenberg, *Steppin' Out*, 149–50.
11. Kuehl, *F. Scott Fitzgerald*, 46.
12. Hutcheon, *A Theory of Parody*, 37.
13. Hearn, 'Fitzgerald and the Popular Magazine Story', 34-5.
14. For an analysis of Taylor's impact on American culture, see Banta, *Taylored Lives*.
15. McCarren, *Dancing Machines*, 20.
16. Ibid., 20.

17. Curnutt, *Introduction to Fitzgerald*, 31–3.

18. This song was featured in the 1919 *Ziegfeld Follies* and was one of three Berlin songs chosen to appear in a 'semi-symphonic arrangement' at Paul Whiteman's 1924 Aeolian Hall concert. See Kimball and Emmett (eds), *The Complete Lyrics of Irving Berlin*, 186–7.

19. Ann Douglas places the membership of the Ku Klux Klan at between 2 and 5 million during the 1920s. See *Terrible Honesty*, 315.

20. See, for example, John A. Higgins's interpretation of 'Myra' as a 'mildly enjoyable . . . farce' despite its 'structural difficulties', reading Myra herself as a *'femme fatale'* in *F. Scott Fitzgerald*, 20. Ruth Prigozy, by contrast, finds the plot 'ingenious', while Kirk Curnutt reads the ending as a justified but failed attempt to 'resolve the inequities between men and women' that earns Myra our sympathy. See Prigozy, 'Fitzgerald's Flappers and Flapper Films', 139; and Curnutt, *Introduction to Fitzgerald*, 85.

21. Douglas, *Terrible Honesty*, 75.

22. See, for example, the Cotton Club in Harlem, and the Plantation Club on Broadway, as discussed in Erenberg, *Steppin' Out*, 254–8.

23. Gilroy, '". . . to be real"', 15–16.

24. See Borshuk, 'An Intelligence of the Body'.

25. Fitzgerald described himself as a 'moralist at heart' in a letter to his daughter, Scottie Fitzgerald, in Fitzgerald, *Letters of Fitzgerald*, 63 [4 November 1939].

26. Sanderson, 'Women in Fitzgerald's Fiction', 143.

27. See Curnutt, 'Introduction', 6.

28. Zelda Fitzgerald, 'What Became of the Flappers?', 399.

29. See Dickson-Carr, *Spoofing the Modern*.

30. See Borshuk, 'An Intelligence of the Body'.

31. Lott, *Love and Theft*, 3, 6.

32. Ibid., 240.

33. North, *The Dialect of Modernism*, 9.

34. Ibid., 59.

35. Lemke, *Primitivist Modernism*, 4.

36. Harding, '"Made for – or against – the Trade"', 114.

37. Dentith, *Parody*, 8.

38. Douglas, *Terrible Honesty*, 348.

39. See Fitzgerald, *In His Own Time*, 447–8; ibid., 456–64.

40. For a discussion of Fitzgerald's parodic plotting and characterization, see Harding, '"Made For – or Against – the Trade"'; for Fitzgerald's self-parodic practices, see Prigozy, 'Fitzgerald's Short Stories and the Depression'.

41. Cohn, *Creating America*, 5.

42. See Turnbull, *Scott Fitzgerald*, 287.

43. Letter from Scott Fitzgerald to Zelda Fitzgerald, in Bryer and Barks (eds), *Dear Scott, Dearest Zelda*, 370 [11 Oct 1940].

44. Mencken, 'Two Years Too Late', 40. Reprinted in Nolte (ed.), *H. L. Mencken's 'Smart Set' Criticism*, 286.

45. West III, *American Authors*, 113.

46. Kirk Curnutt has shown that Fitzgerald would have had access to Freytag's

Technique of the Drama (1865, translated into English in 1895), since Zelda requested to borrow it from him in 1930. See Curnutt, 'The Short Stories of F. Scott Fitzgerald', 298.

47. Harding, '"Made For – or Against – the Trade"', 114.
48. Fitzgerald, *Life in Letters*, 169 [9 Sept 1929].
49. Bryer and Barks (eds), *Dear Scott, Dearest Zelda*, 343 [18 May 1940].
50. May, *The Short Story*, 18–19.
51. Martin Scofield has argued, however, that this exaggerated emphasis on O. Henry's endings is unwarranted, given that endings are universally important in the abbreviated form that characterises the short story. See *The Cambridge Introduction to the American Short Story*, 117–18.
52. Bryer and Barks (eds), *Dear Scott, Dearest Zelda*, 340 [4 May 1940].
53. Stern, 'Will the Real Pat Hobby Please Stand Up?', 320.
54. Cowley, *A Second Flowering*, 31.
55. See, for example, Scofield, *The Cambridge Introduction to the American Short Story*, 108; and Head, *The Modernist Short Story*, 6.
56. See, for example, May, *The Short Story*, 16–19.
57. See Petry, *Fitzgerald's Craft of Short Fiction*, 156; see also Donaldson, 'Scott Fitzgerald's Romance with the South', 7–8.
58. Bullock, 'The Southern and the Satirical', 132.
59. Ibid., 137.
60. Newman, 'All the Sad Young Men', 369.
61. Walton, 'Taps at Reveille', 396.

Chapter 1

1. This description appeared in the magazine version of the story (*Hearst's International*, April 1924), but Fitzgerald revised the story at some point between 1924 and 1926, minimising the similarities to *The Great Gatsby* (1925). West reproduces this revised version in the Cambridge Edition, but includes Fitzgerald's excisions in the Record of Variants. The quotation in the chapter title is taken from Fitzgerald's story 'The Perfect Life' (1929), collected in *The Basil, Josephine, and Gwen Stories*, 134.
2. Fitzgerald, *The Love of the Last Tycoon*, lxxxiv.
3. Letter from Fitzgerald to the Booksellers' Convention, in Turnbull (ed.), *Letters of Fitzgerald*, 459 [early April 1920].
4. West III, 'Annotating Mr. Fitzgerald', 86.
5. West III, 'Explanatory Notes', in *Tales of the Jazz Age*, ed. by West III, 499-528 (523).
6. These films included *How Rastus Got His Turkey* (1911) and *Rastus' Riotous Ride* (1914). One of the flatfoot tapdancing greats was an African American man called King Rastus Brown, a virtuoso who mixed flatfoot tap and shuffle styles. See Stearns and Stearns, *Jazz Dance*, 176, 187. King Rastus Brown never achieved fame outside of the dancing community, and it is unlikely, although not impossible, that Fitzgerald knew him.
7. Bogle, *Toms, Coons*, 4, 8.

8. Turnbull (ed.), *Letters of Fitzgerald*, 522 [18 July 1933]; Nowlin, *Racial Angles*, 12.

9. McCarren, *Dancing Machines*, 190, 160.

10. Lemke, *Primitivist Modernism*, 5; Douglas, *Terrible Honesty*, 526.

11. Erenberg, *Steppin' Out*, 161.

12. Fitzgerald cut this passage when he revised the story for potential (but unrealised) inclusion in *All the Sad Young Men* (1926). West suggests that these cuts were made in order to reduce similarities to *The Great Gatsby* (1925). See West III, 'Introduction', in *Tales of the Jazz Age*, ed by West III, xi–xxviii (xxiv).

13. Douglas, *Terrible Honesty*, 98.

14. Lemke, *Primitivist Modernism*, 6.

15. Fass, *The Damned and the Beautiful*, 220.

16. See Douglas, *The Feminization of American Culture*; see also Sanderson, 'Women in Fitzgerald's Fiction'.

17. As both Sanderson and Sarah Churchwell have noted, this was a gendered narrative, Fitzgerald conceiving of his talent being prostituted out to a commercial audience conceptualised by Churchwell as masculine, jeopardising the (feminine) critical acclaim he sought. See ibid.; and Sarah Churchwell, '"$4000 a Screw"'.

18. Sanderson, 'Women in Fitzgerald's Fiction', 143.

19. Drowne, 'Postwar Flappers', 250.

20. Quoted in Zeitz, *Flapper*, 23.

21. Basil's recourse to the apparent safety of the Tango provides a sense of dramatic irony in light of Rudolph Valentino's erotic Tango exploits, epitomised by the opening sequence to Rex Ingram's hit film, *The Four Horsemen of the Apocalypse* (1921), in which the sensual dips and twists of the Tango culminate in a kiss.

22. See, for example, Roulston, 'Rummaging Through F. Scott Fitzgerald's "Trash"'.

23. Castle and Castle, *Modern Dancing*, 145.

24. See Cook, 'Passionless Dancing'.

25. Golden, *Vernon and Irene Castle's Ragtime Revolution*, 87.

26. Cook, 'Passionless Dancing', 137.

27. Castle and Castle, *Modern Dancing*, 17.

28. Cook, 'Passionless Dancing', 138.

29. Douglas, *Terrible Honesty*, 74, 304; and Wilkerson, *The Warmth of Other Suns*.

30. Quoted in Franks, *Social Dance*, 176.

31. Brown, *Babylon Girls*, 165.

32. Cook, 'Passionless Dancing', 139.

33. See Currell, *American Culture*, 22–32; and del Gizzo, 'Ethnic Stereotyping'.

34. See Driver, *A Century of Dance*, 25–7.

35. In 1934, Fitzgerald wrote to his editor Maxwell Perkins and proposed collecting the stories, suggesting that the public might interpret them 'almost as a novel', in Kuehl and Bryer (eds), *Dear Scott/Dear Max*, 196 [15 May 1934].

36. Ledger, *The New Woman*, 150–76.

37. Ibid., 155; see also Walkowitz, *City of Dreadful Delight*, 45.

38. Erenberg, *Steppin' Out*, 255, 157, 123.

39. Ibid., 255.

40. Morley, *Modern American Literature*, 154; see Berret, *Music in the Works of F. Scott*

Fitzgerald, 124–5 for a discussion of an early draft of *The Great Gatsby* in which Fitzgerald includes both of these songs.

41. Castle and Castle, *Modern Dancing*, 40.
42. Currell, 'Introduction', 2.
43. Crease, 'Jazz and Dance', 76.
44. Irving Berlin's 1910 song, 'Grizzly Bear', instructs readers on how to do the dance, and references Buffalo, a popular destination for elopements: 'Hug up close to your baby / Throw your shoulders t'ward the ceiling / Lawdy, lawdy, what a feelin' / Snug up close to your lady / [. . .] Something nice is gwine to happen / [. . .] Show your darlin' beau / Just how you go to Buffalo / Doin' the Grizzly Bear.' See Kimball and Emmet (eds), *Lyrics of Irving Berlin*, 20.
45. Berret, 'Basil and the Dance Craze', 95.
46. Nowlin, *Racial Angles*, 20.
47. Balkun, '"One Cannot Both Spend and Have"', 132.
48. Castle and Castle, *Modern Dancing*, 33, 146, 150–4, 173–6.
49. Veblen, *The Theory of the Leisure Class*, 20-27.
50. Curnutt, 'Fitzgerald's Consumer World', 115.
51. See Veblen, *The Theory of the Leisure Class*, 20–69.
52. Zelda Fitzgerald, 'What Became of the Flappers?', 398.
53. In its original magazine context in *McCall's*, the joint byline is followed by Scott and Zelda's individual essays in separate columns, each headed by their name, although in much smaller print. See Bruccoli, Smith and Kerr (eds), *The Romantic Egoists*, 132–3.
54. West III, 'F. Scott Fitzgerald, Professional Author', 56.
55. Higgins, *F. Scott Fitzgerald*, 68.
56. Donaldson, *Fool For Love*, 102–3.
57. Higgins, *F. Scott Fitzgerald*, 70.
58. Erenberg, *Steppin' Out*, 207.
59. Ogren, *The Jazz Revolution*, 14.
60. Whiteman and McBride, *Jazz*, 117.
61. Fitzgerald amended the title in his copy of *Hearst's International*, where the story appeared in April 1924, to 'Diamond Dick'; Mangum, *A Fortune Yet*, 50; Higgins, *F. Scott Fitzgerald*, 68.
62. Higgins, *F. Scott Fitzgerald*, 70.
63. Prigozy, 'Fitzgerald's Short Stories and the Depression', 113.
64. Higgins, *F. Scott Fitzgerald*, 136.
65. Harding, '"Made for – or against – the Trade"', 114, 123, 129.

Chapter 2

1. See Martin, 'The First Emotional Bankrupt'; and Balkun, '"One Cannot Both Spend and Have"'.
2. Gale, *F. Scott Fitzgerald Encyclopedia*, 122.
3. Martin, 'The First Emotional Bankrupt', 185.
4. Balkun, '"One Cannot Both Spend and Have"', 131.
5. Nowlin, *Racial Angles*, 20.

6. Fitzgerald, *Life in Letters*, 185 [22 June 1930].

7. Bryer and Barks (eds), *Dear Scott, Dearest Zelda*, 96 [Fall 1930].

8. The passage in square brackets appeared in an earlier draft of the story but was deleted by Fitzgerald before publication.

9. For a fuller exploration of Baker as a modernist muse, see Cheng, *Second Skin*.

10. Daugherty and West III, 'Josephine Baker, Petronius, and the Text of "Babylon Revisited"', 8.

11. Gordon, 'Synesthetic Rhythms'.

12. Bruccoli, *Epic Grandeur*, 289.

13. See Hammond and O'Connor, *Josephine Baker*, 118.

14. Ibid., 118.

15. Baker and Bouillon, *Josephine*, 24–7.

16. Carter, 'Review of *Jazz Cleopatra*', 193.

17. Nowlin, *Racial Angles*, 75.

18. Archer-Straw, *Negrophilia*, 51.

19. Barnwell, 'Like the Gypsy's Daughter', 84.

20. Henderson, 'Colonial, Postcolonial, and Diasporic Readings', [unpaginated].

21. Baker and Bouillon, *Josephine*, 51–2.

22. Brooks, 'The End of the Line', [unpaginated].

23. Brown, *Babylon Girls*, 86, 65.

24. See Brooks, 'The End of the Line', [unpaginated].

25. See, for example, accounts in Archer-Straw, *Negrophilia*, 94–7; and Baker and Chase, *Josephine*, 137.

26. See Cheng, *Second Skin*; and Henderson, 'Josephine Baker'.

27. See Nowlin, *Racial Angles*.

28. Keller, 'The Riviera's Golden Boy', 130.

29. She is with 'Count' Pepito Abatino, her fiancé and manager, who holds a Josephine Baker doll that is costumed in a much more revealing outfit than the demure Baker. The picture is reproduced and discussed in Archer-Straw, *Negrophilia*, 96.

30. Archer-Straw, *Negrophilia*, 97.

31. Mizejewski, *Ziegfeld Girl*, 11.

32. Bruccoli, Duggan and Walker (eds), *Correspondence of F. Scott Fitzgerald*, 406 [26 March 1935].

33. Henderson, 'Colonial, Postcolonial, and Diasporic Readings', [unpaginated].

34. Bruccoli (ed.), *The Notebooks of Fitzgerald*, 131.

35. Henderson, 'Colonial, Postcolonial, and Diasporic Readings', [unpaginated].

36. Martin, '"Remembering the Jungle"', 311.

37. Ibid., 313.

38. Baker and Bouillon, *Josephine*, 55

39. Whiteman and McBride, *Jazz*, 104, 99, 104.

40. Borshuk, 'An Intelligence of the Body', 50.

41. Ibid., 52.

42. See Hutcheon, *The Politics of Postmodernism*, 95–7.

43. Fitzgerald, *Life in Letters*, 182–3 [received 13 May 1930].

44. Warshow, 'The Gangster as Tragic Hero', 99–100.

45. Bruccoli and Bryer, *F. Scott Fitzgerald in His Own Time*, 245.
46. Ibid., 244.
47. Boyd, 'Mostly Flappers', 48.
48. In fact, in the *Post* version of the story, no mention is made of the illustration and, in any case, the final paragraphs of the story are accompanied by an advertisement for Coleman Quick-Lite Gasoline Lamps, rather than a kissing couple. In *Flappers and Philosophers*, Fitzgerald modified the ending to reference the illustration, perhaps calling to the reader's mind the magazine context of the story, despite *Flappers and Philosophers* being a non-illustrated book.
49. In 1936, he wrote to Adelaide Neall, a fiction editor at the *Post*: 'In the last two years I've only too often realised that many of my stories were built rather than written'; see *Life in Letters*, 301 [5 June 1936].
50. Curnutt, *Introduction to Fitzgerald*, 31.
51. Kimball and Emmet (eds), *Lyrics of Irving Berlin*, 288.

Chapter 3

1. The quotation in the chapter title is taken from *Dear Scott/Dear Max: The Fitzgerald–Perkins Correspondence*, 60 [c. 20 June 1922].
2. Kuehl and Bryer (eds), *Dear Scott/Dear Max*, 271–2 [8 May 1922].
3. Ibid., 59 [11 May 1922].
4. See Prigozy, '"Poor Butterfly"'; Graham, *The Great American Songbooks*; and Berret, *Unheard Melodies*.
5. See Giddins, *Visions of Jazz*, 635.
6. Gabbard, 'The Word Jazz', 2.
7. Prigozy, '"Poor Butterfly"', 41.
8. See Graham, *The Great American Songbooks*, 106–10.
9. Ibid., 106.
10. See Bruccoli, *Epic Grandeur*, 28–9, 32, 37, 45, 51, 56, 65. The Triangle Club libretti are collected in Fitzgerald, *Spires and Gargoyles*, 47–100.
11. Turnbull, *Scott Fitzgerald*, 231.
12. Fitzgerald, *The Love of Last Tycoon*, 68.
13. For his own creations, most likely written between 1932 and 1940, see *The Notebooks of Fitzgerald*, 115–37, and for lists of songs, see 287 and 290. Also see intermittent song references in the 'Autobiographical Chart' section of *F. Scott Fitzgerald's Ledger*, 151–89.
14. Mooney, 'Songs, Singers and Society', 228.
15. This discussion is indebted to the excellent overviews of the precariousness of jazz definitions in Savran, *Highbrow/Lowdown*, 22–35; and Evans, *Writing Jazz*, 10–20.
16. Savran, *Highbrow/Lowdown*, 23.
17. Ibid., 28–9.
18. Ogren, *The Jazz Revolution*, 13.
19. Spaeth, *A History of Popular Music in America*, 477.
20. Shaw, *The Jazz Age*, 76
21. Chapman, *Prove It on Me*, 80.

22. See Bogle, *Heat Wave*, 58.
23. Dentith, *Parody*, 194.
24. Carter, *Another Part of the Twenties*, x.
25. Spaeth, *A History of Popular Music in America*, 477.
26. Zinn, *A People's History of the United States*, 382.
27. Hays, 'Class Differences', 216.
28. Fitzgerald, *This Side of Paradise*, 260.
29. See Matthew Bruccoli's Introduction to *The Price Was High*. See also West, 'F. Scott Fitzgerald: Professional Author'.
30. In 1932, Harold Ober made a sworn deposition to the Internal Revenue Service, trying to have Fitzgerald classified as, to all intents and purposes, an employee of the *Post*: 'For the past seven years virtually all of Mr. Fitzgerald's work has been done for and at the request of the Saturday Evening Post. The stories which he first submitted to that magazine were of a type desired by the editors and were accepted, published and paid for and an arrangement made through me that I would submit all of Mr. Fitzgerald's work to the Post. During 1929 and 1930 Mr. Fitzgerald wrote a total of fifteen stories at the request of the editors of The Saturday Evening Post, all of which were copy-righted by that publication and published therein. The arrangement, pursuant to which these stories were written for The Saturday Evening Post, specified the length of each, subject matter, avoidance of certain topics and at an agreed price for each.' Fitzgerald, *As Ever, Scott Fitz-*, 192–3 [26 April 1932].
31. See Hugill, *Shanties from the Seven Seas*, 312–13.
32. There are many variations of these songs: for this version of the chorus see 'A Capital Ship', in *The Mudcat Café Digital Tradition Folk Song Database*, available at <http://mudcat.org/@displaysong.cfm?SongID=11> (last accessed 12 January 2018).
33. Petry, *Fitzgerald's Craft of Short Fiction*, 43–7.
34. Levine, *Highbrow/Lowbrow*, 31.
35. Ibid., 195.
36. See the chapter on 'William Shakespeare in America' in Levine, *Highbrow/Lowbrow*, 11-82.
37. Kammen, 'Introduction', xvii.
38. These five stories were: 'Head and Shoulders' (21 February 1920), 'Myra Meets His Family' (20 March 1920), 'The Camel's Back' (24 April 1920), 'Bernice Bobs Her Hair' (1 May 1920) and 'The Offshore Pirate' (29 May 1920).
39. Graham, *The Great American Songbooks*, 92.
40. The quotation in the section title is taken from Fitzgerald's story, 'Three Acts of Music' (1936), collected in *The Lost Decade*, 8.
41. Berret, *Music in the Works of F. Scott Fitzgerald*, 173.
42. Whilst the story is partly based on Fitzgerald's friends, Nora and Maurice 'Lefty' Flynn, Sara's abandonment of her husband and children recalls Nora Helmer's act of desertion in Henrik Ibsen's 1879 play, *A Doll's House*, which was included in Fitzgerald's first instalment of the reading list he recommended to Sheilah Graham in her 'College of One', albeit with the slightly misremembered title of 'The Dolls House'. See Graham, *College of One*, 204–5.

43. See Kimball and Emmet (eds), *Lyrics of Irving Berlin*, 226, 228–9, 231–2, 254.
44. Ibid., 228.
45. Woollcott, *The Story of Irving Berlin*, 3.
46. Fitzgerald and Mackay had playfully sparred in print in 1925, eight months after she had returned from her trip to Europe and a month before she was to marry Berlin. She had written an article in the *New Yorker* entitled 'Why We Go to Cabarets: A Post-Debutante Explains'. She wrote that society's disapproving elders 'have swallowed too much of Mr. Scott Fitzgerald' when they criticise 'the quality of our taste' in choosing to attend a cabaret. Fitzgerald's riposte is playfully addressed to 'that celebrated intellectual, Miss Ellin Mackay'. Interviewed by the *Chicago Tribune European Edition*, in December 1925, he sardonically empathises that 'people simply have to escape from a milieu largely composed of young women who write articles for the newspapers about the necessity of escaping from such a milieu'. See Mackay, 'Why We Go to Cabarets: A Post-Debutante Explains', 7; and 'Ellin Mackay's Bored Debutantes Are Satirized by Scott Fitzgerald', originally in the *Chicago Tribune European Edition*, 7 December 1925, and reprinted in Bruccoli and Baughman (eds), *Conversations with F. Scott Fitzgerald*, 75.
47. West III, 'Fitzgerald and *Esquire*', 160.
48. The figure of 178 depends on whether certain pieces are classified as essay or fiction. Jackson Bryer counts 178 stories in the Appendix of *The Short Stories of F. Scott Fitzgerald: New Approaches in Criticism*, which includes the nineteen stories identified by Jennifer McCabe Atkinson in 'Lost and Unpublished Stories by F. Scott Fitzgerald', as well as 'Our Own Movie Queen' (1925), which was co-written by Scott and Zelda Fitzgerald, but appeared in print under solely Scott's name.
49. Woollcott, *The Story of Irving Berlin*, 35.
50. Ibid., 152–3.
51. Stern, 'Will the Real Pat Hobby Please Stand Up?', 321–2.
52. Albright (ed.), *Modernism and Music*, 11.
53. Hawthorne, *New York Times Book Review*, 150.
54. Hansen, 'The Boy Grows Older', *Chicago Daily News*, 3 March 1926, 255; Gray, 'Scott Fitzgerald Brilliance Bared in Short Stories', *St. Paul Dispatch*, 20 March 1935, 337; 'Scott Fitzgerald Turns a Corner', *New York Times Book Review*, 7 March 1926, 257; Cowley, *Charm*, May 1926, 271.
55. Fitzgerald, *Life in Letters*, 444 [18 May 1940].
56. West III, 'Introduction', in *Taps at Reveille*, ed. by West III, xxiv.
57. Ibid., xxv.
58. Ibid., xxiv.
59. Warshow, 'The Gangster as Tragic Hero', 99-100.

Chapter 4

1. The quotation in the chapter title is taken from Fitzgerald's story 'Too Cute for Words' (1936), collected in *The Basil, Josephine, and Gwen Stories*, 293.
2. Letter to Scottie Fitzgerald, in Fitzgerald, *Letters of Fitzgerald*, 63 [4 November 1939].

3. See also Berret, 'Broadway Melodies' and *Music in the Works of F. Scott Fitzgerald*.

4. Kunce and Levitt, 'The Structure of *Gatsby*', 101.

5. In the magazine version of the story, which appeared in *The Smart Set* in January 1920, Julie instead sings 'The Blundering Blimp', a song of Fitzgerald's invention which Marcia Meadows performs in 'Head and Shoulders' (*F&P*, 69). Written in October 1919, only a month before he composed 'Head and Shoulders', Fitzgerald's original lyrics in 'Porcelain and Pink' include 'Quiver like a jelly in a shimmy-shakers' dance', but he decided on 'The Imperial Roman Jazz' for the story's inclusion in *Tales of the Jazz Age* (*TJA*, 430).

6. See Berret, 'Broadway Melodies', 299–300.

7. Fitzgerald, *This Side of Paradise*, 18.

8. West III, 'Annotating Mr. Fitzgerald', 88.

9. Hamilton, 'Mencken and Nathan's *Smart Set*', 28.

10. Fitzgerald, *As Ever, Scott Fitz-*, 55 [21 June 1923].

11. Kimball and Emmet (eds), *Lyrics of Irving Berlin*, 262–3.

12. See Dilworth, '*The Great Gatsby* and the Arrow Collar Man'.

13. Kimball and Emmet (eds), *Lyrics of Irving Berlin*, 262–3.

14. Erenberg, *Steppin' Out*, 256.

15. Furia, *The Poets of Tin Pan Alley*, 62; Kimball and Emmet (eds), *Lyrics of Irving Berlin*, 288.

16. Ogren, *The Jazz Revolution*, 149.

17. Wilder, *American Popular Song*, 104.

18. Furia, *The Poets of Tin Pan Alley*, 62.

19. Fred Astaire made a recording of the song for Columbia in 1930 but it did not appear in the 1930 film. He again performed the song, with revised lyrics replacing Lenox Avenue with Park Avenue, in the 1946 film *Blue Skies*.

20. Evans, '"Racial Cross-Dressing"', 393.

21. Seldes, *The 7 Lively Arts*, 96.

22. Erenberg, *Steppin' Out*, 255–9.

23. Dawidoff, 'The Kind of Person', 299.

24. Alexander, *Jazz Age Jews*, 137.

25. Lott, *Love and Theft*, 101.

26. Seldes, *The 7 Lively Arts*, 70.

27. Evans, *Writing Jazz*, 148.

28. See Lears, *No Place of Grace*.

29. Kuehl and Bryer (eds), *Dear Scott/Dear Max*, 30 [29 April 1920].

30. West III, 'Introduction', in *Flappers and Philosophers*, ed. West III, xi–xxxi (xiv).

31. Farebrother, *The Collage Aesthetic*, 1, 9.

32. Ibid., 5; see also Furia, *The Poets of Tin Pan Alley*, 11, in which he compares the verbal collages of e. e. cummings and Cole Porter.

33. Curnutt, *Introduction to Fitzgerald*, 97.

34. Farebrother, *The Collage Aesthetic*, 8.

35. Levine, *Highbrow/Lowbrow*, 33.

36. See ibid., 21.

37. Douglas, *Terrible Honesty*, 356.

38. Savran, *Highbrow/Lowdown*, 66

39. Ibid., 98
40. 'Mr. Fitzgerald's Latest Book', 146.
41. Unidentified clipping in Fitzgerald's Scrapbook #1, in Bryer (ed.), *The Critical Reception*, 56.
42. Ibid., 56.
43. For a discussion of the writing of the story and speculation about Fitzgerald's intentions for its publication (or lack thereof), see West III's introductory comment on 'A Full Life' in *Last Kiss*, 221; as well as Kruse, 'F. Scott Fitzgerald in 1937.'
44. See Kruse, 'F. Scott Fitzgerald in 1937.'
45. Fitzgerald, *A Life in Letters*, 402 [late July? 1939].
46. Savran, *Highbrow/Lowdown*, 77.
47. Berret, *Music in the Works of F. Scott Fitzgerald*, 69.
48. Lemke, *Primitivist Modernism*, 81.
49. Chotzinoff, 'Jazz: A Brief History', 244.
50. Kimball and Bolcom, *Reminiscing*, 88.
51. Ibid., 101.
52. Ibid., 98.
53. Savran, *Highbrow/Lowdown*, 75.
54. Blake et al., *Shuffle Along*, 14.
55. Savran, *Highbrow/Lowdown*, 75.
56. Baker and Bouillon, *Josephine*, 51-2.
57. Kimball and Bolcom, *Reminiscing*, 116.
58. Douglas, *Terrible Honesty*, 384.
59. Ibid., 378.
60. Mizejewski, *Ziegfeld Girl*, 128
61. Croce, *The Fred Astaire and Ginger Rogers Book*, 56.
62. Bruccoli, *Some Sort of Epic Grandeur*, 286.
63. Prigozy, 'Fitzgerald's Short Stories and the Depression', 111.
64. Ibid., 117.
65. Veblen, *The Theory of the Leisure Class*, 49-69.
66. Lanahan, *Scottie*, 87.
67. Although Princeton is not named in 'No Flowers', Bruccoli's introduction to the story in *The Price Was High* asserts that '"No Flowers" is clearly set there; and this story is informed by Fitzgerald's identification with Princeton'; see Fitzgerald, *The Price Was High: The Last Uncollected Stories of F. Scott Fitzgerald*, II, 143.

Chapter 5

1. The quotation in the chapter title is taken from Fitzgerald's essay 'Pasting it Together' (1936), collected in *My Lost City: Personal Essays, 1920-1940*, 148.
2. See Margolies, 'Fitzgerald and Hollywood', 190.
3. Letter to Scottie Fitzgerald, Fitzgerald, *Life in Letters*, 330 [July 1937].
4. *Life in Letters*, 101 [April 1925].
5. Kuehl and Bryer (eds), *Dear Scott/Dear Max*, 255 [25 February 1939].

6. Fitzgerald, *Life in Letters*, 402 [c. late July 1939].
7. See Hannoosh, 'The Reflexive Function of Parody'.
8. Dentith, *Parody*, 193.
9. Veblen, *The Theory of the Leisure Class*, 59.
10. The quotation in the section title is taken from Fitzgerald's essay 'Pasting It Together' (1936), collected in *My Lost City*, 148.
11. Fitzgerald, *Life in Letters*, 107 [c. 24 April 1925].
12. Raubicheck, 'Hollywood Nights', 54.
13. See Cerasulo, *Authors Out Here*.
14. Ibid., 4.
15. Turnbull (ed.), *Letters of Fitzgerald*, 415–16 [Winter 1927].
16. Schulberg, *The Four Seasons of Success*, 97; Margolies, 'Fitzgerald and Hollywood', 199.
17. Schulberg, 'Introduction', in Fitzgerald, *Babylon Revisited*, 9.
18. Miller, 'Avant-garde Trends', 192.
19. Wixson, 'Ragged Edges', 56, 59.
20. Kuehl and Bryer (eds), *Dear Scott/Dear Max*, 88 [c. 20 December 1924].
21. Fitzgerald, *Life in Letters*, 331 [July 1937].
22. Turnbull (ed.), *Letters of Fitzgerald*, 443 [Fall, 1937].
23. See Dixon, *The Cinematic Vision*, 62–6.
24. Conrad, *The Nigger of the 'Narcissus'*, 145–7.
25. Fitzgerald, *Life in Letters*, 256 [23 April 1934].
26. Turnbull (ed.), *Letters of Fitzgerald*, 309 [1 June 1934].
27. Curnutt, 'Literary Style', 36.
28. Wyatt and Johnson (eds), *The George Gershwin Reader*, 52.
29. Cohen, *Silent Film*, 160.
30. Mangion, review of Lise Shapiro Sanders, *Consuming Fantasies*, 240.
31. Boyd, '"Hugh Walpole"', 249.
32. Lehan, 'The Romantic Self', 20.
33. Stern, 'Will the Real Pat Hobby Please Stand Up?', 306.
34. Ibid., 322.
35. West III, 'Introduction', *The Lost Decade*, ed. by West III, xi–xxxii (xvi).
36. It is notable that the film producer Monroe Stahr, protagonist of *The Last Tycoon*, is the only protagonist who manages to marry popular and critical artistic success in Fitzgerald's œuvre, although Fitzgerald planned for him to die prematurely in the novel, as had his model for Stahr, MGM producer Irving Thalberg. Walter Raubicheck and Steven Goldleaf describe Stahr as '[Fitzgerald's] one real artist-hero'. See 'Stage and Screen Entertainment', 310.
37. Letter from Fitzgerald to Arnold Gingrich, quoted in Gingrich, 'Introduction', in Fitzgerald, *The Pat Hobby Stories*, 10 [21 September 1939].
38. Ibid., 10.
39. Ibid., 13, 16.
40. Fitzgerald also wrote two more sequences of stories: one was loosely based on his daughter Scottie, featuring a protagonist named Gwen. Fitzgerald wrote a series of five but struggled to place them in the *Post*, who accepted only two of them. He also wrote four unusual stories based around a medieval count

named Philippe, which were published in *Redbook*. Additionally, three of the stories he wrote shared the same setting of Tarleton, Georgia (based on Zelda's hometown of Montgomery, Alabama): 'The Ice Palace', 'The Jelly-Bean' and 'The Last of the Belles'. Jim Powell, of 'The Jelly-Bean', is also the protagonist of 'Dice, Brassknuckles and Guitar'.

41. Prchal, 'Tune in Next Month', 291.
42. West III, 'Fitzgerald and Esquire', 149.
43. Kuehl, *F. Scott Fitzgerald*, 118.
44. Stern, 'Will the Real Pat Hobby Please Stand Up?', 319, 327.
45. Ames, 'Pat Hobby', 280, 284–5.
46. Higgins, *F. Scott Fitzgerald*, 14; Eble, *F. Scott Fitzgerald*, 62.
47. In a letter to his agent, Harold Ober, Fitzgerald complained that 'I am not very fond of Two for a Penny. It is a fair story with an O. Henry twist but it is niether [sic] 1st class nor popular because it has no love interest. My heart wasn't in it so I know it lacks vitality,' *As Ever, Scott-Fitz-*, 29 [early November 1921].
48. See Furia, *The Poets of Tin Pan Alley*, 49–50.
49. Higgins, *F. Scott Fitzgerald*, 173; Moers, 'Fitzgerald', 528–9.
50. Stern, 'Will the Real Pat Hobby Please Stand Up?', 319.
51. Ibid., 322.
52. Corcoran, 'Identity Crisis', 69.
53. Curnutt, 'The Short Stories of F. Scott Fitzgerald', 306.
54. Margolies, 'Climbing "Jacob's Ladder"', 101.
55. Kuehl, *F. Scott Fitzgerald*, 87; Prigozy, 'Fitzgerald's Short Stories and the Depression', 113, 123.
56. Raubicheck, 'Hollywood Nights', 57.
57. Prigozy, 'Fitzgerald's Short Stories and the Depression', 111–26 (122); Kuehl, *F. Scott Fitzgerald*, 92; Fitzgerald, *Life in Letters*, 301 [5 June 1936].
58. Raubicheck, 'Hollywood Nights', 58.
59. Ibid., 58.
60. Ibid., 61; for a discussion of the Pygmalion myth in Fitzgerald's work, see Chapter 5 of Irwin, *F. Scott Fitzgerald's Fiction*.
61. For example, see Prigozy, 'Fitzgerald's Short Stories and the Depression', 111–26, esp. 122–3.
62. Bruccoli, *Epic Grandeur*, 469–70.
63. Berman, *The Great Gatsby*, 101.
64. Letter to Scottie Fitzgerald, Fitzgerald, *Life in Letters*, 331 [July 1937].
65. See Margolies, '"Kissing, Shooting, and Sacrificing"'.
66. Meyers, 'James Joyce, Subliminal Screenwriter?', 175.
67. McCourt, 'From the Real to the Reel and Back', 8.
68. André Le Vot suggests that the cover of *The Great Gatsby*, by Francis Cugat, may have been inspired by a close-up of Lillian Gish's eyes in the D. W. Griffith film *Enoch Arden* (1911). On seeing Cugat's cover art, Fitzgerald famously incorporated Doctor T. J. Eckleburg into *Gatsby* and begged Perkins, 'For Christ's sake, don't give anyone that jacket you're saving for me. I've written it into the book.' See Le Vot, *F. Scott Fitzgerald*, 154.
69. Puttnam, *Movies and Money*, 109.

70. Cohen, *Silent Film*, 113.

71. Ronald Berman finds traces of Griffith's 'film iconography' in *The Great Gatsby*, and links both Daisy and Myrtle to the Griffith heroines' iconic exaggerated acting style. See Berman, *The Great Gatsby*, 146, 148–9.

72. Erenberg, *Steppin' Out*, 216.

73. See 'Appendix 3: Original Ending for "The Offshore Pirate"' in Fitzgerald, *Flappers and Philosophers*, ed. by West III, 395–6.

74. *F. Scott Fitzgerald's Ledger*, 8–9.

75. Robards, 'California Dreaming', II, 116.

76. This celebrity-infused genre straddling also recalls the biblical movies of Cecil B. De Mille, who converted biblical texts into epic entertainment in such films as *The Ten Commandments*, which moves between the biblical and modern eras.

77. Bilton, 'The Melancholy of Absence', 32.

78. Heywood Broun, in a *New York Tribune* article, c. 1920, pasted into one of Fitzgerald's scrapbooks and quoted by Mizener, *The Far Side of Paradise*, 104.

79. See Curnutt, *Introduction to Fitzgerald*, 31.

80. Margolies, 'Fitzgerald and Hollywood', 199.

81. See, for example, Schulberg's Introduction in Fitzgerald, *Babylon Revisited: The Screenplay*, 12–14; Cerasulo, *Authors Out Here*; and Dixon, *The Cinematic Vision*.

82. Bilton, 'The Melancholy of Absence', 42.

83. Henderson, 'Colonial, Postcolonial, and Diasporic Readings', [unpaginated].

84. Cohen, *Silent Film*, 117.

85. Berman, *The Great Gatsby*, 101.

Conclusion

1. Hutcheon, *The Politics of Postmodernism*, 95–7.

2. Nowlin, *Racial Angles*, 34.

3. Letter from Fitzgerald to Maxwell Perkins, in *Life in Letters*, 67 [c. 10 April 1924].

4. Ibid., 67.

5. Cohen, *Silent Film*, 117.

6. Conrad, *The Nigger of the 'Narcissus'*, 145–7.

7. Bell, 'Plus de Jazz', 94.

8. Mencken, 'Two Years Too Late', 286.

9. Letter to Scottie Fitzgerald, in Turnbull (ed.), *Letters of Fitzgerald*, 63 [4 November 1939].

BIBLIOGRAPHY

Primary Works

Fitzgerald's Short Stories

Fitzgerald, F. Scott, *All the Sad Young Men*, ed. by James L. W. West III, *The Cambridge Edition of the Works of F. Scott Fitzgerald* (Cambridge: Cambridge University Press, [1926] 2013).

—, *The Basil, Josephine, and Gwen Stories*, ed. by James L. W. West III, *The Cambridge Edition of the Works of F. Scott Fitzgerald* (Cambridge: Cambridge University Press, 2009).

—, *A Change of Class*, ed. by James L. W. West III, *The Cambridge Edition of the Works of F. Scott Fitzgerald* (Cambridge: Cambridge University Press, 2016).

—, *The Collected Short Stories of F. Scott Fitzgerald* (London: Penguin, 2000).

—, *Flappers and Philosophers*, ed. by James L. W. West III, *The Cambridge Edition of the Works of F. Scott Fitzgerald* (Cambridge: Cambridge University Press, [1920] 2012).

—, *Flappers and Philosophers: The Collected Short Stories of F. Scott Fitzgerald* (London: Penguin, 2010).

—, *Forgotten Fitzgerald: Echoes of a Lost America*, ed. by Sarah Churchwell (London: Abacus, 2014).

—, *I'd Die for You and Other Lost Stories*, ed. by Anne Margaret Daniel (London: Scribner, 2017).

—, *Last Kiss*, ed. by James L. W. West III, *The Cambridge Edition of the Works of F. Scott Fitzgerald* (Cambridge: Cambridge University Press, 2017).

—, *The Lost Decade: Short Stories from Esquire, 1936–1941*, ed. by James L. W. West III, *The Cambridge Edition of the Works of F. Scott Fitzgerald* (Cambridge: Cambridge University Press, 2013).

—, *The Price Was High: The Last Uncollected Stories of F. Scott Fitzgerald*, ed. by Matthew J. Bruccoli, 2 vols (London: Picador, 1981).

—, *The Short Stories of F. Scott Fitzgerald: A New Collection*, ed. by Matthew J. Bruccoli (New York: Scribner, 2003).

—, *The Stories of F. Scott Fitzgerald*, ed. by Malcolm Cowley (New York: Collier, 1986).

—, *Tales of the Jazz Age*, ed. by James L. W. West III, *The Cambridge Edition of the Works of F. Scott Fitzgerald* (Cambridge: Cambridge University Press, [1922] 2012).

—, *Taps at Reveille*, ed. by James L. W. West III, *The Cambridge Edition of the Works of F. Scott Fitzgerald* (Cambridge: Cambridge University Press, [1935] 2014).

Fitzgerald, F. Scott and Zelda Fitzgerald, *Bits of Paradise*, ed. by Scottie Fitzgerald Smith and Matthew J. Bruccoli (Harmondsworth: Penguin, 1976).

Fitzgerald's Novels

Fitzgerald, F. Scott, *The Beautiful and Damned*, ed. by James L. W. West III, *The Cambridge Edition of the Works of F. Scott Fitzgerald* (Cambridge: Cambridge University Press, [1922] 2013).

—, *The Great Gatsby*, ed. by Ruth Prigozy (Oxford: Oxford University Press, [1925] 1998).

—, *The Love of the Last Tycoon: A Western*, ed. by Matthew J. Bruccoli, *The Cambridge Edition of the Works of F. Scott Fitzgerald* (Cambridge: Cambridge University Press, [1941] 1993).

—, *Tender is the Night*, ed. by Arnold Goldman (London: Penguin, [1934] 1982, 1986, 1998, repr. 2000).

—, *This Side of Paradise*, ed. by James L. W. West III, *The Cambridge Edition of the Works of F. Scott Fitzgerald* (Cambridge: Cambridge University Press, [1920] 2012).

Fitzgerald's Essays and Criticism

Fitzgerald, F. Scott, *My Lost City: Personal Essays, 1920-1940*, ed. by James L. W. West III, *The Cambridge Edition of the Works of F. Scott Fitzgerald* (Cambridge: Cambridge University Press, 2005).

Fitzgerald's Letters

As Ever, Scott Fitz-: Letters between F. Scott Fitzgerald and His Literary Agent Harold Ober, 1919-1940, ed. by Matthew J. Bruccoli and Jennifer McCabe Atkinson (London: Woburn Press, 1973).

Correspondence of F. Scott Fitzgerald, ed. by Matthew J. Bruccoli, Margaret M. Duggan and Susan Walker (New York: Random House, 1980).

Dear Scott/Dear Max: The Fitzgerald–Perkins Correspondence, ed. by John Kuehl and Jackson R. Bryer (London: Cassell, 1973).

Dear Scott, Dearest Zelda: The Love Letters of F. Scott and Zelda Fitzgerald, ed. by Jackson R. Bryer and Cathy W. Barks (London: Bloomsbury, 2003).

Fitzgerald, F. Scott, *A Life in Letters*, ed. by Matthew J. Bruccoli (London: Penguin, 1998).

Scott Fitzgerald: Letters to His Daughter, ed. by Andrew Turnbull (New York: Charles Scribner's Sons, 1965).

The Letters of F. Scott Fitzgerald, ed. by Andrew Turnbull (London: Bodley Head, 1964).

Miscellaneous Works by Fitzgerald

F. Scott Fitzgerald in His Own Time: A Miscellany, ed. by Matthew J. Bruccoli and Jackson R. Bryer (Kent, OH: Kent State University Press, 1971).

F. Scott Fitzgerald: On Authorship, ed. by Matthew J. Bruccoli and Judith S. Baughman (Columbia: University of South Carolina Press, 1996).

F. Scott Fitzgerald's Ledger: A Facsimile (Washington, DC: NCR/Microcard, 1972).

F. Scott Fitzgerald's St. Paul Plays, 1911-1914, ed. by Alan Margolies (Princeton: Princeton University Press, 1978).

Fitzgerald, F. Scott, *Babylon Revisited: The Screenplay*, ed. by Budd Schulberg (New York: Carroll & Graf [1940] 1993).

—, *Conversations with F. Scott Fitzgerald*, ed. by Matthew J. Bruccoli and Judith S. Baughman (Jackson: University Press of Mississippi, 2004).

—, *Spires and Gargoyles: Early Writings, 1909-1919*, ed. by James L. W. West III, *The Cambridge Edition of the Works of F. Scott Fitzgerald* (Cambridge: Cambridge University Press, 2010).

—, *The Vegetable; Or, From President to Postman* (New York: Macmillan, [1923] 1976).

The Notebooks of F. Scott Fitzgerald, ed. by Matthew J. Bruccoli (London: Harcourt Brace Jovanovich/Bruccoli Clark, 1978).

The Romantic Egoists: A Pictorial Autobiography from the Scrapbooks and Albums of Scott and Zelda Fitzgerald, ed. by Matthew J. Bruccoli, Scottie Fitzgerald Smith and Joan Kerr (New York: Charles Scribner's Sons, 1974).

The Thoughtbook of F. Scott Fitzgerald: A Secret Boyhood Diary, ed. by Dave Page (Minneapolis: University of Minnesota Press, [1910–11] 2013).

Films

42nd Street, directed by Lloyd Bacon. USA: Warner Bros, 1933.

All About Eve, directed by Joseph L. Mankiewicz. USA: 20th Century-Fox, 1950.

Blue Skies, directed by Stuart Heisler. USA: Paramount, 1946.

Conductor 1492, directed by Charles Hines. USA: Warner Bros, 1924.

The Chorus Girl's Romance, directed by William C. Dowlan. USA: Metro Pictures, 1920.

Enoch Arden, directed by D. W. Griffith. USA: Biograph, 1911.

Flesh and the Devil, directed by Clarence Brown. USA: MGM, 1926.

The Four Horsemen of the Apocalypse, directed by Rex Ingram. USA: Metro, 1921.

Gold Diggers of 1933, directed by Mervyn LeRoy. USA: Warner Bros, 1933.

How Rastus Got His Turkey, directed by Theodore Warton. France: Pathé Frères, 1911.

The Husband Hunter, directed by Howard M. Mitchell. USA: Fox, 1920.

It, directed by Clarence Badger. USA: Paramount, 1927.

The Off-Shore Pirate, directed by Dallas M. Fitzgerald. USA: Metro Pictures, 1921.

Our Blushing Brides, directed by Harry Beaumont. USA: MGM, 1930.

Our Dancing Daughters, directed by Harry Beaumont. USA: MGM, 1928.

Our Modern Maidens, directed by Jack Conway. USA: MGM, 1929.

Rastus' Riotous Ride, directed by Pat Hartigan. France: Pathé Frères, 1914.

Sherlock, Jr., directed by Buster Keaton. USA: Metro, 1924.

The Shop Girl, directed by George D. Baker. USA: Vitagraph, 1916.

Stop That Shimmie, directed by Eddie Lyons and Lee Moran. USA: Universal, 1920.
The Ten Commandments, directed by Cecil B. De Mille. USA: Paramount, 1923.
Top Hat, directed by Mark Sandrich. USA: RKO, 1935.

Song Lyrics and Libretti

Blues: An Anthology, ed. by W. C. Handy (London: Collier–Macmillan, 1972).
The Complete Lyrics of Ira Gershwin, ed. by Robert Kimball (London: Pavilion, 1994).
The Complete Lyrics of Irving Berlin, ed. by Robert Kimball and Linda Emmet (New York: Alfred A. Knopf, 2001).
Blake, Eubie, Aubrey Lyles, Flournoy Miller and Noble Sissle, *Shuffle Along: The 1921 Broadway Musical Complete Libretto* (Notre Dame, IN: Theatre Arts Press, 2015).

Other

Conrad, Joseph, *The Nigger of the 'Narcissus'*, ed. by Robert Kimbrough, A Norton Critical Edition (New York: Norton, [1897] 1979).
Eliot, T. S., *The Waste Land*, ed. by Michael North, A Norton Critical Edition (New York: Norton, [1922] 2001).
Fitzgerald, Zelda, 'What Became of the Flappers?', in Matthew J. Bruccoli (ed.), *Zelda Fitzgerald: The Collected Writings* (London: Little, Brown and Company, 1992), 397–9.
Hugill, Stan, *Shanties from the Seven Seas: Shipboard Work-Songs and Songs Used as Work-Songs from the Great Days of Sail* (London: Routledge & Kegan Paul, 1961, rev. 1984).
Joyce, James, *Dubliners*, ed. by Terrence Brown (London: Penguin, [1914] 1992, repr. 2000).

Secondary Works

Albright, Daniel (ed.), *Modernism and Music: An Anthology of Sources* (London: University of Chicago Press, 2004).
Alexander, Michael, *Jazz Age Jews* (Princeton: Princeton University Press, 2001).
Ames, Christopher, 'Pat Hobby and the Fictions of the Hollywood Writer', in Jackson R. Bryer, Ruth Prigozy and Milton R. Stern (eds), *F. Scott Fitzgerald in the Twenty-First Century* (Tuscaloosa: University of Alabama Press, 2003), 279–90.
Archer-Straw, Petrine, *Negrophilia: Avant-Garde Paris and Black Culture in the 1920s* (London: Thames & Hudson, 2000).
Baker, Jean-Claude and Chris Chase, *Josephine: The Hungry Heart* (New York: Random House, 1993).
Baker, Josephine and Jo Bouillon, *Josephine*, trans. by Mariana Fitzpatrick (New York: Paragon House, 1988).
Balkun, Mary McAleer, '"One Cannot Both Spend and Have": The Economics of Gender in Fitzgerald's Josephine Stories', in Jackson R. Bryer, Ruth Prigozy and Milton R. Stern (eds), *F. Scott Fitzgerald in the Twenty-First Century* (Tuscaloosa: University of Alabama Press, 2003), 121–38.
Banta, Martha, *Taylored Lives: Narrative Productions in the Age of Taylor, Veblen, and Ford* (London: University of Chicago Press, 1993).

Barnwell, Andrea D., 'Like the Gypsy's Daughter, or Beyond the Potency of Josephine Baker's Eroticism', in Joanna Skipwith, Richard J. Powell and David A. Bailey (eds), *Rhapsodies in Black: Art of the Harlem Renaissance* (London: Hayward Gallery, 1997), 82–9.

Bell, Clive, 'Plus de Jazz', *The New Republic*, 21 September 1921, 92–5.

—, *The Great Gatsby and Modern Times* (Urbana and Chicago: University of Illinois Press, 1996).

Berret, Anthony J., 'Basil and the Dance Craze', *The F. Scott Fitzgerald Review*, 3 (2004), 88–107.

—, 'Broadway Melodies', in Bryant Mangum (ed.), *F. Scott Fitzgerald in Context* (Cambridge: Cambridge University Press, 2013), 293–301.

—, *Music in the Works of F. Scott Fitzgerald: Unheard Melodies* (Madison, NJ: Fairleigh Dickinson University Press, 2013).

Bilton, Alan, 'The Melancholy of Absence: Reassessing the Role of Film in *Tender Is the Night*', *The F. Scott Fitzgerald Review*, 5 (2006), 28–53.

Bogle, Donald, *Heat Wave: The Life and Career of Ethel Waters* (New York: Harper Perennial, 2012).

—, *Toms, Coons, Mulattoes, Mammies, and Bucks: An Interpretive History of Blacks in American Films* (New York: Continuum, 1989).

Borshuk, Michael, 'An Intelligence of the Body: Disruptive Parody through Dance in the Early Performances of Josephine Baker', in Dorothea Fischer-Hornung and Alison D. Goeller (eds), *EmBODYing Liberation: The Black Body in American Dance* (Hamburg: Lit, 2001), 41–57.

Boyd, Alexander, 'Mostly Flappers', in Jackson R. Bryer (ed.), *F. Scott Fitzgerald: The Critical Reception* (New York: Burt Franklin, 1978 [*St Paul Daily News*, 26 December 1920, 6]), 48-9.

Boyd, Thomas A., '"Hugh Walpole Was the Man Who Started Me Writing Novels"', in Matthew J. Bruccoli and Jackson R. Bryer (eds), *F. Scott Fitzgerald in His Own Time: A Miscellany* (Kent, OH: Kent State University Press, 1971), 245–54.

Brooks, Daphne Ann, 'The End of the Line: Josephine Baker and the Politics of Black Women's Corporeal Comedy', *The Scholar and Feminist Online*, 6.1–6.2 (2007–8), available at <sfonline.barnard.edu/baker/brooks_01.htm> (last accessed 9 January 2018).

Brown, Jayna, *Babylon Girls: Black Women Performers and the Shaping of the Modern* (London: Duke University Press, 2008).

Bruccoli, Matthew J., 'Introduction', in Matthew J. Bruccoli (ed.), *The Price Was High: The Last Uncollected Stories of F. Scott Fitzgerald*, vol. 1 (London: Picador, 1981), 9–17.

—, *Some Sort of Epic Grandeur: The Life of F. Scott Fitzgerald*, 2nd rev. edn (Columbia: University of South Carolina Press, 2002).

Bryer, Jackson R. (ed.), *F. Scott Fitzgerald: The Critical Reception* (New York: Burt Franklin, 1978).

—, 'The Critical Reputation of F. Scott Fitzgerald', in Ruth Prigozy (ed.), *The Cambridge Companion to F. Scott Fitzgerald* (Cambridge: Cambridge University Press, 2001), 209–34.

— (ed.), *The Short Stories of F. Scott Fitzgerald: New Approaches in Criticism* (London: University of Wisconsin Press, 1982).

Bullock, Heidi Kunz, 'The Southern and the Satirical in "The Last of the Belles"', in Jackson R. Bryer (ed.), *New Essays on F. Scott Fitzgerald's Neglected Stories* (Columbia: University of Missouri Press, 1996), 130–7.

'A Capital Ship', in *The Mudcat Café Digital Tradition Folk Song Database*, available at <mudcat.org/@displaysong.cfm?SongID=11> (last accessed 12 January 2018).

Carter, Angela, 'Review of Phyllis Rose: *Jazz Cleopatra*', in *Expletives Deleted: Selected Writings* (London: Vintage, 2006).

Carter, Paul A., *Another Part of the Twenties* (New York: Columbia University Press, 1977).

Castle, Irene and Vernon Castle, *Modern Dancing* (London: Harper & Brothers, 1914).

Cerasulo, Tom, *Authors Out Here: Fitzgerald, West, Parker, and Schulberg in Hollywood* (Columbia: University of South Carolina Press, 2010).

Chapman, Erin D., *Prove It on Me: New Negroes, Sex, and Popular Culture in the 1920s* (New York: Oxford University Press, 2012).

Cheng, Anne Anlin, *Second Skin: Josephine Baker and the Modern Surface* (New York: Oxford University Press, 2011).

Chotzinoff, Samuel, 'Jazz: A Brief History', in Karl Koenig (ed.), *Jazz in Print (1856-1929): An Anthology of Selected Early Readings in Jazz History* (Hillsdale, NY: Pendragon, 2002 [*Vanity Fair*, June 1923]), 241-5.

Churchwell, Sarah, '"$4000 a Screw": The Prostituted Art of F. Scott Fitzgerald and Ernest Hemingway', *European Journal of American Culture*, 24:2 (2005), 105–130.

Cohen, Paula Marantz, *Silent Film and the Triumph of the American Myth* (New York: Oxford University Press, 2001).

Cohn, Jan, *Creating America: George Horace Lorimer and the Saturday Evening Post* (Pittsburgh: University of Pittsburgh Press, 1989).

Cook, Susan C., 'Passionless Dancing and Passionate Reform: Respectability, Modernism, and the Social Dancing of Irene and Vernon Castle', in William Washabaugh (ed.), *The Passion of Music and Dance: Body, Gender and Sexuality* (Oxford: Berg, 1998), 133–50.

Corcoran, Mark, 'Identity Crisis in James Joyce's *Dubliners*', *Journal of Franco-Irish Studies*, 2:1 (2011), 57–72.

Cowley, Malcolm, *A Second Flowering: Works and Days of the Lost Generation* (London: André Deutsch, 1973).

—, 'Third Act and Epilogue', in Arthur Mizener (ed.), *F. Scott Fitzgerald: A Collection of Critical Essays* (Englewood Cliffs: Prentice-Hall, 1963 [*The New Yorker*, 30 June 1945]), 64–9.

—, [Untitled Review of *All the Sad Young Men*], in Jackson R. Bryer (ed.), *F. Scott Fitzgerald: The Critical Reception* (New York: Burt Franklin, 1978 [*Charm*, May 1926, 80-1]), 271-2.

Crease, Robert, 'Jazz and Dance', in Mervyn Cooke and David Horn (eds), *The Cambridge Companion to Jazz* (Cambridge: Cambridge University Press, 2002), 69–80.

Croce, Arlene, *The Fred Astaire and Ginger Rogers Book* (New York: Outerbridge & Lazard, 1972).

Curnutt, Kirk, *The Cambridge Introduction to F. Scott Fitzgerald* (Cambridge: Cambridge University Press, 2007).

—, 'Fitzgerald's Consumer World', in Kirk Curnutt (ed.), *A Historical Guide to F. Scott Fitzgerald* (Oxford: Oxford University Press, 2004), 85–128.

—, 'Introduction', in Kirk Curnutt (ed.), *A Historical Guide to F. Scott Fitzgerald* (Oxford: Oxford University Press, 2004), 3–19.

—, 'Literary Style', in Bryant Mangum (ed.), *F. Scott Fitzgerald in Context* (Cambridge: Cambridge University Press, 2013), 34–44.

—, 'The Short Stories of F. Scott Fitzgerald: Structure, Narrative Technique, Style', in Alfred Bendixen and James Nagel (eds), *A Companion to the American Short Story* (Chichester: Wiley–Blackwell, 2010), 295–315.

Currell, Susan, *American Culture in the 1920s* (Edinburgh: Edinburgh University Press, 2011).

—, 'Introduction', in Susan Currell and Christina Cogdell (eds), *Popular Eugenics: National Efficiency and American Mass Culture in the 1930s* (Athens: Ohio University Press, 2006), 1–16.

—, *The March of Spare Time: The Problem and Promise of Leisure in the Great Depression* (Philadelphia: University of Pennsylvania Press, 2005).

Daugherty, Christa E. and James L. W. West III, 'Josephine Baker, Petronius, and the Text of "Babylon Revisited"', *The F. Scott Fitzgerald Review*, 1 (2002), 3–15.

Dawidoff, Robert, 'The Kind of Person You Have to Sound Like to Sing "Alexander's Ragtime Band"', in Elazer Barkan and Ronald Bush (eds), *Prehistories of the Future: The Primitivist Project and the Culture of Modernism* (Stanford: Stanford University Press, 1995), 293–309.

Dentith, Simon, *Parody* (Abingdon: Routledge, 2000).

Dickson-Carr, Darryl, *Spoofing the Modern: Satire in the Harlem Renaissance* (Columbia: University of South Carolina Press, 2015).

Dilworth, Thomas, '*The Great Gatsby* and the Arrow Collar Man', *The F. Scott Fitzgerald Review*, 7 (2009), 80–93.

Dixon, Wheeler Winston, *The Cinematic Vision of F. Scott Fitzgerald* (Ann Arbor: UMI Research Press, 1986).

—, *Fool for Love: F. Scott Fitzgerald*, 2nd rev. edn (Minneapolis: University of Minnesota Press, 2012).

—, 'Scott Fitzgerald's Romance with the South', *Southern Literary Journal*, 5:2 (1973), 3–17.

Douglas, Ann, *The Feminization of American Culture* (New York: Alfred A. Knopf, 1977; repr. London: Papermac, 1996).

—, *Terrible Honesty: Mongrel Manhattan in the 1920s* (London: Picador, 1995).

Driver, Ian, *A Century of Dance* (London: Hamlyn, 2000).

Drowne, Kathleen, 'Postwar Flappers', in Bryant Mangum (ed.), *F. Scott Fitzgerald in Context* (Cambridge: Cambridge University Press, 2013), 245–53.

Dumenil, Lynn, *Modern Temper: American Culture and Society in the 1920s* (New York: Hill and Wang, 1995).

Eble, Kenneth, *F. Scott Fitzgerald* (Indianapolis: Bobbs–Merrill Educational, 1977).

'Ellin Mackay's Bored Debutantes Are Satirized by Scott Fitzgerald', in Matthew J. Bruccoli and Judith S. Baughman (eds), *Conversations with F. Scott Fitzgerald* (Jackson: University Press of Mississippi, 2004 [*Chicago Tribune European Edition*, 7 December 1925]), 75-6.

Erenberg, Lewis A., *Steppin' Out: New York Nightlife and the Transformation of American Culture, 1890–1930* (London: University of Chicago Press, 1981, repr. 1984).

Evans, Nicholas M., '"Racial Cross-Dressing" in the Jazz Age: Cultural Therapy and its Discontents in Cabaret Nightlife', in Henry Jenkins, Tara McPherson and Jane Shattuc (eds), *Hop on Pop: The Politics and Pleasures of Popular Culture* (London: Duke University Press, 2002), 388–414.

—, *Writing Jazz: Race, Nationalism, and Modern Culture in the 1920s* (London: Garland, 2000).

Farebrother, Rachel, *The Collage Aesthetic in the Harlem Renaissance* (Farnham: Ashgate, 2009).

Fass, Paula S., *The Damned and the Beautiful: American Youth in the 1920's* (Oxford: Oxford University Press, 1979).

Franks, A. H., *Social Dance — A Short History* (London: Routledge & Kegan Paul, 1963).

Furia, Philip, *The Poets of Tin Pan Alley: A History of America's Great Lyricists* (Oxford: Oxford University Press, 1992).

Gabbard, Krin, 'The Word Jazz', in Mervyn Cooke and David Horn (eds), *The Cambridge Companion to Jazz* (Cambridge: Cambridge University Press, 2002), 1–6.

Gale, Robert L., *An F. Scott Fitzgerald Encyclopedia* (Westport, CT: Greenwood, 1998).

The George Gershwin Reader, ed. by Robert Wyatt and John Andrew Johnson (Oxford: Oxford University Press, 2004).

Giddins, Gary, *Visions of Jazz: The First Century* (Oxford: Oxford University Press, 1998).

Gilroy, Paul, '". . . to Be Real": The Dissident Forms of Black Expressive Culture', in Catherine Ugwu (ed.), *Let's Get It On: The Politics of Black Performance* (London: Institute of Contemporary Arts, 1995), 12–33.

Gingrich, Arnold, 'Introduction', in F. Scott Fitzgerald, *The Pat Hobby Stories* (Harmondsworth: Penguin, 1967), 7–23.

Gizzo, Suzanne del, 'Ethnic Stereotyping', in Bryant Mangum (ed.), *F. Scott Fitzgerald in Context* (Cambridge: Cambridge University Press, 2013), 224–33.

Golden, Eve, *Vernon and Irene Castle's Ragtime Revolution* (Lexington: University Press of Kentucky, 2007).

Gordon, Terri J., 'Synesthetic Rhythms: African American Music and Dance through Parisian Eyes', *The Scholar and Feminist Online*, 6.1–6.2 (2007–8), available at <sfonline.barnard.edu/baker/gordon_01.htm> (last accessed 9 January 2018).

Graham, Sheilah, *College of One* (London: Weidenfeld and Nicolson, 1967).

Graham, T. Austin, *The Great American Songbooks: Musical Texts, Modernism, and the Value of Popular Culture* (New York: Oxford University Press, 2013).

Gray, James, 'Scott Fitzgerald Brilliance Bared in Short Stories', in Jackson R. Bryer (ed.), *F. Scott Fitzgerald: The Critical Reception* (New York: Burt Franklin, 1978 [*St. Paul Dispatch*, 20 March 1935, 8]), 337-8.

Hamilton, Sharon, 'Mencken and Nathan's *Smart Set* and the Story Behind Fitzgerald's Early Success', *The F. Scott Fitzgerald Review*, 4 (2005), 20–48.

Hammond, Bryan and Patrick O'Connor, *Josephine Baker* (London: Jonathan Cape, 1988).

Hannoosh, Michele, 'The Reflexive Function of Parody', *Comparative Literature*, 41:2 (1989), 113–27

Hansen, Harry, 'The Boy Grows Older', in Jackson R. Bryer (ed.), *F. Scott Fitzgerald: The Critical Reception* (New York: Burt Franklin, 1978 [*Chicago Daily News*, 3 March 1926, 16]), 255-6.

Harding, Brian, '"Made for – or against – the Trade": The Radicalism of Fitzgerald's *Saturday Evening Post* Love Stories', in A. Robert Lee (ed.), *Scott Fitzgerald: The Promises of Life* (London: Vision, 1989), 113–30.

Hawthorne, Hildegarde, [Untitled Review of *Tales of the Jazz Age*], in Jackson R. Bryer (ed.), *F. Scott Fitzgerald: The Critical Reception* (New York: Burt Franklin, 1978 [*New York Times Book Review*, 29 October 1922, 12]), 149-50.

Hays, Peter L., 'Class Differences in Fitzgerald's Works', in Bryant Mangum (ed.), *F. Scott Fitzgerald in Context* (Cambridge: Cambridge University Press, 2013), 215–23.

Head, Dominic, *The Modernist Short Story: A Study in Theory and Practice* (Cambridge: Cambridge University Press, 1992).

Hearn, Charles R., 'F. Scott Fitzgerald and the Popular Magazine Formula Story of the Twenties', *Journal of American Culture*, 18 (Fall 1995), 33-40.

—, 'Colonial, Postcolonial, and Diasporic Readings of Josephine Baker as Dancer and Performance Artist', *The Scholar and Feminist Online*, 6.1–6.2 (2007–8), available at <sfonline.barnard.edu/baker/henderson_01.htm> (last accessed 9 January 2018).

—, 'Josephine Baker and *La Revue Nègre*: From Ethnography to Performance', *Text and Performance Quarterly*, 23:2 (2003), 107–33.

Henson, Kristin K., *Beyond the Sound Barrier: The Jazz Controversy in Twentieth-Century American Fiction* (London: Routledge, 2003).

Higgins, John A., *F. Scott Fitzgerald: A Study of the Stories* (Jamaica, NY: St John's University Press, 1971).

H. L. Mencken's 'Smart Set' Criticism, ed. by William H. Nolte (Washington, DC: Regnery, 1987).

Hutcheon, Linda, *A Theory of Parody: The Teachings of Twentieth-Century Art Forms*, (Urbana and Chicago: University of Illinois Press, [1985] 2000).

—, *The Politics of Postmodernism*, 2nd edn (London: Routledge, [1989] 2002).

Irwin, John T., *F. Scott Fitzgerald's Fiction: 'An Almost Theatrical Innocence'* (Baltimore: Johns Hopkins University Press, 2014).

Kammen, Michael, 'Introduction', in Gilbert Seldes, *The 7 Lively Arts* (Mineola, NY: Dover, 1924, rev. 1952, repr. with an introduction by Michael Kammen, 2001), xi–xxxvi.

Keller, Susan L., 'The Riviera's Golden Boy: Fitzgerald, Cosmopolitan Tanning, and Racial Commodities in *Tender Is the Night*', *The F. Scott Fitzgerald Review*, 8 (2010), 130–59.

Kimball, Robert and William Bolcom, *Reminiscing with Noble Sissle and Eubie Blake*, (New York: Viking, 1973; repr. New York: Cooper Square Press, 2000).

Koenig, Karl (ed.), *Jazz in Print (1856–1929): An Anthology of Selected Early Readings in Jazz History* (Hillsdale, NY: Pendragon, 2002).

Kruse, Horst H., 'F. Scott Fitzgerald in 1937: A Manuscript Study of "A Full Life"', in Jackson R. Bryer, Ruth Prigozy and Milton Stern (eds), *F. Scott Fitzgerald in the Twenty-First Century* (Tuscaloosa: University of Alabama Press, 2003), 153–72.

Kuehl, John, *F. Scott Fitzgerald: A Study of the Short Fiction* (Boston: Twayne, 1991).

Kunce, Catherine and Paul M. Levitt, 'The Structure of *Gatsby*: A Vaudeville Show, Featuring Buffalo Bill and a Cast of Dozens', *The F. Scott Fitzgerald Review*, 4 (2005), 101–28.

Lanahan, Eleanor, *Scottie: The Daughter of . . . The Life of Frances Scott Fitzgerald Lanahan Smith* (New York: HarperCollins, 1995).

Le Vot, André, *F. Scott Fitzgerald: A Biography*, trans. by William Byron (Harmondsworth: Penguin, 1985).

Lears, T. J. Jackson, *No Place of Grace: Antimodernism and the Transformation of American Culture, 1880–1920* (New York: Pantheon, 1981; repr. London: University of Chicago Press, 1983, 1994).

Ledger, Sally, *The New Woman: Fiction and Feminism at the 'Fin de Siècle'* (Manchester: Manchester University Press, 1997).

Lehan, Richard, 'The Romantic Self and the Uses of Place in the Stories of F. Scott Fitzgerald', in Jackson R. Bryer (ed.), *The Short Stories of F. Scott Fitzgerald: New Approaches in Criticism* (London: University of Wisconsin Press, 1982), 3–21.

Lemke, Sieglinde, *Primitivist Modernism: Black Culture and the Origins of Transatlantic Modernism* (Oxford: Oxford University Press, 1998).

Levine, Lawrence W., *Highbrow/Lowbrow: The Emergence of Cultural Hierarchy in America* (London: Harvard University Press, 1988).

Lott, Eric, *Love and Theft: Blackface Minstrelsy and the American Working Class* (Oxford: Oxford University Press, 1993).

McCabe Atkinson, Jennifer, 'Lost and Unpublished Stories by F. Scott Fitzgerald', *Fitzgerald/Hemingway Annual*, (1971), 32–63.

McCarren, Felicia, *Dancing Machines: Choreographies of the Age of Mechanical Reproduction* (Stanford: Stanford University Press, 2003).

McCourt, John, 'From the Real to the Reel and Back: Explorations into Joyce and Cinema', in John McCourt (ed.), *Roll Away the Reel World: James Joyce and Cinema* (Cork: Cork University Press, 2010), 1–11.

Mackay, Ellen, 'Why We Go to Cabarets: A Post-Debutante Explains', *The New Yorker*, 28 November 1925, 7–8.

Mangion, Carmen M., review of Lise Shapiro Sanders, *Consuming Fantasies: Labor, Leisure, and the London Shopgirl, 1880–1920* (2006), *Journal of British Studies*, 47:1 (2008), 239–41.

Mangum, Bryant, *A Fortune Yet: Money in the Art of F. Scott Fitzgerald's Short Stories* (London: Garland, 1991).

Margolies, Alan, 'Climbing "Jacob's Ladder"', in Jackson R. Bryer (ed.), *New Essays on F. Scott Fitzgerald's Neglected Stories* (Columbia: University of Missouri Press, 1996), 89–103.

—, 'Fitzgerald and Hollywood', in Ruth Prigozy (ed.), *The Cambridge Companion to F. Scott Fitzgerald* (Cambridge: Cambridge University Press, 2001), 189–208.

—, '"Kissing, Shooting, and Sacrificing": F. Scott Fitzgerald and the Hollywood Market', in Jackson R. Bryer (ed.), *The Short Stories of F. Scott Fitzgerald: New Approaches in Criticism* (London: University of Wisconsin Press, 1982), 65–73.

Martin, Quentin E., 'The First Emotional Bankrupt: F. Scott Fitzgerald's Josephine Perry', *The F. Scott Fitzgerald Review*, 1 (2002), 177–95.

Martin, Wendy, '"Remembering the Jungle": Josephine Baker and Modernist Parody', in Elazar Barkan and Ronald Bush (eds), *Prehistories of the Future: The Primitivist Project and the Culture of Modernism* (Stanford: Stanford University Press, 1995), 310–25.

May, Charles E., *The Short Story: The Reality of Artifice* (London: Routledge, 2002).

Mencken, H. L, 'Two Years Too Late', in William H. Nolte (ed.), *H. L. Mencken's 'Smart Set' Criticism* (Washington, DC: Regnery, 1987 [*The Smart Set*, December 1920]), 286.

Meyers, Jesse, 'James Joyce, Subliminal Screenwriter?', in John McCourt (ed.), *Roll Away the Reel World: James Joyce and Cinema* (Cork: Cork University Press, 2010), 174–85.

Miller, Linda Patterson, 'Avant-garde Trends', in Bryant Mangum (ed.), *F. Scott Fitzgerald in Context* (Cambridge: Cambridge University Press, 2013), 191–202.

Mizejewski, Linda, *Ziegfeld Girl: Image and Icon in Culture and Cinema* (London: Duke University Press, 1999).

Mizener, Arthur, *The Far Side of Paradise: A Biography of F. Scott Fitzgerald* (Cambridge, MA: Riverside Press, 1951).

Moers, Ellen F., 'Fitzgerald: Reveille at Taps', *Commentary*, 34 (1962), 526–30.

Mooney, Hughson F., 'Songs, Singers and Society, 1890–1954', *American Quarterly*, 6:3 (1954), 221–32.

Morley, Catherine, *Modern American Literature* (Edinburgh: Edinburgh University Press, 2012).

'Mr. Fitzgerald's Latest Book', in Jackson R. Bryer (ed.), *F. Scott Fitzgerald: The Critical Reception* (New York: Burt Franklin, 1978 [*Princeton Alumni Weekly*, 11 October 1922, 40–1]), 146-7.

Newman, Frances, '*All the Sad Young Men:* One of the Wistful Young Men', in Matthew J. Bruccoli and Jackson R. Bryer (eds), *F. Scott Fitzgerald In His Own Time: A Miscellany* (Kent, OH: Kent State University Press, 1971 [*New York Herald Tribune Book Review*, 25 April 1926]), 368–70.

North, Michael, *The Dialect of Modernism: Race, Language, and Twentieth-Century Literature* (New York and Oxford: Oxford University Press, 1994).

Nowlin, Michael, *F. Scott Fitzgerald's Racial Angles and the Business of Literary Greatness* (Basingstoke: Palgrave Macmillan, 2007).

Ogren, Kathy J., *The Jazz Revolution: Twenties America and the Meaning of Jazz* (New York: Oxford University Press, 1989).

Parker, Dorothy, 'Once More Mother Hubbard – As Told by F. Scott Fitzgerald', in Matthew J. Bruccoli and Jackson R. Bryer (eds), *F. Scott Fitzgerald In His Own Time: A Miscellany* (Kent, OH: Kent State University Press, 1971 [*Life*, 7 July 1921]), 447-8.

Petry, Alice Hall, *Fitzgerald's Craft of Short Fiction: The Collected Stories, 1920–1935* (London: UMI Research Press, 1989).

Prchal, Tim, 'Tune in Next Month: Fitzgerald's Pat Hobby and the Popular Series', in Jackson R. Bryer, Ruth Prigozy and Milton R. Stern (eds), *F. Scott Fitzgerald in the Twenty-First Century* (Tuscaloosa: University of Alabama Press, 2003), 291–300.

Prigozy, Ruth, 'Fitzgerald's Flappers and Flapper Films of the Jazz Age: Behind the Morality', in Kirk Curnutt (ed.), *A Historical Guide to F. Scott Fitzgerald* (Oxford: Oxford University Press, 2004), 129–61.

—, 'Fitzgerald's Short Stories and the Depression: An Artistic Crisis', in Jackson R. Bryer (ed.), *The Short Stories of F. Scott Fitzgerald: New Approaches in Criticism* (London: University of Wisconsin Press, 1982), 111–26.

—, '"Poor Butterfly": F. Scott Fitzgerald and Popular Music', *Prospects*, 2 (1977), 40–67.

Puttnam, David, *Movies and Money* (New York: Vintage, 2000).

Raubicheck, Walter, 'Hollywood Nights: The Filmmaker as Artist in "Crazy Sunday"', *The F. Scott Fitzgerald Review*, 7 (2009), 53–64.

Raubicheck, Walter and Steven Goldleaf, 'Stage and Screen Entertainment', in Bryant Mangum (ed.), *F. Scott Fitzgerald in Context* (Cambridge: Cambridge University Press, 2013), 302–10.

Robards, Brooks, 'California Dreaming: Dream Sequences in Hollywood Musicals, Melodramas and Horror Movies', in Paul Loukides and Linda K. Fuller (eds), *Beyond the Stars: Studies in American Popular Film*, 5 vols (Bowling Green, OH: Bowling Green State University Popular Press, 1990–6), II, 114–29.

Roulston, Robert, 'Rummaging Through F. Scott Fitzgerald's "Trash": Early Stories in the *Saturday Evening Post*', *Journal of Popular Culture*, 21:4 (1988), 151–63.

Sanderson, Rena, 'Women in Fitzgerald's Fiction', in Ruth Prigozy (ed.), *The Cambridge Companion to F. Scott Fitzgerald* (Cambridge: Cambridge University Press, 2001), 143–63.

Savran, David, *Highbrow/Lowdown: Theater, Jazz, and the Making of the New Middle Class* (Ann Arbor: University of Michigan Press, 2009).

Schulberg, Budd, *The Four Seasons of Success* (London: Robson, 1974).

—, 'Introduction', in Budd Schulberg (ed.), *Babylon Revisited: The Screenplay* (New York: Carroll & Graf [1940] 1993), 7–14.

Scofield, Martin, *The Cambridge Introduction to the American Short Story* (Cambridge: Cambridge University Press, 2006).

'Scott Fitzgerald Turns a Corner', in Jackson R. Bryer (ed.), *F. Scott Fitzgerald: The Critical Reception* (New York: Burt Franklin, 1978 [*New York Times Book Review*, 7 March 1926, 9]), 257-8.

Seldes, Gilbert, *The 7 Lively Arts* (Mineola: Dover, 1924, rev. 1952, repr. with an introduction by Michael Kammen, 2001).

Shaw, Arnold, *The Jazz Age: Popular Music in the 1920s* (New York: Oxford University Press, 1987).

Spaeth, Sigmund, *A History of Popular Music in America* (London: Phoenix House, 1948, repr. 1959).

Stearns, Marshall and Jean Stearns, *Jazz Dance: The Story of American Vernacular Dance* (New York: Macmillan, 1968; repr. London: Collier Macmillan, 1979).

Stern, Milton R., 'Will the Real Pat Hobby Please Stand Up?', in Jackson R. Bryer (ed.), *New Essays on F. Scott Fitzgerald's Neglected Stories* (Columbia: University of Missouri Press, 1996), 305–38.

Turnbull, Andrew, *Scott Fitzgerald* (London: Vintage, 1962, repr. 2004).

Veblen, Thorstein, *The Theory of the Leisure Class*, ed. by Martha Banta (Oxford: Oxford University Press, 2009).

Walkowitz, Judith R., *City of Dreadful Delight: Narratives of Sexual Danger in Late-Victorian London* (London: Virago, 1992).

Walton, Edith H., 'Taps at Reveille: Scott Fitzgerald's Tales', in Matthew J. Bruccoli and Jackson R. Bryer (eds), *F. Scott Fitzgerald In His Own Time: A Miscellany* (Kent, OH: Kent State University Press, 1971 [*New York Times Book Review*, 31 March 1935]), 395–6.

Ward, Christopher, 'Paradise Be Damned! by F. Scott Fitzjazzer', in Matthew J. Bruccoli and Jackson R. Bryer (eds), *F. Scott Fitzgerald In His Own Time: A Miscellany* (Kent, OH: Kent State University Press, 1971 [*The Triumph of the Nut and Other Parodies*, New York: Henry Holt, 1923]), 456-64.

Warshow, Robert, 'The Gangster as Tragic Hero', in *The Immediate Experience: Movies, Comics, Theatre and Other Aspects of Popular Culture* (London: Harvard University Press, 1962; rev. edn 2001), 97–103.

West III, James L. W., *American Authors and the Literary Marketplace Since 1900* (Philadelphia: University of Pennsylvania Press, 1988).

—, 'Annotating Mr. Fitzgerald', *The American Scholar*, 69:2 (2000), 82–91.

—, 'Explanatory Notes', in James L. W. West III (ed.), *Flappers and Philosophers* (Cambridge: Cambridge University Press, 2012), 351–80.

—, 'Explanatory Notes', in James L. W. West III (ed.), *Tales of the Jazz Age* (Cambridge: Cambridge University Press, 2002), 499–528.

—, 'F. Scott Fitzgerald, Professional Author', in Kirk Curnutt (ed.), *A Historical Guide to F. Scott Fitzgerald* (Oxford: Oxford University Press, 2004), 49–68.

—, 'Fitzgerald and *Esquire*', in Jackson R. Bryer (ed.), *The Short Stories of F. Scott Fitzgerald: New Approaches in Criticism* (London: University of Wisconsin Press, 1982), 149–66.

—, 'Introduction', in James L. W. West III (ed.), *Flappers and Philosophers* (Cambridge: Cambridge University Press, 2012), xi–xxxi.

—, 'Introduction', in James L. W. West III (ed.), *The Lost Decade: Short Stories from Esquire, 1936-1941* (Cambridge: Cambridge University Press, 2013), ix–xxxii.

—, 'Introduction', in James L. W. West III (ed.), *Tales of the Jazz Age* (Cambridge: Cambridge University Press, 2002), xi–xxviii.

—, 'Introduction', in James L. W. West III (ed.), *Taps at Reveille* (Cambridge: Cambridge University Press, 2014), ix–xxxi.

Whiteman, Paul and Mary Margaret McBride, *Jazz* (New York: J. H. Sears, 1926; repr. New York: Arno, 1974).

Wilder, Alec, *American Popular Song: The Great Innovators, 1900–1950*, ed. by James T. Maher (New York: Oxford University Press, 1972).

Wilkerson, Isabel, *The Warmth of Other Suns: The Epic Story of America's Great Migration* (New York: Random House, 2010).

Wixson, Christopher, 'Ragged Edges: The Curious Case of F. Scott Fitzgerald's *The Vegetable*', *American Drama*, 15.2 (2006), 48–60.

Woollcott, Alexander, *The Story of Irving Berlin* (London: G. Putnam's Sons, 1925).

Zeitz, Joshua, *Flapper: A Madcap Story of Sex, Style, Celebrity, and the Women Who Made America Modern* (New York: Three Rivers, 2006).

Zinn, Howard, *A People's History of the United States* (New York: HarperCollins, 1980; 4th rev. edn 2003, repr. 2005).

INDEX

214 / F. Scott Fitzgerald's Short Fiction